Neo-Victorianism and

Bloomsbury Literary Studies series
Also available in the series:
Active Reading, Ben Knights
Adapting Detective Fiction, Neil McCaw
Beckett and Decay, Kathryn White
Beckett and Ethics, Russell Smith
Beckett and Phenomenology, Ulrika Maude
Canonizing Hypertext, Astrid Ensslin
Character and Satire in Post War Fiction, Ian Gregson
Coleridge and German Philosophy, Paul Hamilton
Contemporary British Fiction and the Artistry of Space, David James
Contemporary Fiction and Christianity, Andrew Tate
Contemporary Women Writers Look Back, Alice Ridout
Dickens, Christianity and 'The Life of Our Lord', Gary Colledge
Ecstasy and Understanding, Adrian Grafe
English Fiction in the 1930s, Chris Hopkins
Incarnation of Language, Michael O'Sullivan
Intention and Text, Kaye Mitchell
Lacan and the Destiny of Literature, Ehsan Azari
Magical Realism and Deleuze, Eva Aldea
Male Jealousy, Louis Lo
Mapping World Literature, Mads Rosendahl Thomsen
Marginality in the Contemporary British Novel, Nicola Allen
Measureless Time of Joyce, Deleuze and Derrida, Ruben Borg
Modernism and the Post-Colonial, Peter Childs
Money, Speculation and Finance in Contemporary British Fiction, Nicky Marsh
Palimpsest: Literature, Criticism, Theory, Sarah Dillon
Recalling London, Alex Murray
Seeking Meaning for Goethe's Faust, J. M. van der Laan

Neo-Victorianism and the Memory of Empire

Elizabeth Ho

Bloomsbury Literary Studies

BLOOMSBURY
LONDON · NEW DELHI · NEW YORK · SYDNEY

Bloomsbury Academic
An imprint of Bloomsbury Publishing Plc

50 Bedford Square	1385 Broadway
London	New York
WC1B 3DP	NY 10018
UK	USA

www.bloomsbury.com

Bloomsbury is a registered trade mark of Bloomsbury Publishing Plc

First published 2012
Paperback edition first published 2013

© Elizabeth Ho 2012

Elizabeth Ho has asserted her right under the Copyright, Designs and Patents Act, 1988, to be identified as Author of this work.

All rights reserved. No part of this publication may be reproduced or transmitted in any form or by any means, electronic or mechanical, including photocopying, recording, or any information storage or retrieval system, without prior permission in writing from the publishers.

No responsibility for loss caused to any individual or organization acting on or refraining from action as a result of the material in this publication can be accepted by Bloomsbury or the author.

British Library Cataloguing-in-Publication Data
A catalogue record for this book is available from the British Library.

ISBN: HB: 978-1-4411-6155-0
PB: 978-1-4725-2552-9
ePDF: 978-1-4411-9778-8
ePUB: 978-1-4411-8770-3

Library of Congress Cataloging-in-Publication Data
Ho, Elizabeth.
Neo-victorianism and the memory of empire/Elizabeth Ho.
p. cm. – (Continuum literary studies)
Includes bibliographical references and index.
ISBN 978-1-4411-6155-0 (hardcover: alk. paper) – ISBN 978-1-4411-9778-8 (ebook pdf) – ISBN 978-1-4411-8770-3 (ebook epub)
1. Postmodernism (Literature) 2. Literature, Modern–21st century–History and criticism. 3. Postcolonialism and the arts. 4. Literature, Modern–20th century–History and criticism. 5. English literature–19th century–Influence. 6. Imperialism in popular culture. 7. Literature and society–English-speaking countries. I. Title.
PN98.P67H6 2012
809'.9113–dc23
011047844

Typeset by Deanta Global Publishing Services, Chennai, India
Printed and bound in Great Britain

Contents

Acknowledgments   vi

List of Figures   viii

Introduction: Neo-Victorianism and Improper Postcolonialisms   1

Chapter 1: Neo-Victorianism and "Ripperature": Alan Moore's *From Hell*   27

Chapter 2: Neo-Victorianism Down Under: Peter Carey's *Jack Maggs*   55

Chapter 3: Neo-Victorianism South of Nowhere: Margaret Atwood's *Alias Grace*   81

Chapter 4: "Far-Flung" Neo-Victorianism: Hong Kong and Jackie Chan's Neo-Victorian Films   113

Chapter 5: Neo-Victorianism and Science Fiction: "Steampunk"   141

Chapter 6: The Neo-Victorian-at-Sea: Toward a Global Memory of the Victorian   171

Notes   203

Bibliography   217

Index   235

Acknowledgments

This book has a long prehistory and I am grateful to all the people and institutions that have played a role in its conception and development that I may have omitted. This book was begun at Rutgers University under the guidance and supervision of Ed Cohen, Carolyn Williams and Marianne DeKoven. Together they taught me new ways to be a Victorianist and then encouraged me to turn towards the contemporary. I am grateful for the support and advice they offered long after the dissertation was finished. I am also grateful to my much-missed colleagues and graduate students in the English Department at Texas A&M University who helped me refine old ideas and travel new ground. In particular, I would like to thank Bob Griffin, Shona Jackson, Kate Kelly, Jimmie Killingsworth, David McWhirter and Paul Parrish. I would like to thank my wonderful colleagues in the English Department at Ursinus College; collectively they helped me create much-needed time and offered support and good cheer as this project neared completion. A special thank you needs to go to Joyce Lionarons who guided me through the final stages towards publication.

This book has benefited from its rehearsal at different conferences and venues: namely, the "Neo-Victorianism: The Politics and Aesthetics of Appropriation" conference at the University of Exeter; the "Fashioning the Neo-Victorian" conference at the University of Erlangen-Nuremberg; A.S.A.P. 2 at the University of Trier; and the New Modern British Studies Working Group at Texas A&M University. The Melbern G. Glasscock Center for Humanities Research at Texas A&M generously provided research funds for my chapter on Margaret Atwood and my fellowship there resulted in invaluable feedback from my colleagues. I am thankful for the camaraderie, the challenging questions and thoughtful suggestions from the audiences at all of these gatherings. In particular, I am grateful to Marie-Luise Kohlke, one of the many great people I have met as this book travelled – her comments have played an important role in shaping the final draft of this book.

Acknowledgments

I wish to thank Chris Staros and Chris Ross at Top Shelf Productions and Clara Yim at the *South China Morning Post* for providing me with the images that accompany this project. Special thanks must also go to Colleen Coalter and David Avital at Continuum for their belief in this project and patience in answering my every question – it has been a pleasure working with them.

Over the years, many friends have contributed engaging intellectual discussion, sound advice, scoldings and emotional support, often all at the same time. They are Kim Bartel, Amy Benson, Desirée Garcia, Chris Pizzino, Scott Maisano, Ilan Mitchell-Smith, Mike Rubenstein, Susan Tomlinson, Jessica Westerhold and Jenny Worley.

I owe an enormous debt to Deborah Barkun, Jane Elliott, Meredith Goldsmith, Stephanie Kerschbaum, Mary Ann O'Farrell and Susanna Throop. They were always ready to read large portions of the manuscript, make copious comments and perform meticulous editing; they shielded me from criticism and often from myself; they offered friendship, mentoring and kind counsel often over delicious dinners. They are the smartest women I know and inspire me daily to be a better scholar, teacher and colleague.

Finally, I must thank my sister, Helen Ho, and my parents for their love and unflagging support, especially when my work kept me from them. The biggest thank you is reserved for my husband, Nathan Bridgeman, who always knew that I could do this and to whom this book is dedicated.

Portions of Chapter 1 were published as "Post-Imperial Landscapes: 'psychogeography' and Englishness in Alan Moore's graphic novel: *From Hell: A Melodrama in Sixteen Parts*" in *Cultural Critique* (2006) 63, Spring, pp. 99–121. An earlier version of Chapter 2 appeared as "Peter Carey's *Jack Maggs* and the trauma of convictism" in *Antipodes* (2003) 17, 2, pp. 124–32.

List of Figures

FIGURE 1 "Queen Victoria statue splashed by red paint" by Chinese artist Pun Sing-lui, Victoria Park, Hong Kong (1996), 16 September, reproduced by permission of *South China Morning Post*. 2

FIGURE 2 "Gull and Thatcher's enterprise culture." *From Hell* (1999), 10, p. 20 © Alan Moore & Eddie Campbell. 28

FIGURE 3 "Gull in the twentieth century." *From Hell* (1999), 8, p. 40 © Alan Moore & Eddie Campbell. 30

FIGURE 4 "Queen Victoria as clip art." *From Hell* (1999), 2, p. 19 © Alan Moore & Eddie Campbell. 35

FIGURE 5 "Gull's map of London." *From Hell* (1999), 4, p. 19 © Alan Moore & Eddie Campbell. 46

FIGURE 6 "Saint Paul's Cathedral: picture postcard?" *From Hell* (1999), 4, p. 38 © (Alan Moore & Eddie Campbell. 51

Introduction

Neo-Victorianism and Improper Postcolonialisms

Every year in Hong Kong, pro-democracy demonstrations and memorials of the Tiananmen Square massacre are held in Victoria Park, the ex-colony's largest outdoor public gathering space. A bronze statue of Queen Victoria sitting on an ornate throne still dominates the landscape of the park, an anachronistic blip in the international image of the territory. Commissioned in 1887 for Victoria's Golden Jubilee to stand proudly in the city center, it was one of hundreds of statues raised around the British Empire from Malta to British Columbia to Cape Coast, Ghana. Around the world, statues of Queen Victoria served to legitimize the authority of the British Empire in visible, tangible ways, anchoring monumental sites of memory to individual, collective, and political identities.[1] Queen Victoria's presence in the territory has never been erased, even as Hong Kong achieved its complicated postcoloniality when it was returned to China in 1997 and symbolically signaled the end of the British Empire. In fact, whenever recent administrations needed a reminder of Hong Kong's colonial legacy as they built the territory's neo-colonial relationship with China, Queen Victoria's statue regained its prominence in the postcolonial landscape.

For example, in 1996, just before Hong Kong's reunification with China, Queen Victoria was "vandalized" by the mainland-trained performance artist and Hong Kong resident Pun Sing-Lui. In a powerful gesture of defiance and frustration, Pun covered the statue with several cans of red paint and proceeded to dent the monarch's nose with a hammer (see Fig. 1). He waited patiently for the press and the police to arrive and claimed his performance was a protest against the "dull, colonial culture" (Wan, 1996, p. 3) in Hong Kong before undergoing court-mandated psychological evaluation and imprisonment for twenty-eight days.

Significantly, the government interpreted Pun's act of memory as mental imbalance rather than as a legitimate objection to the quality of Hong Kong's postcolonial culture. Denounced by the public, the government and

FIGURE 1   Queen Victoria statue splashed by red paint. © South China Morning Post

art critics, Pun offered this rationale for his shocking performance in an interview with Mariana Wan in the *South China Morning Post*:

> I smashed this statue. The message is loud and clear: I am saying no to colonial culture. I do not hold anything against Queen Victoria personally. What I am against is the era the statue represents; an era of colonialism. A lot of people do not know why this statue is in the park. Or if they know they are not aware of its significance . . . In Hong Kong, nobody thinks hard on the significance of the statue of Queen Victoria. A lot of artists and people said they had fond feelings towards this statue; that as children, they had played under it. This I find very strange. I don't know whether that is due to the fact that Hong Kong has neglected its education on historical and cultural matters . . . A museum is a perfect place for it so that people, the future generations, can reflect on the history of Hong Kong. Not a park. (Wan, 1996, p. 15)

For Pun, "smashing" the statue constitutes an act of recovery, a chance to say "no to colonial culture" and to confront in the present all that Victoria stands for, namely, "an era of colonialism." He finds it "strange" that Hong Kong "artists and people . . . do not know . . ." or "are not aware" and do not "think hard" or, have *forgotten* what Victoria stands for. Lacking knowledge, rigor and a hermeneutics of suspicion, Hong Kong people have confused Victoria with childhood, a safe memory that equates Victoria – and one could argue the nineteenth century in general – with "fond feelings" that impede access to the nineteenth century as an "era of colonialism." However simple and childishly belligerent Pun's act of recovery is, his statement also reveals a desire to enable Hong Kong to recover *from* its colonial past and present naïveté. Although the present has "neglected its education on historical and cultural matters," Pun remains hopeful that the removal of the statue to a "museum" might help "future generations . . . reflect on the history of Hong Kong." Only by excising the memory of empire from public space and thus integrating it into historical, narrative time can people safely "reflect" on the past suggesting "future generations" that have integrated its colonial legacy or put it to rest. What Pun fails to recognize in his anticolonial statement, however, are the complexities in the narrative of recovery beyond the one he has imposed that progresses naturally from childish nostalgia to mature critical reflection. In the same interview, Pun also denied any symbolic significance behind his use of the color red and supported the return of Hong Kong to China. Thus, Pun misses the opportunity to address Hong Kong's unfinished legacy of imperialism, Victoria's obfuscation of China's imperial games, and the image of Hong Kong "artists and people... playing" under the statue as a different act of memory and recovery from his own: one that constitutes an underlying and under-represented desire to trouble the postcolonial or perhaps even pleasurably and "playfully" defer the possibility of a post-imperial identity to retain the benefits of colonial rule.

Pun's remodeling of Queen Victoria with her nose "out of joint" (Lee, 1996, p. 8) as the *South China Morning Post* gleefully announced, creates an appropriate image for the ways in which "the Victorian" uncannily and persistently reappears "out of joint" in a literary and popular culture with a markedly global reach. As such, Pun offers a particularly visible instance of the "neo-Victorian:" a term originally coined by Dana Shiller to describe a rapidly growing phenomenon in contemporary fiction that was "at once characteristic of postmodernism and imbued with a historicity reminiscent of the nineteenth-century novel" (Shiller, 1997, p. 538). Shiller was among the first to distinguish neo-Victorianism as an entrenched literary phenomenon beyond the domain of "historiographic metafiction" (Hutcheon, 1998a, p. 105), the genre in which neo-Victorianism's characteristics such as intertextuality and historicity have traditionally been discussed, or the recent "historical turn" (Keen, 2006, p. 167) in contemporary fiction, which details an unspecified and general interest in any past in the present. A. S. Byatt's Booker Prize-winning novel, *Possession* (1990), initially the most well-known and respected example of literary neo-Victorianism, has since been eclipsed by the popularity of the nineteenth century as a period of return in the present and the expansion of neo-Victorianism to other locations, fields and media. Representing a huge literary, cultural and academic industry, neo-Victorianism is now a term that links together the literary postmodernism of John Fowles' *The French Lieutenant's Woman* (1969) and the popularity of Michel Faber's scandalous serial epic *The Crimson Petal and The White* (2002), or the postauthentic aesthetics of the BBC "reality" series, *Victorian Farm* (Elliot, 2009) and the melodramatic Hollywood pastiche, *Sweeney Todd* (Burton, 2007). And, while critics have agreed that a certain meta-critical apparatus or self-reflexivity regarding the adaptation of the Victorians are requirements for a text to be considered neo-Victorian, setting it apart as "*more* than historical fiction set in the nineteenth century" (Heilmann and Llewellyn, 2010, p. 4), *Possession* sits comfortably alongside a range of other less conventional and more playful examples of the neo-Victorian such as online games like *Orphan Feast* (Robox Studios, 2007); web comics like Pab Sungenis's *The New Adventures of Queen Victoria* (2006 – present); graphic novels such as *Chester 5000 XYV* (Fink, 2011), an erotic steampunk/robot love story; role-playing

Introduction 5

games like *Space: 1889* (Chadwick, 1988); bands like The Tiger Lillies and Rasputina; and fashion trends from the popularity of the corset in contemporary fashion to steampunk "cosplay" conventions. As these disparate examples and versions of "the Victorian" suggest, regardless of the audibility of its appropriative faculties, neo-Victorianism is a deliberate misreading, reconstruction or staged return of the nineteenth century in and for the present across genres and media. The proliferation of neo-Victorian texts and the consolidation of neo-Victorianism into a legitimate field of studies, made evident online journal *Neo-Victorian Studies*, have made recent neo-Victorian scholars wary of the formation of a neo-Victorian canon governed by a similarity in recuperative impulses that results in an "aesthetics of the politically correct" (Gutleben, 2001, p. 11). Along the same lines, Eckart Voigts-Virchow has argued, a little tongue-in-cheek, that the hermeneutics of the subcultural, the popularity of queering the Victorian for example, has made neo-Victorian authors nostalgic for the Victorian mainstream (Voigts-Virchow, 2009, p. 122). However, the same wariness and urgency to address the "widest adaptive and appropriative impulses" (Heilmann and Llewellyn, 2010, p. 32) available in neo-Victorianism have prompted even wider and more varied study of the questions: why the Victorian? Why now?

In answer to these questions, I argue that "the Victorian" (after this no longer encased in scare quotes) has become a powerful shorthand for empire in the contemporary global imagination – so much so that Pun turns to the most visible symbol of Victoriana to express his hatred of the "era of colonialism." Regardless of the actual reality of history or the complexities of historiography, we, like Pun, remember or misremember the nineteenth century as the apex of the British imperial project. The overwhelming narrative told by Pun, neo-Victorian novels, popular culture and Victorian Studies is that the nineteenth century should be remembered as the "high noon of empire" (Gikandi, 1996, p. 190). I contend that the return to the Victorian in the present offers a highly visible, highly aestheticized code for confronting empire again and anew; it is a site within which the memory of empire and its surrounding discourses and strategies of representation can be replayed and played out. Pun's striking and specific "rewriting" of *the* icon of the British Empire complements the ever-growing number of neo-Victorian texts produced within and without the West concerned, however ambivalently, with the aftermath of the empire and its reappearance in processes of globalization. For the locations I explore in this book – post-imperial Britain, the former settler colonies of Australia and Canada, the "last" colony of Hong Kong and locations such as Japan and China that have been influenced by Western imperialism – the nineteenth-century British past cannot be thought of as separate from neo-imperial presents and futures. In terms of a recovery from that imperial past, neo-Victorianism offers those situated in various postcolonial moments and specific locations a powerful conceptual and aesthetic vocabulary for exploring the past – which, in turn, offers ways of coping with the temporal palimpsests of the present.

To the examples of neo-Victorianism I have listed above, therefore, can be added an equally concentrated number of postcolonial neo-Victorian examples. A line of influence can be traced from Jean Rhys's *Wide Sargasso Sea* (1966) to D. M. Thomas's 2000 novel, *Charlotte: The Final Journey of Jane Eyre* (1847), which audaciously rewrites the ending of *Jane Eyre*, claiming that Brontë "was an extraordinary liar" (Thomas, 2000, p. 118); Michael Redhill's novel, *Consolation*, long-listed for the 2007 Booker Prize, recovers the story of a British immigrant's arrival in 1850s Toronto and his daguerreotypes of the city as a balm for the tragedies of the urbanized present; recently, a Smithsonian museum put on a mid-career retrospective of British-Nigerian artist Yinka Shonibare, displaying his neo-Victorian tableaux in the medium of Dutch and Indonesian fabric sculptures; a dramatic cricket match stages the economic exploitation of an Indian village by the Raj in *Lagaan: Once Upon A Time in India* (Gowariker, 2001), a Bollywood musical. Beyond the confines of the former British Empire, neo-Victorianism seems entrenched in Japan according to the popularity of the *manga* collections, *Emma: A Victorian Romance* (Mori, 2002–8) and *Black Butler* (Toboso, 2007 – present), and the prevalence of the "Gothic Lolita" fashion phenomenon. Finally, *Princess Kaiulani* (Forby, 2009), a biopic of the last heir to the throne of Hawaii, makes explicit connections between her education in Victorian England and the island chain's colonization by the U.S. Thus far, the discussion of neo-Victorian production has been limited primarily to contemporary British literature and film as part of a larger conversation about Britain's post-imperial anxieties.[2] My book complicates existing critical work on neo-Victorianism by exploring its global popularity and asks the timely, often overlooked question: what new access to postcolonial experiences is gained when the Victorian goes around the world?

The "N-word" and the "V-word"

In general, the study of neo-Victorianism has been dominated by its literary resonances with the formal aesthetics and political aims of postmodernism, hence its subordination to "historiographic metafiction" and the genre's ability to disrupt teleology and readmit lost voices and texts. John Kucich and Dianne F. Sadoff's influential introduction to the volume of essays devoted to the "Victorian afterlife" in the present encapsulates the centrality of the nineteenth century to theorizing about postmodernism. Kucich and Sadoff use the term "post-Victorian" to describe postmodernism's overdetermined obsession with the Victorian age as a narcissistic mirror held up to reflect its own origins. Borrowing from Frederic Jameson, they cite the nineteenth century as a "crucial historical break" or "rupture" (Kucich and Sadoff, 2000, p. x) from which postmodernism triumphantly emerges.[3] Similarly, Tatjana Jukić describes the neo-Victorian as a means by which to chart the changes in postmodernism. She claims we have "twisted" our perception of the "second half of the nineteenth century" and its relationship to "story-telling" so as to "fit the current angle of postmodernist poetics, thus reflecting not only the Victorians, but also the internal growth of postmodernism itself" (Jukić, 2000, p. 88). Inherent in her discussion as well is the notion that the continual reappearance of the Victorian in postmodern literature is a refutation of postmodernism's proclamation of "the end of history." Following Jukić's argument, Cora Kaplan notes that the sheer number of neo-Victorian narratives indicates our constantly shifting relationship to history as a "conceptual monad, not so much lost as permanently restless and unsettled" (Kaplan, 2007, p. 3). Thus, as a genre so preoccupied with subverting temporality and so capable of disrupting the totalizing narratives of historical teleology, neo-Victorianism remains firmly embedded in the poetics and politics of postmodernism. Such readings have also generated an important critical vocabulary for neo-Victorianism: parody versus pastiche, for example, index the strength of a text's participation in neo-Victorianism; while simulacra and simulation form much of the genre's aesthetic economy. Without jettisoning these important postmodernist concerns, my book explores the restaging of the nineteenth century not only for consumption and as the moment of "rupture" or "origins" for postmodernism but as a means to rethink postcolonial politics and experience. Within the new context of postcolonialism I am proposing, neo-Victorianism can be viewed as a strategy with which to incorporate and work through persistent anxieties and uncertainties that emerge in the wake of the British Empire's dissolution. After all, while we may all participate in what Jameson calls the "whole world system of a present-day multinational capitalism" (Jameson, 1991, p. 37) that underpins postmodernism, for a great many of us, it is the experience of empire and after that informs our national, cultural and political identities.

Approaching neo-Victorianism as a global, Anglophone project, this book moves away from reading the returns to the nineteenth century as strictly an articulation of the internal logic and development of postmodernism. In many ways, I take up the challenge laid down by Kaplan in her book, *Victoriana: Histories, Fictions, Criticism* (2007), in which she refers to Jane Campion's 1993 film *The Piano* as an important example of "global Victoriana". (Kaplan, 2007, p. 10). Kaplan concludes with a reminder that neo-Victorianism "participat[es] in a much wider, transnational as well as national debate, reaching beyond the boundaries of Britain's former empire: a debate about historical memory and the direction of the political future in which we, as readers and citizens, do have a voice and a role to play" (ibid., p. 162). Kaplan is very interested in what she calls the "Empire at home" and neo-Victorianism's capability for examining the impact of empire on Britain but does not, other than her single chapter on Campion's film, move outward to explore other neo-Victorian sites of production. In some ways, my book provides a necessary corrective to the omission of the postcolonial from neo-Victorian scholarship. Situating neo-Victorianism within a postcolonial agenda, rather than a more conventional postmodern understanding of the loss of historicity, reveals how neo-Victorian narratives supplement and enhance postcolonial theory as a memorial practice at a time when our geopolitical conditions call for new ways of engaging with history.

Recent scholars interested in the afterlife of the Victorian in the present have used the terms "post-Victorian," "retro-Victorian" and "Victoriana."[4] Read through the lens of postmodernism, the prefix "neo" best carries the burden of neo-Victorianism's aesthetic and political functions. An anxiety about genre can be seen in discussions of whether the "neo" indicates true innovation in form and content or whether it is merely historical fiction, at best historical fiction plus.[5] Critics caution us to strike a balance between the sometimes uncritical pleasures of looking back to the Victorian age, the market forces involved in corralling those pleasures, and neo-Victorianism's political capacity to recuperate the suppressed voices and histories of the past.[6] For Ann Heilmann and Mark Llewellyn, the latest to address neo-Victorianism's scope and archive, the "neo" refers to a necessary "metafictional mode" (Heilmann and Llewellyn, 2010, p. 5); to be considered neo-Victorian, a text must add some new knowledge or understanding of either the Victorians themselves or how contemporary fiction adapts and appropriates the past, preferably both. They offer a comprehensive survey of neo-Victorianism as a means to explore our unfinished literary, thematic and ethical business with the nineteenth century and the nineteenth-century novel, using a constantly telescoping distance between "them" to think about and solve the problems of "us." Like Heilmann and Llewellyn, I would like to stress the semantic link that emerges between "neo-Victorianism" and other "neo's" like neo-Conservatism and neo-liberalism, for example, which involve political movements that do not simply look back to the past but reiterate and replay it in more diverse, complicated and troubling ways (ibid.). For my project, the term "neo-Victorian" also carries a different political charge because of the ability of the prefix "neo" to evoke current shifts and aggregations in the international dynamics of power. As the following chapters will make clear, manifold concerns about empire drive postcolonial neo-Victorianism into the new millennium; while neo-Victorian narratives in the late-twentieth-century exhibit a need to recover and recover from the atrocities of empire in the past, postmillennial examples of neo-Victorianism demonstrate an imperative to delineate neo-imperial and neo-colonial arrangements in a globalized present.

As much critical energy has been devoted to expanding the definition of the Victorian as crafting the complexities of the "neo." Each version of the Victorian told in contemporary fiction has been aided, in part, by the exciting and interdisciplinary trajectory of Victorian Studies and its agenda of canon-busting and the study of "Other Victorians" enabled by gender studies and postcolonial theory. That early neo-Victorian novels by Byatt and David Lodge tended to be set in academia or, like Fowles' novel, geared toward academic readers underscores the reliance of neo-Victorianism's content on academic writer such as Michel Foucault (1990)or Raymond Williams rereading nineteenth century culture and history as much as Victorian literature itself. Just as Victorian Studies has debated whether "Victorian" means periodization (the "long nineteenth century" versus the dates of Queen Victoria's reign) or a conceptual field, so too has neo-Victorian studies sought to push its own boundaries.[7] As Heilmann and Llewellyn caution, just as "not all narratives published between 1837 and 1901 are Victorian" (Heilmann and Llewellyn, 2010, p. 6), neither are all narratives set between 1837 and 1901 considered neo-Victorian. This allows them a generous amount of slippage, facilitating discussions of "neo-nineteenth century" (ibid., p. 29) texts featuring Saartje Baartman, the so-called "Hottentot Venus," for example, which inhabits the same temporal landscape as the jealously guarded, definitely not neo-Victorian, Jane Austen camp. While I am interested in novels published after 1990, treating *Possession* as a watershed text, others move backward and forward to examine less identifiable examples of neo-Victorianism: in *Victorians in the Rearview Mirror* (2007), Simon Joyce, for example, explores how Bloomsbury modernists looked back at the Victorians and Heilmann, in particular, has pushed for how the neo-forties novel might have its predecessors in modernist *and* neo-Victorian fiction.[8] The journal, *Neo-Victorian Studies*, solicits papers that interpret neo-Victorianism as widely and interdisciplinarily as possible and encourages submissions that are not "restricted to geographical British contexts or those of the British Empire and its one-time colonies." The journal welcomes essays "dealing with nineteenth-century Asian, African, North and South American contexts, among others."[9] While such endeavors are vital to the health of the field, they point to the ways in which an under-examined memory of empire encodes itself into the V-word of neo-Victorianism. While neo-Victorian studies interrogates what is gained when it re-evaluates or even jettisons the term "Victorian," blind spots occur over the colonizing potentials of the same terminology. When the Victorian stands in for empire, it also reveals how neo-Victorian studies might be seen as implicated in its own "Victorian" project to colonize *all* historical fiction set in the nineteenth century, regardless of geographical or cultural differences, for academic and nonacademic consumers. Just as neo-Victorian fiction engages in a meta-dialogue with its own appropriative impulses and strategies, a postcolonial approach can elicit a similar self-awareness within neo-Victorian scholarship.

Improper Postcolonialisms

In arguing that the Victorian functions as a metonym or code for the vestiges of empire "out of joint" in the present, I build on the work of critics like Anne McClintock, Simon Gikandi and Rey Chow, who all argue emphatically that colonialism has not yet ended and that the survival of colonialism in the decolonized present persists in the form of palpable continuities as well as ruptures. As Gikandi argues, colonialism continues as a "state of mind" and as an "undecideability" in the present that arises from the "inevitable conjuncture between the desire for decolonization and the reality of the colonial archive" (Gikandi, 1996, p. 2). Similarly, Rey Chow discusses the need for postcolonial politics to address the "ideological legacies" and the "cultural effects of colonialism" and to understand postcoloniality as "marked by events that may be technically finished but that can be fully understood only with consideration of the devastation they left behind" (Chow, 1998a, p. 151). Gikandi's emphasis on the psychological after-effects of colonialism and Chow's sensitivity to its "ideological" aftermath remind us that the neo-colonial "state of mind" has direct political consequences helping justify the exploitation of third world labor or military invasions. This book seeks to understand neo-Victorianism as an expression of such colonial hauntings in which the international reappearance of the nineteenth century works as a kind of traumatic recall. In postcolonial neo-Victorian texts, the legacy of empire asserts itself as an obstacle toward imagining a viable future so that we remain, as Derek Gregory has asserted, stuck in the "colonial present" (Gregory, 2004, p. 7). As many of the texts in my archive demonstrate, the stubborn memories and physical and political remnants of empire(s) continue to exist often in debilitating ways in the quotidian, supposedly decolonized present.

Postcolonial neo-Victorianism offers a rich repository of a global English heritage that implies the after-effects of colonial settlement, imperial policies, and the survival of "civilizing" institutions; however, it also acknowledges and reckons with colonial brutality and atrocities. Thus, neo-Victorianism contains at its heart a powerful ambivalence: its agenda includes "writing back" to empire – a reinterpretation of canonical Western texts and a critique of entrenched master narratives – as an act of revision, however, neo-Victorian texts simultaneously give voice to feelings of regression and return that manifest themselves in often noncontestatory, even celebratory evocations of the nineteenth century. Thus, at first glance, postcolonial neo-Victorian texts can appear mainstream in the hands of writers like Peter Carey and Margaret Atwood who subtly attend to subaltern experiences of empire and are supported by the apparatus of the Booker Prize, which maintains Britain as the imperial (literary) center. As centripetal narratives, however, Carey and Atwood's work, like many examples of postcolonial neo-Victorianism, explore how the dominant culture romanticizes, naturalizes, and authorizes narratives and structures of empire as it struggles to come to terms with their continuances in the present. The genre highlights the persistent problems of colonial relations but does not often erase them. Neo-Victorianism emphasizes these *improper* postcolonialisms defined by a present still haunted and seduced by colonial structures or privilege and suggests that decolonization may be a profound forgetting of the conditions of colonialism that preceded it.

As the chapters in this book illustrate, this ambivalence toward the nineteenth-century past is particularly well suited to exploring the muddy contours of settler postcolonialisms. Canada, and other postcolonial settler colonies like Australia, New Zealand, and South Africa, unsettles contemporary postcolonial theories that tend to privilege rather stark temporal and spatial understandings of the marginalized and the colonized. Doing the Victorian in ex-settler colonies therefore reveals other ways to put pressure on the "post" in postcolonialism. As a powerful memorial practice, neo-Victorianism can restage and dramatize white European complicity in the nineteenth century in and for the present. In particular, it frames the act of settlement as the subsequent propagation of an ideology of whiteness in the establishment of the foundational myths of nation. As an interrogative practice, neo-Victorian readings help open up the concept of "writing back to empire" to include more complex questions of race beyond the hypersignification of raced bodies: as Alfred J. López asks, "what happens to whiteness after empire" and "to what extent do white cultural norms or imperatives remain embedded in the postcolonial or postindependence state as part – acknowledged or not – of the colonial legacy" (López, 2005, p. 4)? In the case of Australia and Canada, official multiculturalism is one of the most important and ongoing experiments dealing with race relations in the aftermath of colonialism. Neo-Victorianism can help us address the drastically altered status of whiteness in the postcolonial world but more importantly, it allows us to see the residue of imperialism in current policies like multiculturalism, which are supposed to enable the Other and pave the way for an antiracist future, but which nonetheless serve as perpetual reminders of the racialized past.

However, the approach to neo-Victorianism I propose faces, as one of its drawbacks, the continued maintenance of Britain as its center. As Antoinette Burton has argued, even after the "imperial turn" (Burton, 2003, p. 2) across disciplines, the exceptionalism of the British Empire as *the* example of "empire, nation, race, colony and globe" (ibid., p. 20) remains. The danger of negotiating even critical returns to the *imperium* is that "Britain – and England within it – tends to remain the fixed referent, the a priori body upon which empire is inscribed" (ibid., p. 5). In order to subject this centrality to critique, I shift to the periphery and highlight the ways in which "England" problematically remains a persistent fantasy in global, Anglophone neo-Victorianism. In my discussion of neo-Victorian Australian texts like Peter Carey's *Jack Maggs* (1997), for example, "England" functions as a dogmatically "fixed referent" in the Australian imaginary emerging as a trauma for the contemporary Anglo-Australian demographic, and restricting its position with respect to the colonial past. A functioning map remodeled on neo-Victorian production would retain Britain as the "a priori body upon which empire is inscribed" (ibid.) but the relationship of Australia to England would be spatially recast, unsettling the metaphor of the land "down under." At stake are more nuanced understandings of nation in a globalized present: does "nation" in recent decades always have to be considered imperial? What political and imaginative work does its fiction of cohesion and unity still perform?

In this book, I offer a neo-Victorian remapping in which Australia, Canada and Hong Kong – all locations whose processes of decolonization are by no means complete and whose foundational myths are cemented in the nineteenth century – gain primacy over ostensibly "proper" postcolonial sites such as India and the Caribbean, locations that follow a separatist narrative from that of "Greater Britain." The improper locations addressed in this book reorient themselves imaginatively toward Britain so as to negotiate neo-colonial relationships: Canada, for example, recovers a memory of Britain to maneuver against a neo-colonial relationship with the U.S.; while Hong Kong, one of Britain's final colonies, occupies a wildly oscillating position in the neo-Victorian map as it disavows and yet is seduced by its British foundations and by continued articulations of colonial discourses that bespeak its rediscovered relationship to China. My consideration of neo-Victorian science fiction superimposes new technologies onto old geographies like China and Japan to explore the relationship between the imperial past and neo-imperial presents and futures. Guided by location, I construct a cartography of problematic postcolonialisms that decenters conventional understandings of the imperial world and emphasizes physical and psychical dislocations, unbounded and overlapping spaces, layered temporalities and unfinished experiences. In a postcolonial context, neo-Victorianism disorders progress-oriented narratives that lead naturally from decolonization to independence and provokes new cartographies of the postcolonial world.

Considered in the light of the cartography I offer, neo-Victorianism emphasizes the continued relevance of postcolonial theory at a particular moment when empire is evoked again as a way of making sense of globalization and to mediate the dominant fantasy that our geo-political situation has been a single-super power world. Seeking to understand the U.S. as a uni-power, some scholars have drawn analogies between the U.S. hegemony and the British Empire, tracing, in the discourse of U.S. power, the iconography and vocabulary of Victorian imperialism.[10] A similar, gradually increasing, set of analogies emerge in the wake of the massive leaps in China's modernization process, its territorial holdings and treatment of ethnic minorities, and the European Union's internal politics, economic might (and woes) and expansion eastward. Conversely, postcolonial theory functions as a reminder of past empires, as caution and conscience against discussions about globalization that portray it as ahistoric, flat and universal.[11] In some ways, the cartography of neo-Victorianism's ability to remind us of long-standing systems of power that operate in the present also offers a counterargument to globalization's often singular narrative. Quite simply, does "thinking globally," as part of the popular adage goes, require thinking about empire? It strikes me that the return to the Victorian shares with postcolonial studies an interest in maintaining the centrality of empire and its mechanisms not only in the definition and establishment of the postcolony, but also in the salutary and forgetful discourses surrounding globalization. Neo-Victorianism offers a corrective to the political blindness to the will of empire in the present that refutes postcolonial scholarship and the project of decolonization, both of which have accomplished so much in the recovery and reinstatement of local experiences and histories subsumed by empire. By fixing the Victorian to a memory of empire, neo-Victorianism creates a useful fiction: one that questions the idea of the emergence of postmodernism and transnational capitalism as the origins of globalization by reinscribing the stubborn concept of nation, thus avoiding what Loomba et al. have called the "eclipse" (Loomba et al., 2005, p. 8) or, the forgetting of, postcolonialism. Whether neo-Victorianism serves as a successful strategy to combat the dilemmas of globalization remains to be seen, and I explore these implications in the final chapter of this book.

For the locations, like Hong Kong, still disconnected from the utopian promise of the postcolonial state, the memory of the Victorian in the present begs the question: to what extent can we refute, deny or even expel everything that is colonial? Can it be excised from living memory and public space to the sanitized interior of the museum, as Pun so desires? Implicit in Pun's iconoclastic act is another question: can we expel colonialism's progenitor, the West? When is it acceptable and appropriate to recover from the colonial past? Is it only the "future generations" who get to recover? Who performs the recovery – the "artists" or the "people?" What can that recovery mean and what forms can it take beyond the narrow progression described by Pun? These are the themes that *Neo-Victorianism and the Memory of Empire* pursues.

Past Recovery: Methods of Remembering

Neo-Victorianism participates in a discourse of memory and recovery, and its textual strategies allow postcolonial cultures to make sense of a disjunctive moment in which the memory of empire continues to affect the present. Neo-Victorian novels tend to be populated by amnesiac, traumatized, mad and mourning characters, and many examples (*Jack Maggs*, *Alias Grace*,

Sarah Waters' *Affinity* (2002) and Julian Barnes's 2005 novel, *Arthur and George*, to name a few) revisit the murky origins of psychoanalysis as a discipline in the nineteenth century. While some critics have read these characters and novels as illustrative of postmodern challenges to the master narratives of history, I believe this conspicuous trend in neo-Victorianism marks a shift to new arguments about memory's relationship to nation or, the formations of collective and individual identities that make up the postcolonial state (of mind). My work intersects here with Kate Mitchell's reading of neo-Victorian fiction as "memory texts" that both "communicate memory – that which is already known through a variety of media about the Victoria era, for example – and offer themselves *as* memory" (Mitchell, 2010, p. 32).[12] Refining Mitchell's framework of cultural memory, I argue that the shift in neo-Victorianism from the rubric of history to the vocabulary of memory offers not just a rehearsal of postmodernism's political concerns about the detotalization of history but also an opportunity to theorize and represent more accurately the experience of postcolonialism. Thus, I consider melancholia, nostalgia and trauma as a social index of collective dis-ease in the present and not just extrapolations from psychoanalytic interpretations of individual disorders.

An urgent need to seek new ways of understanding and expand the vocabulary for expressing how the past impinges on the present has led to the eclipse of history by memory. We have entered into a situation where local memory – defined as dynamic, fluid, under constant revision and always in the now – is intimately linked to the articulation of what Andreas Huyssen calls "quality time" (Huyssen, 2003, p. 27) or, the privileging of alternate temporalities. This proliferation of mnemic strategies and practices responds to the processes of modernity and technological innovation, large-scale global movements from immigration and decolonization and profound historical traumas. Populations are torn or tested in such a way that memory becomes the driving force behind political, cultural and personal decisions. For such populations, neo-Victorian texts reflect these profound reorderings of memory in culture, and can manage the transmission of memories of empire, which is, in turn, an interrogation of their use-function in the present. At the same time, memory's perceived irrationality, unpredictability and power to rise unbidden in the present also speaks to an overwhelming sense that dis-ease, disorder and pathology are the regulating norms when considering the past and its relationship to the present. Despite – and because – of this negativing, the collapse in the distinction between history and memory points to new use-functions of memory in social, cultural and political spheres.

Rather than rehearse the history/memory debate, I acknowledge their entanglement and ask instead: why are neo-Victorian texts asking us to think about history as memory (and vice versa) and how do they theorize both? In my reading, neo-Victorianism's preoccupation with memory helps recast postcolonial theory as a memorial practice. Thus, neo-Victorianism highlights how postcolonial theory and fiction together generate new arrangements and rearrangements of temporality that register primarily through the operations – and failures – of memory. Each geographical location covered and therefore each nuance, experience and legislated version of postcolonialism discussed in this book seeks to articulate a new kind of temporality that can bring the colonial past and mentality into the present. Neo-Victorianism offers what postcolonial theory has long called for: a way of thinking about history differently, a way of making it accountable to the present – and a way of being with the past in the present.

While each chapter contains its own critical apparatus determined by its specific geographical location, the memorial practices and pathologies exhibited by each location are united by their status as "structure(s) of relation to the past" (Bal, 1999, p. xi), to use Mieke Bal's term. Bal argues that rather than debating the differences between "ordinary" and "traumatic" memories, between narrative memory and a radical resistance of memory to integration, between normal and pathological, it is more useful to distinguish between "varying moods and specific colorings of memory" (ibid.). For Bal, a given culture's proximity to and participation in an event "colors" its "structure of relation" to that event. I borrow Bal's idea to address the way in which the structure of relation to the nineteenth-century past in my project changes according to where one stands in relation to the serial collapse of empire. In other words, one's physical relationship to and investments in the "imperial turn" construct and influence one's method of remembering: as each chapter in my book moves outward from Britain toward the former outposts of empire, the shades, "moods" and "colorings of memory" change dramatically.

For example, as I have already noted, discussions of post-imperial Britain's structure of relation to the past tend to revolve around melancholia, a persistent diagnosis that Raymond Williams revealed in the conflict between the country and the city, past and present. More recently, this diagnosis has been renewed by Ian Baucom, who defines Britain's post-imperialism by drawing on Freud's theory of mourning and melancholia. The diagnosis is writ large in national terms: essentially a narcissistic identification with the "object-love," in this case, nation as defined by empire, melancholia sets in when the subject cannot relinquish the lost object or cannot find adequate compensation for its loss (Baucom, 1999, p. 84). Similarly, Paul Gilroy uses the term "postcolonial melancholia" to describe a post-imperial Britain unwilling and unable to face the loss of national greatness and prestige. Faced with a racially diverse population from the post-colonies as a daily reminder of the "hidden, shameful store of imperial horrors" (Gilroy, 2005, p. 94) and exacerbated by an unsettled economic and political climate (white) Britain has refused to work through its feelings of guilt and shame and has turned instead to active forgetfulness and silence punctuated by racist violence and debilitating nostalgia for a prior cohesion based on racial homogeneity. Gilroy calls for "healthier patterns" (ibid., p. 99) of mourning that must address the horrors and inequities of imperial and colonial history if Britain is to move toward multiculturalism and respect for diversity and difference. Neo-Victorianism, however, can be resistant to "healthier patterns" of recovery, opting sometimes to problematically embrace the pleasure of return, as I discuss in Chapter 1. Approaching methods of remembering as a structure of relation to the past allows for a critical examination – rather than a judgment – of modes like nostalgia, which can be organized, skillfully manipulated and constructed to forge continuities between individual identity and the collective. That neo-Victorianism in Britain peaked at the same time as Margaret Thatcher's radical modernization of Britain's post-imperial identity, shored up by the "heritage industry" and a growing culture of preservation suggests a collective desire to embrace the contradictions between critical memory and nostalgia in support of nationalist ideologies.

In Britain, the manipulation of national melancholia for political purposes is particularly visible and critically contested – part of its "memoro-politics," Ian Hacking's term for the politicization of memory based on claims of "forgotten pain" or "eroded memory" (Hacking, 1995, p. 213). The twinned concerns of this book – recovery *of* the past and recovery *from* the past – represent the entanglement of new technologies of memory and justice. Increasingly, the language of memory tends to be deployed for political reasons in the postcolonies. And, if this deployment privileges pathological memory – ranging from Derrida's "archive fever" to a host of theorists identifying the present's "wound culture" (Seltzer, 1998, p. 275) or "trauma culture" (Kaplan, 2005) – it is because the appeal to memory is central to ideas of reparation, political and economic compensation, the righting of injustice, the demand for witness and apology, all concerns in the postcolonial world. No wonder that the project of nation in the present should be focused around the rhetoric and the hope that psychoanalysis – even it is only in the guise of popular psychology – will enable the nation to move beyond itself, to "get over" or recover from a particular history or historical event in order to move forward to multiculturalism for example, or to a nonracist future.[13] The conventional usage of this language of memory and healing, however, does not acknowledge how individuals and groups in the habitus of the "post" still resist recovery and continue to invest in the colonial, even when these identities and structures are debilitating and often contradictory and static. The question of who, or which group, participates in recovery and controls its interpretation as integration, or even as forgetting, becomes particularly contentious in some of the locales discussed in this book.

Neo-Victorian authors satisfy both a postcolonial and postmodern agenda by offering their rewritings of the nineteenth century to fill the gaps of an incomplete archive whose lack of artifacts, traces and documents have created a situation of trauma in the present. They emphasize that the dominant structure of relation to the nineteenth century past in a global context *is* trauma to dramatize the politics of recovery, to disrupt the smoothness of the national narrative, and to insist on multiple readings of foundational myths and national origins.[14] Cathy Caruth defines trauma as an "event that . . . is experienced too soon, too unexpectedly, to be fully known and is therefore not available to consciousness until it imposes itself again, repeatedly, in the nightmares and repetitive actions of the survivors." (Caruth, 1996, p. 4). For Caruth, the crux of recovery lies in the "crisis of truth" that trauma produces. Essentially an impossibility of witnessing, trauma is a piece of the past blasted from history and narrative; it "cannot be placed within the schemes of prior knowledge" (Caruth, 1995, p. 153) and was not integrated into narrative memory when it occurred. It is a memory that "has no place," Caruth continues, "neither in the past, in which it was not fully experienced, nor in the present, in which its precise images and enactments are not fully understood" (ibid.). This "crisis of truth" (ibid., p. 6) calls into question popular notions of recovery, like the one articulated by Pun for example, and clinical notions of recovery that identify stages of transference, mourning and reconnection that eventually allows the patient to be reabsorbed into "commonality" or the collective.[15]

Trauma becomes a textual characteristic of neo-Victorianism as it describes a radical presence of the past in the present or, a piece of past experience that has been severed from narrative memory and returns in the form of flashbacks. Significantly for this project, neo-Victorianism's structure of address between a past Other and witnessing present articulates *postcolonial* trauma. As Caruth suggests, the act of witnessing trauma is not just listening to the Other of one's past self, but also "the story of the way in which one's own trauma is tied up with the trauma of another, the way in which trauma may lead, therefore, to the encounter with another, through the very possibility and surprise of listening to another's wound" (Caruth, 1996, p. 8). However, while Caruth's definition clears a space to listen to the trauma of postcolonial Others, she does not address the dangers of that narrative being co-opted or colonized by the listener, a problem of telling and retelling that neo-Victorianism stages in its self-reflexive textuality. Meanwhile, achieving a post-imperial identity also depends on the structure of trauma as postcolonialism in theory and practice seems haunted by a fear of repetition: that the return to a homeland or the developing national consciousness that constitutes the modernity of the "post" might offer forms of what Gikandi calls "imperial normativity" (Gikandi, 1996, p. 199) again. Neo-Victorianism offers a way of mediating this terror of repetition in its retelling of the past that is paradoxically also a "departure and a difference" (Caruth, 1995, p. 106).

Neo-Victorian texts deliberately evoke a "crisis of truth" in their exploration of the unfinished legacy of empire to explore the implications of "recovery:" defined as both a "getting better" and a necessary forgetting. In what ways does recovery in a neo-Victorian text mean an involuntary or even a deliberate retraumatizing of the present, issues inherent in what Dori Laub terms "bearing witness" (Laub, 1992, p. 57)? Or is it the imperative of the neo-Victorian text to simply affect change in the cultural conditions under which an event may be remembered or retold or in which silence might be condoned or when witnessing and listening may occur?

As I have demonstrated, the neo-Victorian project of recovering the memory of empire disrupts imperial chronology and emphasizes that postcolonialism is an entanglement of cartographic and temporal identities. On the one hand, neo-Victorianism stresses the uncomfortable critical position that the power of place is very much ingrained in the present. It asserts that there will always be a center; it might compete with or offer different models of being or it might unabashedly function like the old one. And so, old geographical understandings of center and periphery may still apply. On the other hand, neo-Victorianism also weakens the privileged position of remembering as recovery and stresses other narratives of mis-remembering for their communal power as an alternative to the power of place. These methods and strategies of remembering are deployed differently and are differently inflected by various ex-colonial sites, each with their own agenda of unsettling conventional understandings of recovery. In this book, I present a more expansive and inclusive account and theorization of how neo-Victorianism works in a global context that illuminates the question of usable and disposable pasts in the imagination of post-imperial futures.

Patel and Pun, or, A Chapter Review

A. S. Byatt's *Possession: A Romance* – an English novel written about English literature for English readers (and English majors) – is a fitting point of departure for a new approach to postcolonial neo-Victorianism. As the quest to possess the newly discovered love letters between Victorian poets Randolph Henry Ash and Christabel LaMotte becomes public, James Blackadder, the novel's stodgy English professor, reluctantly confronts English literature's global implications. In order to defend Britain's right to hold the letters in its national archive against greedy (and wealthier) American critics and buyers, Blackadder is forced to appear on a talk show hosted by the novel's only postcolonial character, Ms. Shushila Patel. Instructed to reduce Ash to a three minute sound-byte as "the sexiest property in town" (Byatt, 1990, p. 435), Blackadder flounders through lengthy descriptions of the importance of Ash to British literary study, gently informing Ms. Patel that "[y]ou can't understand the twentieth century without understanding him" (ibid., p. 433). However, Ms. Patel proves to be the wrong audience:

> Ms Patel looked politely baffled. She said, "I'm afraid I never heard of him until I got into this story. I did a literature course in my degree, but it was in modern American literature and post-colonial English. So tell me why we should still care about Randolph Henry Ash?" (ibid.)

Muddling through his justifications, Blackadder asks himself, quite poignantly if inappropriately, "why do the English always have to apologise?" (ibid.) Byatt dismisses Shushila Patel as the "politely baffled" reader of *Possession's* very English concerns, despite (and because of?) her more "worldly" education and a different experience of empire. However, she practices the more appropriate reading strategies for the "improper" postcolonialisms that this book's archive offers. Despite being "politely baffled," the iconoclasm of her question connects her with Pun. In addition, she embodies the skepticism and intellectual rigor that Pun believes is missing in the Hong Kong public playing in the shadow of Queen Victoria.

In *Possession*, the answer to Blackadder's question, "why do the English always have to apologise" – or, a desire to shed the colonial guilt inherent in the English memory of empire – is occluded by the romance of the novel and by Byatt's masterful ventriloquism and manipulation of Victorian and postmodern conventions. It is clear, however, that access to postcolonial experience must be mediated by different literatures – for example, the "modern American literature" and "post-colonial English" of Shushila Patel's education – and different phenomenologies of time and memory other than those lovingly celebrated in Byatt's novel.[16] Guided by these other literatures and locations, my archive for this book also acknowledges that the pains and pleasures of return are sought through less official, more seductive and illegitimate channels than canonical literature, like the performance art of Pun Sing-Lui, for example. As Pun's vandalism of the Queen Victoria statue demonstrates, neo-Victorianism privileges media that function as technologies of memory, re-enacting the past by actively re-making it for the present. And if, as I have argued, different geographical locations have different structures of relation to their nineteenth century pasts, it makes sense that neo-Victorianism's postcolonial concerns are enabled and enhanced by genres that are particularly suited to rearrangements of temporality and new cartographies. Science fiction and visual genres like film and graphic novels manipulate temporality and sequentiality, and are even responsible for generating and resisting expectations of what the Victorian *should* look like and thus govern how it should be remembered. Operating under different economies than the novel, the distribution of these genres, especially film, can transcend language, national boundaries or specific market niches in favor of communal memories of the nineteenth century via the visual. In addition, particular media and forms are linked to particular locations: neo-Victorian texts produced in Australia and Canada tend to be literary novels but, they are, more importantly, Booker Prize-winning or nominated novels, capable of competing on a global scale and bringing recognition to marginalized national literatures.[17] Such novels also depend on – and thus reflect the continued desire for – the structures of center and periphery as it is Britain that continues to validate postcolonial production and thus manage the definition of postcolonialism itself.[18] Foregrounding the proliferation of neo-Victorianism across location, genres, and media allows me to address the cultural, historical and political conditions under which the Victorian reappears and to be site-specific in my analysis of the imaginative functions it performs for the present.

Byatt's casual dismissal of an entire strand of postcolonial thought emphasizes that empire begins at home. Thus, I begin with neo-Victorian texts produced in Britain with a chapter that reveal occlusions from standard stories of Englishness. In Britain, neo-Victorianism interrogates the cultural policies of Margaret Thatcher and Tony Blair. Both administrations have given consistent attention to the crisis of post-imperial British identity: significantly, Thatcher recalled "Victorian values" as she reinvented national institutions, while Blair projected visions of a "New Britain" in tandem with his radical modernization or "rebranding" of the British state. In these chapters, I argue that neo-Victorianism becomes a rival engagement with the anxieties generated by the breakdown of traditional notions of Englishness that Thatcherism and Blairism also struggled to address. If, as I have argued, the British structure of relation to their nineteenth-century past is melancholic, then the strategies of circumventing but also indulging in melancholia have turned British neo-Victorianism into a battleground for voicing and maintaining a silence about a hegemonic Englishness. To track the anxieties about appropriate approaches to Britain's post-imperial identity, my first chapter addresses the phenomenon of "Ripperature," or fictionalized accounts of Jack the Ripper.

Alongside Thatcher and Blair's official rewritings of the national story was an increased production in "Ripperature." Remembering Jack the Ripper's brutal murders of at least five prostitutes in the East End in 1888 forms an unlikely avenue of return in contrast to Thatcher's recycling of "Victorian values," and forms a critique of how Englishness in the present is manipulated, packaged and sold, both at home and abroad. The first chapter focuses on three contemporary examples of Ripperature: Alan Moore's serialized graphic novel *From Hell: A Melodrama in Sixteen Parts* (1988–98); Iain Sinclair's "metaphysical detective novel" (Emilsson, 2002, p. 271) *White Chappell, Scarlet Tracings* (1987) and Peter Ackroyd's skewed tribute to the Whitechapel murders, *Dan Leno and the Limehouse Golem* (1994). All three authors use scenes of "psychogeography," a regenerative remapping of London according to ritual and violence, in order to create an alternate cartography to the "official" London made up of secularized, tourist landmarks signifying a stable and homogenized Englishness. While Sinclair and Moore, in particular, express anxiety about using Ripperature as a countermyth to the overly celebratory scopic and rhetorical mood of Thatcher's "Victorian values," Ackroyd's postmodern pastiche, on the other hand, elides the powerful feminist critiques of serial killings and Englishness in favor of masculinist and Anglophilic popular versions of the Ripper mythos. Despite its status as a compromised genre within neo-Victorianism as my reading of its gendered politics suggests, Ripperature challenges and resists the dominant discourse of heritage by portraying nostalgia, rather than Ripperature, as a form of violence that butchers the national past.

While Ripperature remains ambivalent about the heritage industry for its uncritical celebration of Englishness, Australian author Peter Carey attempts to break the lure of England that still endures in the contemporary Australian imagination. Chapter 2 examines Carey's third Australian neo-Victorian novel *Jack Maggs* (1997), a revision of Dickens's portrayal of the convict in *Great Expectations* (1861) and of Australia as England's antipodean other. *Jack Maggs* can be mistaken as nostalgia for a national past based on British racial and cultural homogeneity; however, I demonstrate that the novel responds to the way in which England, usually regarded as irrelevant or at opposite poles to Australia, is, in fact, still the trauma at the heart of efforts to define Australia as "home." The novel also intervenes in the unresolved self-hatred stemming from the double trauma of Australia's foundation: the stigma of convict ancestry and aboriginal dispossession. By telling the story of a transported convict's return "home" to London and of his subsequent mesmerism by the English author Tobias Oates (a character based on Dickens himself), the novel recasts the relationship of the colonized to the colonizer as an overwhelming, irrational need to embrace and identify with the aggressor. At the same time, the novel reflects on Carey's self conscious position as a white postcolonial author heavily promoted on the global Anglophone cultural markets, which informs the novel's ironic portrayal of Jack Maggs' position as a would-be Australian author. The novel's solution to the trauma of colonization is to privilege a model of prosperous and domestic citizenship that tentatively transcends "nation" and encompasses the many singularities of what it means to be Australian. In *Jack Maggs*, Carey's method of recovery detaches the Victorian from its moorings in empire and Englishness in order to bequeath a version of "old" Australia, reimagined as not "English," to those unable to recognize themselves in the "new" Australia of official multiculturalism.

Canada, a companion site to Australia, brings to the forefront neo-Victorianism's ability to recover and confront the vestiges of empire in post-imperial policies like multiculturalism. Written during a highly fractious Quebec Referendum that threatened to unravel Canada's status as a unified nation, Margaret Atwood's novel *Alias Grace* (1996) represents the culmination of her exploration of Anglo-Canadian domesticity. The novel fictionalizes the history of Grace Marks, "one of the most notorious Canadian women of the 1840's" (Atwood, 1996, p. 461), imprisoned for murdering her English employer and his mistress. Grace's supposed amnesia about the murders and her subsequent diagnosis of "double consciousness" (ibid., p. 433), the Victorian precursor to multiple personality disorder, is used by Atwood to pathologize, in order to critique, the rhetoric of multiculturalism, the perceived break up of Canada, and the pressure that bordering the U.S. puts on Canadian identity. In this chapter, I argue, Atwood diagnoses Anglo-Canadian settler postcolonialism as haunted by white cultural norms, which play out in the racialization of Grace Marks' Irishness and in the deliberate absence of race (rather than ethnicity) in the novel. By making clear the politics of Grace's victimhood, *Alias Grace* deconstructs white Anglo-Canada as a power bloc and presents whiteness as historically and culturally determined rather than fixed. Atwood's version of the Victorian recovers a history of how Anglo-Canadian foundational myths and its contemporary identity crises are defined by what Richard Dyer has called "the invisibility of whiteness" (Dyer, 1997, p. 3). The implications of whiteness within Canadian multiculturalism revealed by Atwood's neo-Victorian project address the denials of the multiplicities within Canada's "post"-colonialism that have yet to be worked through.

In Chapter 4, I shift my attention to Hong Kong, now a "special administrative region" of China, and examine how the memory of the Victorian can be employed in addressing neo-colonial anxieties inherent in the asymmetrical configurations of power the ex-colony continues to face. Neo-Victorian production from and about Hong Kong almost exclusively recovers the Opium Wars as the foundational story of Hong Kong; dwarfed by these competing imperial narratives, "Hong Kong" frequently disappears as a subject in its own right.[19] This chapter focuses on the global/local figure of Jackie Chan who, like Pun, provides a comic and anarchic reversal to the Opium narrative in his neo-Victorian movies: *Project A* (1984); *Shanghai Noon* (2001); its sequel, *Shanghai Knights* (2003). Chan's popularity as an action star makes Hong Kong's "improper" postcolonialism palpable for Western and overseas Chinese audiences in ways that literature cannot. Drawing on Rey Chow's concept of "portability" (Chow, 1993, p. 176), her extended metaphor for the articulation of a positive, postcolonial identity for Hong Kong, I argue that Chan's movies readdress Hong Kong's history as a significant *entrepôt* for the largest migration of Chinese overseas and can simultaneously address the traumatic exodus from Hong Kong in the years leading up to reunification with China. As a postcolonial performer on the global stage, the iconic and "portable" Jackie Chan provides a way for Hong Kong to recover a memory or narrative of its own origins outside of its triangulated relationship with Britain and China and settle its anxieties about the Chinese diaspora. Chan's global circulation and thus the "portability" of the memory of Hong Kong establishes a concept of Chineseness (rather than Englishness, in this case) disinterred from myths of homeland and of Hong Kong as a "home" paradoxically based on continual movement and states of transit. Hong Kong generated colonial discourses well into the late-twentieth century only to be enfolded back into an ongoing Chinese imperial narrative; Jackie Chan's use of the Victorian as a memorial practice allows us to see more clearly Hong Kong's situation *between* empires.

The implicit movement toward the U.S. and China as the new imperial centers in the previous chapters suggests that neo-Victorianism can be particularly effective in exploring alternate histories and geographies of empire. Using Jackie Chan's 2004 multicultural adaptation of Jules Vernes' *Around the World in 80 Days* (1873) as an introduction to Chapter 5, I explore examples of neo-Victorian science fiction, especially "steampunk," an offshoot of cyberpunk in which technological advances of the present are projected backward into the nineteenth century. Steampunk's strengths lie in its reimagination of the British Empire within neo-imperial systems and flows, structures and agendas, and its ability to reflect anxieties about contemporary geographies of power. The study of steampunk also enhances neo-Victorianism's ability to trouble the cartography of empire because its rearrangement of time *and* space privileges competing industrial and technological center to Britain, such as China and Japan, examining them as spaces of anxiety. Therefore, in this chapter, I re-evaluate two canonical examples of neo-Victorian science fiction, *The Difference Engine* (1991) by William Gibson and Bruce Sterling and *The Diamond Age or, A Young Lady's Illustrated Primer* (1995) by Neal Stephenson, and examine the neo-"Victorientalist" anxieties manifested by their imagined geographies. Finally, I turn to Otomo Katsuhiro's *anime* film, *Steamboy* (2004), as Japan's ambivalent relationship to Western technology complicates and revises the "Victorientalism" in its Western predecessors. Via steampunk, I examine how race is entangled with technology and how places and people are understood insofar as they correspond to an imagined geography of development centered on an idealized Victorian or Europeanized past. Neo-Victorianism's partnership with steampunk, I argue, allows us to connect the imperial project from the Victorian past with the potential neo-empires of the present and future.

My book concludes by examining a sea change in postmillennial neo-Victorian fiction. In the final chapter, I explore the "neo-Victorian-at-sea," my term for the recent emergence of neo-Victorian texts, such as Matthew Kneale's *English Passengers* (2000) and Amitav Ghosh's *Sea of Poppies* (2008), that are based on the sea voyage rather than the narratives of foundation and settlement of conventional neo-Victorian texts. The enclosure of the ship and the routes and rhythms of sail create new contact zones with the Victorian that significantly revise the structures of relation to the past. Drawing on Gilroy's *The Black Atlantic* (1993), I read the neo-Victorian-at-sea as an intervention in conventional neo-Victorianism's territorialism and status as national literature. Instead, the shift toward the ocean establishes a global memory of the Victorian attuned to transnationality and globalization. The neo-Victorian-at-sea reframes British imperialism as a fluid and shifting political space freeing the genre from the referent of Britain. Without Britain as an anchor, however, the neo-Victorian-at-sea presents us with an unbounded globality that offers a rejuvenation of the field but also threatens to unravel the genre itself. I explore new directions for neo-Victorianism in David Mitchell's *Cloud Atlas* (2004) and China Miéville's *The Scar* (2002), the second volume of his Bas-Lag trilogy. While these novels depart significantly from generic norms, they nonetheless adhere to neo-Victorian tropes. Mitchell and Miéville's turn to the neo-Victorian and the sea demonstrates that the future of neo-Victorian studies might lie in the attempt to interrogate, if not eliminate, its links to nation and Britain, in particular, so as to retain the genre's potential to reveal colonial relations in a globalized, neo-imperial world and to search for commonalities beyond those defined by center/periphery models and economies.

Reading neo-Victorianism as part of a global politics rather than a "pathology" of memory by which history is occluded, my book legitimizes and values the ways in which the Victorian is consistently misread, misremembered, stereotyped and forcefully adapted to give expression to desires for identification, consolation, compensation and reparation in the present. By displaying a range of relationships to the colonial past in high and low forms, I argue that neo-Victorianism allows the present to imaginatively confront empire again and weigh the consequences of working through that past – or not – in locations and identities that cannot yet be called postcolonial in the interests of a post-imperial future. My approach calls for a need to complicate the anarchic and creative acts of recovery made by cultural writers like Pun. At the same time, I want to trouble the knowledge of readers like Shushila Patel, a product of empire and well-versed in postcolonial theory; and to include Blackadder, the apologist whose sensitivity to the Victorian lends him a renewed relevance in the present. For this crowded stage of readers, ethical re-engagements with the nineteenth century become an imperative for the recovery of "future generations," however inconsistent or difficult. As postcolonial writers continue to "play" under the sign of Victoria, the meaning of original events and their significance for the present can be changed and the past can be reconfigured in order to refigure the future.

Chapter 1

Neo-Victorianism and "Ripperature": Alan Moore's *From Hell*

In the graphic novel *From Hell: A Melodrama in Sixteen Parts* (1988–98), Alan Moore devotes an entire chapter to Jack the Ripper's final masterpiece, the violent mutilation of Mary Jeanette Kelly. In Moore's version, Sir William Gull, Royal Physician in Extraordinary to Queen Victoria is identified as the Ripper and Kelly's death marks the zenith of Gull's madness and fulfillment of his mythological beliefs.[1] Eddie Campbell's black and white illustrations offer primarily abstract close-ups of a knife hitting arteries, organs, and flesh, and of Gull lovingly arranging Kelly's body into the chaos that was captured in the infamous crime scene photographs of what was presumably Kelly's corpse. The energy required to kill Kelly causes the boundaries of time to dissolve: Gull hallucinates about his days as a young surgeon performing an autopsy in an operating theater, but also forward in time to the present as his exertions cause him to burst into the twentieth century. In an ecstatic hallucinatory state, Gull suddenly finds himself triumphantly brandishing a scalpel in the middle of a contemporary open-walled office (see Fig. 2). This scene of the 1880s bleeding into the "enterprise culture" of the 1980s offers an example of Moore's explicit use of Jack the Ripper to comment on the present's relationship to the past. Moreover, it illustrates how the graphic novel and its ability to hold text and image, past and present, in critical tension becomes a privileged form to address the potentialities and anxieties in the shifts in temporality that neo-Victorianism requires.

In this scene, Gull accuses the workers around him of being "numbed" by the "shimmering numbers and . . . lights" of the twentieth century. "Think not to be inured to history," he announces, "its black root succours you. It is INSIDE you. Are you asleep to it, that cannot feel its breath upon your neck, not see what soaks its cuffs? See me! Wake up and look upon me! I am come amongst you. I am with you always!" As Gull remains invisible to the present, he delivers his final condemnation: "You are the sum of all

FIGURE 2 Gull and Thatcher's enterprise culture. *From Hell* © Alan Moore & Eddie Campbell

preceding you, yet you seem indifferent to yourselves. A culture grown disinterested even in its own abysmal wounds" (Moore and Campbell 1999, 10: p. 2).[2] Gull accuses the twentieth century not only of its loss of historical memory, but also of the tendency in celebrations of the national past to gloss over the dark spots of the Whitechapel murders or Britain's imperial history. Desensitized by the "shimmering numbers . . . and lights," the office workers take no notice as Gull hugs Kelly's broken body to himself.

Emblematic of neo-Victorianism's agenda, the nineteenth century depicted in *From Hell* deliberately intervenes in celebratory misreadings of the Victorian as seen in heritage films and in the recuperative fantasy of A. S. Byatt's Booker Prize-winning novel, *Possession* (1990). The aristocratic Gull's "work" on East End prostitutes articulates his own sense of himself as an apocalyptic theorist while Campbell's graphics of the twentieth century mirror Margaret Thatcher's recovery of the "Victorian values" of thrift, a heavy work ethic, morality and capitalism at the same time that she restructured the economics of the welfare state (see Fig. 3).[3] Moore and Campbell create a nineteenth-century nightmare born out of the values admired by "emininent neo-Victorians" such as Thatcher and neo-Conservative historians like Gertrude Himmelfarb. If Moore launches his criticism of Thatcherism on the grounds of Ripperature – fictionalized accounts of the Whitechapel murders and Jack the Ripper – it is because of the genre's ability to strike a delicate balance between heritage, as it is often packaged, and its potential to retain a catalog of hypocrisy, misogyny, violence, poverty and prurience often excised from the national past.

From Hell began its serial run in 1988 to mark the centenary of the Whitechapel murders: the series ended in 1996 and the second appendix "The Dance of the Gull Catchers" was not released until 1998. The series was gathered into its current book form in 1999 to coincide conspicuously with Britain's lackluster millennium celebrations. With the inclusion of the second appendix, the novel looks back to the Thatcher administration and ahead to that of Tony Blair's New Labor. Like Thatcher, Blair attempted to "rebrand" Britain from its global reputation as a "backwards-looking place, an old country living off its capital" (Leonard, 1997, p. 17) to a "young country" and a "Creative Britain," two of Blair's terms for Britain's general renewal. Blair's policy was one of what critics have described as "retrolution" or, "disguising the future as the past in order to make it palatable" (Blake, 1988, p. 144). Jack the Ripper speaks both for and against Blairite cultural policies. On the one hand, he epitomizes modernity: as Moore has theorized in *From Hell's* first appendix, "the idea that the 1880s embody the essence of the twentieth century, along with the attendant notion that the Whitechapel murders embody the essence of the 1880s, is central to *From Hell*" (Moore and Campbell 1999, I: p. 14). On the other hand, he can be included in "Cool Britannia," Blair's awkward phrase for the cultural rejuvenation of his New Britain, because Jack the Ripper is capable of branding Britain both at home and in the global marketplace. However, the Ripper also appears as an English hero opposed to modernization and multiculturalism, part of English heritage and evidence of what Patrick Wright has described as "living in an old country" (Wright, 1985, p. 2). As an unconventional form of neo-Victorianism, I argue, Ripperature interacts with and intervenes in the cultural policies of Thatcher and Blair, tracing anxieties and confusion over the breakdown of traditional notions of Englishness that those policies hoped to address. Jack the Ripper's survival past the millennium, in particular in the movie version of *From Hell* (2001), addresses the uneasy

FIGURE 3 Gull in the twentieth century. *From Hell* © Alan Moore & Eddie Campbell

tension between Englishness as an ethnicity under siege and the supposedly more inclusive, multicultural, but equally problematic "British" identity. The co-optation of *From Hell* by Hollywood requires us to think about global neo-Victorianism or, the global dissemination of Jack the Ripper in service of Britain's ideological needs, and to consider the forces shaping Britishness within that global context.

From Hell began serialization within a larger context of Ripperature such as Iain Sinclair's *White Chappell, Scarlet Tracings* (1987), an experimental, melancholic narrative that telescopes between Thatcherite London and a surreal fictionalization of Gull's life. Moore shares with Sinclair an interest in Stephen Knight's "Final Solution," the subtitle of Knight's book, which advanced the theory of a vast conspiracy connecting the Duke of Clarence; Walter Sickert, the painter; Royal Physician, Dr William Withy Gull; and his coachman and accomplice, Netley. Moore and Sinclair's work also keep company with Peter Ackroyd's *Dan Leno and the Limehouse Golem* (1994), a novel that references without representing the Whitechapel murders, but nonetheless has been adopted by fans into the Ripperature canon.[4] Although *From Hell* provokes more interest and discussion as a neo-Victorian text, I will also treat the triumvirate of Moore, Sinclair and Ackroyd as part of a proliferation of Ripperature and "Ripperology," or theories about Jack the Ripper's identity, that appeared at the same time as the twinned discourses of Thatcherism and Blairism, both of which attempted to recapture, defend and perform Britain's centrality in the world and Englishness on the home-front. The Whitechapel murders are a contested site in recent British cultural discourse from postmodern novelists to academic feminists. For example, Judith Walkowitz's influential article, "Jack the Ripper and the Myth of Male Violence" was published in *Feminist Studies* in 1982 and her book length study of urban violence against women, *City of Dreadful Delight*, was published in 1992. Jane Caputi's *The Age of Sex Crime* (1987) addresses copycats of Jack the Ripper throughout the history of serial murder and his subsequent reputation as the "father" of "modern sex crime" (Caputi, 1987, p. 4). There was also a particular density of less critical Ripper narratives and artifacts, which included movies; television documentaries; souvenirs; and memorabilia in the form of commemorative Jack the Ripper t-shirts, keychains, mugs and tea towels.[5] The arc of Ripperature's career, I argue, mirrors the increased attention to heritage display and practices in Britain that generated a fierce debate over what gets to count as heritage and contestation over the meaning of continuity and belonging. This concentrated moment of Ripperature appears when Englishness, gender and whiteness were visibly attached to heritage, what

Stuart Hall has called "*the* Heritage" undeniably constructed for *someone*: "for those who 'belong' – a society which is imagined as, in broad terms, culturally homogenous and unified" (Hall, 2005, p. 26). Considered as heritage work, Ripperature in the 1980s can be remarkably blind to the transformations of Englishness or what neo-Victorianism has the potential to recover. It is a form of neo-Victorianism that desires to be divorced from empire and other accusations made against the memory of British heritage itself, and yet, unable to escape collusion with the forces of contemporary capitalism represented by the heritage industry.

As a national character, Jack the Ripper was resurrected at a period when, according to Stuart Ward, "ideas about British character... became difficult to sustain as the external props of the imperial world was progressively weakened" (Ward, 2001, p. 12). Today, Jack the Ripper is undeniably English, entrenched as part of British heritage: on a drink coaster set depicting things and places English that I came across, Jack the Ripper was the first in a series that includes Windsor Castle, Henry VIII, Edinburgh Castle, William Shakespeare, Winston Churchill and Sherlock Holmes. In their original moment, however, the Whitechapel murders were a colonial monad and, therefore, potentially available for critique and rescue in the postcolonial present. Those suspected of being the Ripper ranged from a Jewish butcher, German body snatchers, a Malay sailor and other foreigners excluded from normal conceptions of Englishness. In fact, the editor of the *East London Observer* noted, "it was repeatedly asserted that no Englishman could have perpetrated such a horrible crime..." (1888). In his coverage of sex crime and the nineteenth-century media, Christopher Frayling implies that by attempting to understand and market the Ripper within the context of a media tradition that employed mainly Gothic conventions, the late-Victorian media had actually created a distinctly masculine and English character. "Criminologists," he continues, "may write of *Jack l'Eventreur*, or *Giacomo-lo-Squarciatore*, but [the Ripper] only makes sense in an English setting, in the culture which produced the Mysteries of London, Sherlock Holmes... and Dr. Jekyll and Mr. Hyde..." (Frayling, 1986, p. 206). Thus, Jack the Ripper can be read as a specifically English fantasy absorbed over the centuries into the contemporary attention to what Raphael Samuel has called "island stories" (Samuel, 1999, p. xi), more diminutive, national narratives that ostensibly no longer have empire as their reference point. By the Ripper centenary in 1988, when *From Hell* began, Britons and tourists alike were eager to celebrate the Whitechapel murders and to claim Jack the Ripper as an Englishman. In this chapter, I claim Ripperature and the Ripper mythos as a neo-Victorian discourse, one that invents and contributes to a post-imperial fantasy of deviant, daring, and heroic Englishness, and one that occludes both the memory of empire and the feminist readings of the Whitechapel murders.

Ripperature and Gender: Margaret Thatcher's "Queenliness"

The 1980s marked a surge in feminist readings of the Whitechapel murders against the glorification of misogynist sex crime in the cult of the serial killer. Judith Walkowitz's work, for example, has been instrumental in pointing out that the continual invocation of the Ripper myth has justified and increased the violence against women in the metropolis. At the same time, she unraveled the competing discourses, narratives and genres that structure both the Whitechapel murders and our contemporary view of Victorian femininity and sexuality. Serial killing is not, as Caputi emphatically asserts, inexplicable, mysterious, or part of some "explosion . . . of extrinsic evil" but rather, a "logical step in the procession of patriarchal roles, values, needs and rule of force" (Caputi, 1987, p. 3). It is almost impossible for recent work, historical or fictional, to ignore the misogynistic implications of the Whitechapel murders since the publication of such feminist texts in the 1980s. What feminist Ripperology has done, as Walkowitz has shown, is to "exorcize that ghost from women's consciousness, by historicizing Jack the Ripper." Only by "retuning to the scene of the crimes and investigating how the story of Jack the Ripper was constructed out of the fissures and tensions of class, gender, and ethnic relations in 1888" (Walkowitz, 1982, p. 544) can the myth be exposed. These feminist readings contribute to the redefinition of Englishness: if we can consider Jack the Ripper as one articulation of the myth of the free-born Englishman, then he renders unimaginable, in the most distressing ways, the liberties of the free-born Englishwoman. However, as Moore's gender anxious text demonstrates, by pitting Jack the Ripper, a potent symbol of violent misogyny against Margaret Thatcher, the most powerful woman in British politics, any countermovement that engages Thatcher on the ground of gender are rendered problematic at best, and misogynistic at the very worst.

According to Marina Warner's study of power, allegory and the female form, it was sometimes necessary to point out to British children that Margaret Thatcher and the queen were not the same person (Warner, 1985, p. 44). The conflation of femininity, royal pomp and circumstance, ritual and symbolism with real political power has lent Margaret Thatcher a certain "queenliness" (ibid.) that links her bodily to the nation. However, it seems apt to ask: with which queen – Elizabeth II or Victoria – is Margaret Thatcher confused with? Even without her misreading of the Victorian in her elaboration of "Victorian values," Thatcher's similarity to Queen Victoria is undeniable: both women occupied multiple and conflicting positions on the scales of femininity and political power. Both women possessed the masculine attributes of military power and the authority of the state and simultaneously embodied the maternal and fulfilled the demands of domesticity. Both women oversaw – although in very different terms – Britain's imperial height and demise. The discursive power Heather Nunn attributes to Thatcher – her "bellicose leadership," which "upheld an aggressively phallic economy of control," and her femininity, which was a "potential point of excess of collapse of that systematic control and order" (Nunn, 2002, p. 18) – reproduces almost exactly Adrienne Munich's description of Queen Victoria's "secrets."[6] Ripperature's tendency to play with images of female power dramatizes the tension involved in launching an attack on Thatcher in any gendered terms: can there be a critical stance taken against the role of women in relation to the power of the state that does not lapse into antifeminist stereotyping and aggression or portraying women as mere victims?[7]

From Hell settles on Gull as the sole killer, acting on orders from Queen Victoria to quietly and effectively silence the scandal of Prince Eddy's secret marriage to Annie Crook. Moore's Queen Victoria is vengeful and threatened, a paste-board figure that authorizes Gull to remove the "four whores of the apocalypse" (Moore and Campbell 1999, 3, p.15) who have dared to blackmail the Crown for the measly sum of £10. In Moore's version, the five Ripper victims were not chosen at random but were rather a systematic elimination of Annie's unfortunate friends. Unable to call Gull back once the order has been issued, Victoria helplessly submits to the brutality of the murders, which escalate with Gull's increasing insanity. Like Pun's vandalism of the Queen Victoria statue, Campbell undoes the romance of Victoria by reducing her to an iconic figure: lacking in animation, shrouded in cross-hatching, she exists merely as clip art (see Fig. 4).

Instead, Victoria is represented by a network of Freemasons, thus reducing male power to secret trials and courts, role-playing and games, and parodies the kind of male-bonding and camaraderie seen in the "post-heritage" films like *The Full Monty* (Cattaneo, 1997) or *Trainspotting* (Boyle, 1996) that explore the redefinition of traditional masculinity after the decline of heavy industry under Thatcher.[8] The attention to male bonding in Ripperature mirrors the phenomenon of the "New Lad" in the 1990s and is part of a highly scripted masculinity with an emphasis on heterosexuality, hedonism

FIGURE 4 Queen Victoria as clip art. *From Hell* © Alan Moore & Eddie Campbell

and sexism.[9] Alison Light argues that changes in the emotional and ideological understanding of sexuality and feminism in postwar Britain created a "realign[ment] of sexual identities which was part of a redefinition of Englishness" (Light, 1991, p. 8). While this "realignment" certainly worked in Thatcher's favor, it also underscores the perceived weakness of masculine power and the fear that post-imperial identity would continue to be apologetic, inclusive and full of empathy – in other words, feminized. *From Hell* offers a reading of the sustained interest in Jack the Ripper in contemporary British culture as a backlash against this feminization of Englishness and English politics that the Victoria-as-Thatcher allegory represents.

Iain Sinclair takes up the question of masculinity and female power in more problematic ways in *White Chappell, Scarlet Tracings*. Sinclair's gang of book dealers offer a snapshot of post-imperial masculinity: "Iain Sinclair," the narrator, who "thought of himself as the Late Watson" (Sinclair, 1987, p. 15) rather than the more heroic or memorable Holmes; Jamie, or "the Old Pretender" who had "plenty of relatives in decayed mansions, inhabited by domestic animals and uncontrolled vermin" (ibid., p. 13); Dryfield, whose name is recycled from the archives of the Whitechapel Library, and finally Nicholas Lane, wracked by violent bouts of "copious vomiting" that leaves him emaciated "like a cancer inherited from a centuries old act, now flowering" (ibid., p. 41), who is laden with the physical effects of his companions" more psychical pain. Obsessed with Ripperology, they believe that the murders hold divinatory and prophetic powers that can re-enchant the present. Trafficking equally in books and drugs, the book dealers operate in the "bleak days of enterprise zone capitalism" (ibid.) in the fringe economy outside of the norms and confines of "enterprise culture." Involved in shady, unethical practices, the men are deeply un-nostalgic for national treasures, ready to ship them off to American buyers, a far cry from the stewardship of the National Trust. Sinclair portrays post-imperial masculinity as exhausted, alienated and under siege, drastically revising the "princes of industry" (quoted in Corner and Harvey, 1991, p. 7) championed by Thatcher. However, an insidious nostalgia pervades the novel in an underlying desire to return to a more authentic masculinity located in the past and represented by the fictionalization of Gull's life.

To the book dealers, Ripperature becomes a rival conspiracy to match Thatcher's manipulation of heritage. It is all consuming, an unwavering commitment to a crime whose solution, like London's labyrinth, can only be glimpsed but not solved. The letters of the names of the Ripper's victims make a recognizable "sentence" that hints at, but cannot provide, meaning: "Mary Ann Nichols, Annie Chapman, Elizabeth Stride, Catherine Eddowes, Marie Jeanette Kelly. MANACESCEMJK. MANAC. ES.CEM. JK. MANAC ES CEM, JK" (Sinclair, 1987, p. 51). As Sinclair, the narrator, asks, "But what does it matter? This version is far more fun than the so-called truth . . ." (ibid., p. 66). However, this kind of postmodern play with "truth" violates the historical content of the Whitechapel murders feminists scholars like Walkowitz and Caputi are trying to recover. Focusing on the "fun" of Ripperology means that *White Chappell, Scarlet Tracings* tends to mythologize, rather than historicize, the Ripper victims. Jack the Ripper exacerbates the conundrum faced by post-imperial (white) masculinity: who is the one to identify with, the white male serial killer or the women, lower classes and the colonial other?[10]

There are very few female characters that appear in the novel's present to counteract the misogyny described in the novel's nineteenth-century past. Rather, it is eerily repeated in the way female characters are often exotic dancers hired by Joblard to compliment his bizarre experiments in time travel. Instead, Sinclair offers the transvestite figure of Gull, cross-dressed as his wife, Lady Gull, in a deliberate echo of Margaret Thatcher. S/he is the only representation of female power in the novel: "though her hands are heavily ring'd, they are powerful; her face is powdered, her lips savage, her eyebrows quite alarming. [Inspector Abberline] thinks of an owl: feathered, immobile, calm, razor claws, hidden beneath a Japanese wrapper" (Sinclair, 1987, p. 171). Disrobing and removing her theatrical make-up reveals genitalia, "thick but unaroused, a knotted rope-end. Flattened nipples painted around with star-shapes, mapped skin: Sir William Withey Gull" (ibid., p. 173). This scene illustrates Thatcher's own transvestic properties: her self-comparison to Winston Churchill; the campy, manly Spitting Image puppet; and her claiming of the nickname the "Iron Lady."[11] Thatcher crossed easily between the domestic sphere of the Tory Woman, a figure that recalled the Victorian "angel of the house," and the public sphere of aggressive, masculine politics. Pursuing this reading demonstrates how Sinclair ultimately denies his novel any positive representation of female power. The memory of Gull coupled with a critique of Thatcher links patriarchy with misogyny and stresses the difficulty of dissent.

This anxiety about female power expresses itself more problematically in *Dan Leno and the Limehouse Golem*. The foil to male impersonator Elizabeth Cree, Ackroyd's female Ripper figure, is transvestite performer Dan Leno, the star of the London stage. Leno's cross-dressing talents on the stage are recognizable, enjoyable burlesques of the traditional dame figure of pantomime: the novel allows Leno to move in and out of his cross-dressing parts with relative ease and stability, as "he played so many parts he hardly had time to be himself. And yet, somehow, he was always himself" (Ackroyd, 1994, p. 108). Unlike Leno, Lizzie's cross-dressing – and by extension, Thatcher's – appears pathological, forming the outward expression of the schizophrenia that makes her both a killer and a very good actress. If Elizabeth Cree is the serial killer and it is finally revealed that the Golem is a woman, the novel sidesteps the very issues that make the cultural repetition of the Ripper murders deeply problematic for feminist critics, readers, viewers and authors alike. One could accuse Ackroyd of valorizing a version of the past that maintains rather than dispels what Walkowitz has described as the "modern myth of male violence against women" (Walkowitz, 1982, p. 544) thereby equating heritage with the violence of Jack the Ripper. Caputi notes the distressing tendency among some male academics to refer to Jack the Ripper (and other male serial killers) as a "hero," as a "doer," a "man of action and record-breaking accomplishments" (Caputi, 1987, p. 61) and a "mythic master criminal" (ibid., p. 38) who has evaded capture forever. Whether intended or not, this same tendency in the novel to heroize the murderer with theatrics firmly lands *Dan Leno and the Limehouse Golem* into a genealogy of Ripperology that is Jack worship, as opposed to the feminist insights of Walkowitz, Caputi and others. By displacing the deeply misogynist elements of the Whitechapel murders, Ackroyd has inadvertently made Jack the Ripper more palatable, even enjoyable. Ultimately, Ackroyd's novel functions as a defense and preservation of things English, even Jack the Ripper. In order to mask the contemporary sexual politics at play, the Limehouse murders are made to function discursively in place of the Whitechapel murders: the Golem becomes, like the Ripper, a bogeyman, convenient scapegoat and legend amongst petrified Londoners. Through heavy-handed allusion and intertextual play, the 1880s in *Dan Leno and the Limehouse Golem* becomes, in a way that is very different from *White Chappell, Scarlet Tracings* and *From Hell*, a displacement that masks the novel's own antifeminist project.

Ripperature and Heritage: Melancholic Narratives and a Critique of Neo-Victorianism

In "Dance of the Gull Catchers," the second appendix to *From Hell*, which forces readers to reinterpret their pleasurable response to what had been an all-encompassing, highly satisfying tying up of all the loose-ends of the Whitechapel murders, Moore traces the history of Ripperology.

While Campbell depicts a group of Ripperologists in period dress running around in circles and chasing an elusive gull with nets, Moore writes that only the "choreography" (Moore and Campbell, 1999, II, p. 1) of the dance, the genealogy of Ripperology is mappable. The "rest," as Moore tells us with his own net in hand, is "dodgy pseudo-history" (Moore and Campbell, 1999, II, p. 3). The popularity of this "pseudo-history," Moore continues, "the purpose of all art, all writing, on the murders, fiction and non-fiction" is perhaps "simply to participate" (Moore and Campbell, 1999, II, p. 3). Despite an unflattering comparison, neo-Victorian scholars can also be considered "gull catchers" as we too "endlessly cross-track and over-print the [academic] field" (Moore and Campbell, 1999, II, p. 1) in pursuit of the Victorian. While the unsolved nature of the Whitechapel murders reflect postmodern concerns about historiography, Moore's emphasis on the "participation" in "dodgy pseudo-history" emphasizes the ways in which postmodernism and neo-Victorianism dovetail with arguments about heritage: all offer the nation a "simulacra" of the past; all are interested in superficiality, surfaces and hyper-realities. Postmodernism, neo-Victorianism and the heritage industry, it can be argued, "conspire" (Hewison, 1987, p. 135) to keep us sheltered from both past and present. What *From Hell* also details is the enjoyable complicity of participation in this conspiracy: the letters that the killer supposedly sent to Scotland Yard are written by a cross-section of English society, from a "woman in Bradford" (Moore and Campbell, 1999, 9, p. 35) to school children in dorms. Finally, the signature "Jack the Ripper" extends over and unites the skyline of London (ibid., p. 36). Ripperature and Ripperology invite "participation" in, or the production of, what Raymond Williams has called "knowable communities" of Englishness. Ripperature evokes acceptable and well-known images of Victorian England as "home:" Williams has remarked that the city's "romantic atmosphere" and its characteristics of "fog, the gaslight, the hansom cabs, the street urchins" (Williams, 1973, p. 227) vies with the countryside for nostalgic identification.[12] While Ripperature articulates a collective or communal sensibility, its meta-narrative structure makes it well aware of its culpability in the nationalistic ideologies it seeks to critique.

The graphic novel's visuality makes it a particularly appropriate medium with which to launch a critique against the heritage industry and neo-Victorianism itself. Such a critique is encoded into *From Hell* as Inspector Abberline laments over the crowds gathering to buy souvenirs, "four women get killed and it's like the start of a new industry! . . . only the start mind you" (Moore and Campbell, 1999, 9, p. 2). Eddie Campbell's stark black and white illustrations are often reproduced from late-nineteenth century photographs of London and address the appetite for visual culture that opened a market for Victorian photographs in the 1970s and 1980s.[13] The pleasure of "old photographs" (Samuel, 1994, p. 337), according to Samuel, generates a "hallucinatory sense of oneness with the past" (ibid., p. 334) as, through reproduction of images and our own narcissistic projection, the past *seems* to measure up to the desires of the present. The graphic novel's unique format exploits this fantasy of wholeness: as each panel in a comic depicts a single moment in time, the active participation of the reader is required in creating "closure" and thus meaning across what Scott McCloud calls, the "the limbo of the gutter" (McCloud, 1994, p. 65), or the gaps between one panel and the next. Suggestively, McCloud deems this act of closure, "your special crime, each of you committing it in your own style" (ibid., p. 68). As we aid and abet Gull in his brutality, the women's bodies that literally litter the gutters of *From Hell* underscore even further that this desire for closure is an act of violence and that uncritical heritage, by extension, can be considered a crime scene. Instead of emphasizing the pleasure of collecting Victoriana and the fantasies of authenticity and origins that are gained from such nostalgic identification, Moore and Campbell interject such scopophiliac tendencies with necrophilia. Comforting and recognizable old photographs of urban heritage – of London's high streets and city life – are juxtaposed against criminal evidence, the chilling *tableaux mordants* of the autopsy and crime scene photographs taken of the victims' bodies that haunt the pages of the text with their radical dismemberment and incompletion. These photographs become the text's "punctum" or "wound" (Barthes, 1980, p. 27), the fragments of an unassimilable history, themselves an accusation that the present's relationship to the past is not historical enough. The crime scene photographs disrupt the narrative of images that have come to signify the Victorian as a golden age and destabilize notions of Englishness that "old photographs" supply.

Moore and Campbell's deliberate evocation of "old photographs," I argue, demonstrates how heritage tends to reduce history to texts and objects that function as myths and mere curios of continuity. *From Hell*, more so than *White Chappell, Scarlet Tracings*, which accepts and revels in post-imperial detritus, reveals an intense anxiety about a historical field dominated by *things* elevated to the level of clue, allowing nothing to be dismissed or discarded. Moore's decision to treat history as a crime scene neither reconsecrates the past like Sinclair nor does it restore (and reinvent) the fading English character of the East End, like Ackroyd. According to Mike Pearson and Michael Shanks, the "dialectic of the crime scene" is a "surplus and a simultaneous dearth of meaning" (Pearson and Shanks, 2001, p. 61) and this overwhelming contradiction generates a sense of anxiety in *From Hell* that runs through the text and spills over into the extensive footnotes that make up the first appendix, a supplemental archive of coincidences, inconsistencies, extraneous details, bibliographical information and the simple demarcation of what is "fact" and "fiction." For example, Chapter 7 of the graphic novel is entitled "A Torn Envelope" after one of the supposed clues found on victim Annie Chapman's body. It turned out that this clue, upon which many Ripper theories initially rested, was "meaningless" (Moore and Campbell 1999, I, p. 23), part of the "insignificant pieces of debris" that litter the Ripper field, like "a new black bonnet, a chalk scrawl, a ginny kidney" (ibid., I, p.24). These objects have become powerful talismans, objects of desire capable of providing meaning where before there was none.

The narrative that can be constructed from the debris and clues of the Ripper's historical field portrays Gull as a constant in time, a malevolent spirit that links random events into a conspiratorial whole. Recalling the theories of James Hinton on the architecture of time, Moore constructs a history based on repetition: in 1788, the Monster, Renwick Williams, terrorizes London; a hundred years later in 1888 Gull commits the Whitechapel murders; fifty years after Gull, the Halifax slasher strikes; twenty five years later in 1963, also autumn, the infamous "Moors Murderers," Myra Hindley and Ian Brady, are attending a showing of the movie, *The Ripper*, in Manchester; and finally, the Yorkshire Ripper, Peter Sutcliffe, hallucinates a visit from Gull, demanding a sacrifice of prostitutes for a "garden . . . in a high place, sewn with dismal little flowers" (Moore and Campbell, 1999, 14, p. 18). The manipulation of temporality at the end of the graphic novel creates a masterpiece of alternate history, heavily edited for its patterned effect and entirely absorbing – except that Moore calls into question the pleasures of such a return and the melancholic structure of relation to the past that makes up British neo-Victorianism.

While Ripperature has the capability of achieving the goals of the global neo-Victorian that I am arguing for, it remains tethered to a problematic Englishness and fetishizes London without necessarily addressing it as a crisis zone of Englishness that still persists at the heart of the former empire. In *Dan Leno and the Limehouse Golem*, for example, Ackroyd celebrates London's history of theatricality, musicality and spectacle, which, at its zenith in the late nineteenth century, still exists in his conception of contemporary London. According to Ackroyd, it is in the Cockney, the working class, the residuum of music-hall slang and culture that the "perpetual, infinite, London would one day be found" (Ackroyd, 1994, p. 246). To Ackroyd's description of this theatrical, essentially English London, Julian Wolfreys floats the answer, "perhaps it's because they're aware they [Londoners] live in what in the nineteenth century was perceived generally as the greatest city on the planet . . ." (Wolfreys, 1998, p. 257). The celebration of Englishness in Ackroyd obfuscates the history of London as the center of empire; in the novel, Ackroyd is quick to assert the uniqueness of London's position, that the Golem was "some flagrant confirmation of its status as the largest and darkest city of the world" (Ackroyd, 1994, p. 88) and fosters the arrogant, though rather naïve, notion that it is the "first of its kind upon the globe" (ibid., p. 163). In contrast, Moore's graphic novel intervenes in the uninterrupted and at times uncritical expression of Englishness.

Ackroyd's novel illustrates how the cult of Jack the Ripper offers a different structure of relation to the past: a melancholia consisting of pleasurable and uncritical return. Calling on the twinned pleasures of serial reading and serial killing, Kate Lonsdale argues that the simultaneous pleasure and anguish of Ripperology is akin to "Freud's *fort da* game of disappearance and return, the pleasure of these solutions is in the constant capture and release, release and capture" (Lonsdale, 2000, p. 102). With reference to Freud, Lonsdale implies that Ripperature and Ripperology are essentially melancholic discourses. In Freudian terms, mourning and melancholia are both "reaction[s] to the loss of a loved person, or the loss of some abstraction which has taken the place of one, such as one's country, liberty, an ideal and so on" (Freud, 1917, p. 310). In the mourning process, the mourner will slowly withdraw all libidinal attachments to the lost object and invests them elsewhere. The melancholic, however, refuses to break the attachment and the lost object is subsequently elevated to the level of the ideal. Nostalgia arises when the melancholic is unable to find a suitable object worthy of forming a lasting attachment to and so pines for what is lost and therefore unattainable. Paul Gilroy's diagnosis of Britain's postcolonial melancholia is helpful here. The feelings of "discomfort, shame, and perplexity" (Gilroy, 2005, p. 90) that arise from being confronted with the physical realities of empire results in an "imperiled Englishness" (ibid., p. 118) that exhibits itself in simultaneous celebration and eruptions of racist violence, although in the case of Ripperature, one can add to the list a celebration of violence against women. Once these feelings are evoked, Gilroy continues, the "unsettling history" of empire is "diminished, denied and then, if possible, actively forgotten" (ibid., p. 90). Uncritical Ripperature, and by extension, uncritical neo-Victorianism, happily "forgets" and disavows feelings of "discomfort, shame and perplexity" and avoids confronting and acknowledging the realities of empire and after that Gilroy attributes to a successful post-imperialism.

In light of this, it seems inappropriate to discuss these three examples of Ripperature within the rubric of postmodern historiography rather than to view them as melancholic narratives. According to Freud, "there is no doubt that the greater pleasure was attached to the second act" (Freud, 1922, p. 14) – the return to *da* or "there." The refrain of Ackroyd's novel – a rousing "here we are again!" – provides such an example of enthusiastic return: murders occur repeatedly on the same locations and the "golem's" iterations through time, emptied even of Ripperature's ambivalence toward Englishness and gender, are unabashed indulgences in a continuous English tradition and heritage. In *Dan Leno*, the theater is "better than any memory" (Ackroyd, 1994, p. 19) and becomes a thinly disguised metaphor for heritage. To leave it is "like being expelled from some wonderful garden or palace" to be faced instead with "the dirty bricks of house fronts, the muck of the narrow streets, and the shadows cast by the gas lamps in the Strand . . . and some page from a magazine lying in a puddle of filth" (ibid., p. 53). *White Chappell, Scarlet Tracings* poses a more hesitant question: "on . . . or back?" (Sinclair, 1987, p. 57). The novel seems unwilling to relinquish the pleasures of Englishness and nostalgia inherent in its approach to Ripperology and this can be seen, as I will discuss later, in the narrator's melancholic performance of psychogeography, a post-imperial flâneurism that obsessively tracks the "there." The novel is seduced by the enigmatic Joblard, who holds the disturbing notion that to exorcise the present of the overwhelming weight of the past, the Ripper's crimes will have to be repeated and re-enacted: "[u]nless we can exactly repeat the past, we will never make it repent; it will escape us. Nothing is exorcised. It goes on forever" (Sinclair, 1987, p. 151). Despite the desire for exorcism, itself a kind of recovery, a compulsion to repeat drives the novel's temporal scheme.

Only Moore attempts, however problematically, to both exhaustively recover the history of the Whitechapel murders and to recover *from* them. In "Dance of the Gull Catchers," Moore describes his encounter with John Morrison, a Ripperologist who "allegedly" (Moore and Campbell, 1999, II, p. 19) sleeps with Mary Kelly's tombstone under his bed. Morrison wants a time machine to "alter Mary's awful fate" (ibid., p. 18) but Moore warns, "there'd be no coming back. You'd be trapped in the past" (ibid.). Again, the comparison between Ripperologist and neo-Victorianist is unflattering but apt and Moore's warning extreme but appropriate. Indeed, Moore's own venture into the East End is plagued by uncanny repetition: in the rearview mirror of his taxi he sees the Masonic echo in the sign "Widowson" (ibid., p. 19) on a lorry. Moore models his construction of history for an Englishness trapped by the constraints of urban geography and heritage on "Koch's snowflake" (ibid., p. 23), a mathematical construct that describes an infinitely long, infinitely convoluted line circumscribing a finite space. Like Gull's vision of the Masonic pentagram embracing London, the story can't extend beyond the "initial circle" (ibid.) circumscribed by the facts of the Whitechapel murders. Moore tries to write himself out of the web that history has made for him by attempting a *coup d'etat*: the woman mutilated beyond recognition in 13 Miller's Court, he masterfully argues using Campbell's visual sleight of hand, was *not* Mary Kelly, who escaped Gull's plot and returned to Ireland where she lived out her days, the happy mother of four daughters. Although attempting to undo the repeated violence against the five victims that accompanies each telling of the Ripper story, Moore can only substitute another body, another woman, in Kelly's place. The novel's anxiety about exploitation extends into the second appendix of the graphic novel where Kelly's double, the exotic dancer in The Ten Bells pub, awaits. "Koch's snowflake," therefore, reflects the ethics of neo-Victorianism's project: in what ways is its extension beyond the "finer crenellations" (ibid.) of the Victorian an act of liberation or another act of violence?

Post-Imperial Landscapes: Ripperature, Psychogeography, and Englishness

Recovery in *From Hell* also occurs in other acts of reclamation such as Moore and Campbell's meticulous attention to the "psychogeography" of London. Iain Sinclair was one of the first writers to imaginatively employ psychogeography in an immense travelogue about his attempt to "cut a crude V into the sprawl" (Sinclair, 1997, p. 1) of London and to "vandalize dormant energies by an act of ambulant signmaking" (ibid.). Sinclair's "ambulation" through London woke the "dormant energies" of a city (and a country) he believes has been sold "down river," a title of another one of his travelogues, by Thatcher. He defines psychogeography as a "grid of energies" (ibid., p. 127) mapped across London, an "occult mapping of the city" (ibid.) anchored by sites and icons of violence, mysticism or "ancient taint" that "still exercises a powerful influence on any imagination that allows itself to float over the streets in a willed discrimination of archetypes" (ibid.). Sinclair constructs psychogeography as a political countermovement to

Thatcherite policies, carried out by her henchmen, the "developers, clerks, eco freaks and ward bosses" (ibid., p. 146), who are hoping to curtail or erase the remaining traces of historical change in order to remove disruptions and destabilizing "lived" elements from official versions of the past. Reading *From Hell's* visual and more thoughtful approach to psychogeography, however, reveals the way in which the movement both comments on and works against the way in which English space is produced as heritage. Like Sinclair, Moore and Campbell attempt to remap touristic London as a landscape of alternative desire where glimpses of some originary trauma and suffering can still be felt. The graphic novel depicts London as a city full of locations that are "empowered by suffering," where "despair and terror . . . reverberate[d] in the soil and stones for ever more" (Moore and Campbell, 1999, 4, p. 27). However, by drawing attention to the violence out of which sanitized tourist locations are forged, Moore also forces us to reread Sinclair's psychogeography as shot through with the misogynistic desire to "cut a crude V' into Thatcher's London. *From Hell's* psychogeography also confronts its own limitations: while the graphic novel's reclamation of lost or contested territory attempts to destabilize the hegemony that Englishness maintains over the more inclusive category of Britishness, it does so by establishing and reinforcing the frontiers of whiteness.

In one of the most powerful and arguably English sequences in *From Hell*, William Gull acts as a psychic tour guide and takes his dull-witted coachman and accomplice Netley on a tour of the psychogeography of London. This section of the text is paired with a second segment in a later chapter where Gull hallucinates himself as a spirit, a zeitgeist even, making links through time and charting the fluxes in history. While the second psychogeographic journey maps the temporal architecture of the first, I would like to stress the heavily touristic nature of psychogeography in Chapter 4 as it addresses the negotiated constructions of official and unofficial versions of Englishness. Netley drives Gull to a long list of obscure as well as national moments, "Battle Bridge where matriarchy fell with Boadicea; London Fields where Saxons praised the moon's assassin . . . Northampton Square bought with Masonic gold, and Bloomsbury St George where Hawksmoor raised his pagan mausoleum . . ." (Moore and Campbell, 1999, 4, p. 19) with a short lunch of steak and kidney pie in Earl's Court. The pair concludes their tour at St Paul's Cathedral, the center of the pentagram that Gull maps across London. As they travel, Gull marks the locations they have visited on a large map of the city, the authoritative and concrete detail of Campbell's reproduction visibly confronting the more invisible elements of Gull's myth-map (see Fig. 5).

FIGURE 5 Gull's map of London. *From Hell* © Alan Moore & Eddie Campbell

"Maps," as Gull tells a suitably confused Netley, "have a potency; may yield a wealth of knowledge past imagining if properly divined. Encoded within this city's stones are symbols thunderous enough to rouse the sleeping gods . . ."(Moore and Campbell, 1999, 4, p. 19). The journey is Gull's attempt to apprentice the illiterate Netley in the ability to "read" London as a "literature of stone, of place-names and associations. Where faint echoes answer back from off the distant ruined walls of bloody history" (ibid., p. 9). It is hard not to read this lengthy segment of the text as a parody of the Ripper Walking Tours that are eager to profit on the pleasures of retrieval, re-enactment and immediacy. But Gull's tour also crafts a different map of desire that addresses the compound identity of Englishness and forces us to think critically about the kinds of violence in the historical past neo-Victorianism chooses to appropriate and ignore.

In *From Hell*, the map traced by Gull provides a geographical and anthropological "deep map" (Pearson and Shanks, 2001, p. 64) of London; one that allows for the simultaneity in the "deep" layers of historical formation that can begin to address the ineffable nature of the metropolis. Moore's "deep map" reveals a polyglot, unstable notion of Englishness: the deeper one goes, the more a distinctly non-Anglo-Saxon history is revealed. The duo stop briefly at Earl's Court, which Gull notes, "was once called Billingswell, after 'Belino's Well,' sacred unto the solar God-king Belinos, Son of King Lud" (Moore and Campbell, 1999, 4, p. 17). Other depth-related stories haunt this section of the graphic novel, from the more superficial burial of John Williams, the Ratcliff Highway murderer, at a crossroads "with a stake thrust through his heart" (Moore and Campbell, 1999, 4, p. 29) to the "stripe of ash" that the Iceni queen Boadicea left after burning London to the ground rather than surrender it to the Romans, a "cold black vein in London's geologic strata, token of one woman's wrath" (ibid., 4, p. 8). These are sites that the official "monumentality" of London would rather not contain: they stress the excess, the residual and the local that can disrupt or at least provoke a re-evaluation of national belonging or "consensus" (Lefèbvre, 2001, p. 220). As the modern City of London has been remapped and reconstructed by the officials of history to contain secularized tourist landmarks, Moore's "deep map" of London offers an alternative to the supposedly stable version of Englishness that such monuments offer.

Monuments, according to Henri Lefèbvre, contain "the element of repression" which represents the struggle to guarantee a sense of "membership" or submission to "a generally accepted Power and a generally accepted Wisdom" (Lefèbvre, 2001, p. 221). "To the degree that there are traces of violence and death, negativity and aggressiveness in social practice," Lefèbvre continues, "the monumental work erases them and replaces them with a tranquil power and certitude which can encompass violence and terror" (ibid., p. 222). Visited by Gull and Netley, a place like the Tower of London becomes synonymous in the present with the power and stability of the British monarchy; its keep and vaults are symbolic repositories of English history. Described by Samuel as "Britain's leading tourist attraction" today, rivaling both the Tour d'Eiffel and the Empire State Building internationally, and "one of the sights of London from at least the reign of Elizabeth I" (Samuel, 1999, p. 105), the Tower has been "multifunctional" as a "military fortress, a royal palace, a state prison, a zoo, a jewel house, a museum, an army barracks, an arsenal, the place where all gold, silver and copper coin was struck . . . and not least 'the Repository of the antient Records of this nation'"(ibid., p. 104). Only in the nineteenth century, however, was the "rehistoricization" (ibid., p. 108) of the Tower in its present, tourist-friendly form. Driving past its walls, Gull describes a violent and supernatural history of the Tower:

> This tower must HUM, a dynamo of blood and history . . . built on the "white mound" named in pagan myths where Britain's founder, Brutus, late of Troy, lies mouldering. Guided by Moon Goddess-sent dreams, Brutus seized Britain from its rulers, Gog and Magog, raising New Troy . . . "Troy Novantum" . . . here pledged to DIANA. Here Bran's head's buried; Celtic God whose name means "Blessed Raven." His birds nest here still. "Tis said London's destroyed if they depart. Their population is therefore restored occasionally: ravens imported from elsewhere that

seem to stay "til death. The "Sol Tower" of the Sun King Lud stood here, rebuilt by Romans; Normans; Britain's conquerors. Here died Jane Grey, Judge Jeffreys; Anne Boleyn; Guy Fawkes; The Little Princes . . . infant sacrifices even Druids might admire. Here, in 1817, a keeper and his wife perceived a cylinder of viscous azure light, thick as an arm, that hovered briefly, then was gone. Another sentry saw a bear-like apparition slide beneath the jewel-room door. He fell into a fit and died shortly. Perhaps some places do indeed possess vitality. They dream and feed, and propagate themselves. (Moore and Campbell, 1999, 4, p. 28)

For Gull, the Tower reveals a misogynistic, pagan history and taps into some of the more obscure, mythical foundational stories of the city of London. Although depicted as a nodal point of dense supernatural energies, we can read through Gull's obsession with myth and see instead continuing stories of violence and sacrifice in the name of national stability.

Fixed markers, often phallic landmarks like the obelisk on the Thames embankment known as Cleopatra's Needle, anchor much of Gull's tour. Plagued by calamities and disaster in its journey back 'home' to England as an imperial prize, the Needle anchors a long history of struggle that stretches back "fifteen hundred years before Christ's birth" when the stone was "etched with hieroglyphic prayers that Atum, Egypt's sun god might increase his sovereignty" (Moore and Campbell, 1999, 4, p. 20). While the shipwrecks and deaths that accompany the Needle's journey are a jab at England's imperialist games, the Needle is also a dark tribute to Gull's alternate cartography, for buried underneath the Needle, Gull claims, is "a map; daguerrotypes of our epoch's most lovely women . . . and a razor" (ibid.). The seductiveness of psychogeography lies in its potential for unveiling counterhegemonic stories like the vanity of dragging an obelisk from Alexandria to London as imperial spoils. But its drawback can be found in the "willed discrimination" of sites and archetypes described by Iain Sinclair, as it can also lead to Gull's misogynistic template. In Gull's mind, the killing of the five prostitutes reaffirms male power over a matriarchy "hinged on childbirth's mystery" (ibid., p. 8). Perhaps, he tells Netley, "men rebelled . . . a few at first, a small conspiracy . . . who by some act of social magic, or politics, or force, cast women down that men might rule" (ibid.). For Gull, the city's landmarks are symbols of this original "conspiracy" and justify his brutality: the domination of a male sun over a female moon can be seen in sites as varied "Half-Moon Lane," named for Herne, "who usurped Diana's role as leader of the lunar hunt" and ultimately to St Paul's Cathedral where Diana is "chained" by a "web of ancient signs, that woman might abandon useless dreams of liberty" (ibid., p. 35).

Such "porno-tropics" (McClintock, 1995, p. 22) as the Needle, to borrow from Anne McClintock, illustrate the ways in which women's bodies "served as the boundary markers of imperialism" (ibid., p. 24) conveniently guarding seas, oceans and unknown "virgin" territory with their often monstrous and highly sexualized bodies. For McClintock, the feminization of the land is a "traumatic trope" recurring in "the aftermath of male boundary confusion" and is invariably a "strategy of containment" (ibid., p. 24). The "male loss of boundary," she argues, is compensated for "reinscribing a ritual excess of boundary, accompanied, all too often, by an excess of military violence" (ibid.). Gull's ritualistic murders are his strategy of containment, an attempt to restore London's contested terrain to its rightful masculine ownership: "[o]ur suffragettes demand that women vote and have equality," he angrily notes, "they'd drag us back to that primordial nursery, the rule of instinct and the tyranny of mother's milk! We can't have that" (Moore and Campbell, 1999, 4, p. 30). His unfettered and leisurely movement through and remapping of London radically curtails, through violent dismemberment, the very difficult journeys that his victims make through the streets every day in the endless search for money, food and lodging.

St Paul's Cathedral is the center of Gull's psychogeographic tour. Its architecture, symbolism and history offer an intense concentration of the mythology that Gull has been tracing: it is the center of masculine power within which Gull believes that the "unconscious, the Moon and Womanhood are chained" (Moore and Campbell, 1999, 4, p. 37). Moore's research reveals that embracing the dome's structure are five iron chains supposedly used to capture and maintain the presence of various gods. St Paul's Cathedral is meant to function as an official "*lieu de memoire*," described by Pierre Nora as a site of disappearance where "continuity persists" but only because they are saturated with "the sense that memory has been torn" (Nora, 1989, p. 7). As Ian Baucom has suggested, *lieux de memoire* are often elegiac locations where an "identity-preserving, identity-enchanting, and identity-transforming aura lingers, or is made to appear" (Baucom, 1999, p. 19) and so are often highly contested. So, St Paul's dome appears as a landmark in many sentimental London stories including the fairy tale of the Charles and Diana royal wedding. Yet, Iain Sinclair also describes the Cathedral as an empty stage for shameless national spectacles, drawing attention to the ideological processes through which fantasies of retrieval and stability are evoked and constructed. For Sinclair, St Paul's is both a

"Thatcherite temple" and the "ultimate heritage operation," its site managed by "security personnel in ecclesiastical drag manning the cash registers" (Sinclair, 1997, p. 172). Moore's St Paul's is cheekily empty, devoid of tourists in his version of the nineteenth century.

Within St Paul's, Gull spreads his map of London on the ground and tells Netley to align the sites that they have visited with a ruler. A reluctant and nauseous Netley completes what Gull reveals to be a pentagram with St Paul's at the center and is suddenly made privy to Gull's plan to "reinforce" the "lines of power" according to the "ancient ways" of sacrificing "Diana's priestesses"(Moore and Campbell, 1999, 4, p. 37), thus commencing a deadly and deliberate repetition of the past. Gull's all-encompassing symbolism and his assertion that the story of female sacrifice that he will carry out is "written . . . inked in blood long dry . . . engraved in stone" and dictated by the "streets wherein you grew" brings the past up. Netley vomits his lunch with an immense "hwurrr . . . urr . . . urwulsh" (ibid.) upon the steps of St Paul's as he recognizes the role he is to play and the coercive, oppressive history of the city that Gull has sketched. This amazingly cinematic sequence ends with a dark relief of St Paul's dome rising over a blackened London, a parody of a picture postcard (see Fig. 6). The darkened London sites of Gull's psychogeography, so reminiscent of the preconservation, soot-covered monuments of London in the 1980s, coupled with Netley's explosive reaction, raise the same questions as heritage: what, in the post-imperial landscape, is to be enthusiastically preserved or violently expelled?

If psychogeography can draw our attention to misogyny and the violence of heritage, it surprisingly does not admit representations of race – even as it is preoccupied with London, celebrated in the present as a multicultural space that is supposedly more cosmopolitan, vibrant and racially tolerant. Sinclair, for example, has been criticized for neglecting the multiethnic fabric of the city he traverses. In *White Chappell, Scarlet Tracings*, as in his nonfiction, Sinclair ignores the East End's racial makeup. His book dealers search for environments where the past in all its energetic decay can still be felt:

> Southwark holds its time, with the City, with Whitechapel, with Clerkenwell, holds the memory of what it was: it is possible to walk back into the previous, as an event, still true to this moment. The Marshalsea trace, the narrative mazetrap that Dickens set, takes over, the figures of fiction outliving the ghostly impulses that started them. The past is a fiction that absorbs us. It needs no passport, turn the corner and it is with you.

"...engraved in stone"

FIGURE 6 Saint Paul's Cathedral: picture postcard? *From Hell* © Alan Moore & Eddie Campbell

> The things they do are natural, you do those things. Detached from this shadow you are nothing, there is nothing. You have no other existence. (Sinclair, 1987, p. 63)

This is an oft-quoted example of Sinclair's psychogeography, but its elegiac tone reveals a memory of an indigenous Englishness pitched forgetfully and dramatically against an expansive British Empire.[14] Instead, the past *does* require a "passport" to denote the long histories of immigration and ethnicity that are also anchored to the same sites. Thus Sinclair can be accused of preserving and "collud[ing] in the very norms of Thatcher's Britain." His version of the East End is "governed, quite plainly, by a corporate white male consciousness" (Brooker, 2000). Sinclair inadvertently creates a version of Englishness as exclusive as Thatcher's. Ackroyd's psychogeography makes even fewer claims toward multiculturalism: centered around the "spiritual center" (Ackroyd, 1994, p. 270) of the Reading Room of the British Museum, *Dan Leno and the Limehouse Golem* is informed by an archive reserved only for men like George Gissing who sits "far away" from the "two long tables reserved for ladies," not because he was "in any sense a misogynist" but because he was "still young enough to maintain the illusion that the pursuit of knowledge must be a cloistered and self-denying activity . . ." (ibid., p. 110). *From Hell's* psychogeography points out how hegemonic Englishness is constructed, but while it destabilizes Englishness, it cannot racialize it. If psychogeography forms an important element of Ripperature, it serves to point out that neo-Victorianism in Britain can often remain ineffective in its recovery of histories of race and ethnicity.

Jack the Ripper™

"Dance of the Gull Catchers," set in what remains of Whitechapel, reminds us that the colonizing efforts of reclamation and regeneration, masked as New Labor's modernization, continues.[15] The mining of the Ripper quarry and the "tireless, sinister enthusiasm" of the Gull catchers have obscured the "reality" (Moore and Campbell, 1999, II, p. 22) of the Whitechapel murders. This reality of "five murdered paupers, one anonymous assailant," Moore wryly notes, has been "dwarfed by the vast theme-park we've built around it" (ibid.), and the final panels of the text acknowledges the economics and psychic exchange of the "gull catchers" return to the past. The appendix closes with two iconic figures of Whitechapel, 1998, part of a changing East End "where redevelopment . . . looms ominously just beyond the century's brim" (ibid., p. 24). In The Ten Bells, the pub that has remained standing because of its association with the Whitechapel murders, an exotic dancer simulates masturbation to "jack, jack, jack your body" (ibid.) in front of an audience of gull catchers including Moore himself. The pub's exploitative atmosphere creates an eerie continuity between past and present. Outside, Moore notes, the renovated Christ Church, whose steeple has dominated the action of the graphic novel, sits like a "horrifying geriatric," its "chin wiped," "cleaned up" and "made presentable," or "rebranded" to borrow from Blair again, for "smart young visitors" (ibid.). If neo-Victorianism requires careful choices about what kind of Victorian is depicted, *From Hell's* appendix clearly asks us to consider the context of neo-Victorianism's present as well.

One of the panels from the 1998 second appendix features a billboard advertisement for *From Hell*, the movie; spot-lit, it dwarfs the background of Christchurch. This panel anticipated the "Hollywoodification" of the graphic novel, as *From Hell* was one of the first of its genre to be adapted into a screenplay; the film was directed by the Hughes brothers (of *Menace to Society* (1993) fame) in 2002. The Hughes brothers' version took some large liberties with Moore's plot: it melded the characters of Inspector Abberline and R. J. Lees, the royal psychic, into one lead character, and rather than depicting the complexities of Moore's plot and the unknowability of history, the Hughes brothers stressed solutions and linearity with Abberline privately witnessing, at each crucial moment, Gull's punishment and demise. The adaptation of *From Hell* effectively turned the post-imperial landscape of the graphic novel into a neo-imperial one: the Hughes brothers painstakingly reproduced the East End of London in the city of Prague which suggested that the remnants of "authentic" (and economically viable) Englishness could no longer be found at its original site; at the same time, the mockney performances of American actors Johnny Depp and Heather Graham in lead roles affirmed that "Englishness" was both easily translatable and performed.[16] Thus, Jack the Ripper's most recent guise has been in support of Britain's image abroad, or rather, selling Britain to an American audience. In his review of the movie *From Hell*, Iain Sinclair notes that "after Tony Blair's sterling support for America's Afghan adventure, Brits can expect to be upgraded from sneering villains and movie spooks to Byronic antiheroes (like the Celtic Hannibal Lecter)" (Sinclair, 2002). Indeed, Ian Holm, as the impeccably polite and instructive Sir William Gull, certainly fits the bill. Sinclair's reading may be far-fetched but it does show a continued mapping of national characteristics onto the unlikely, gendered, but elastic figure of one of the world's most notorious serial killers.

Although the movie opens with a shot of St Paul's Cathedral against a blood-red sky and a swooping descent into the underworld of the East End, it noticeably omits Gull and Netley's travel sequence and the graphic novel's lengthy scenes of psychogeography. These scenes of Englishness are excised from the text to produce what the Hughes brothers have called their "ghetto story" (quoted in Sinclair, 2002). But, once excised, the Hughes brothers have actually created a more racially diverse version of the East End than Moore's. As I have argued, psychogeography can make invisible, despite its emphatic pedagogy of all-encompassing vision and nomadic randomness, the large immigrant population and diverse racial makeup of the city. In the Hughes' movie, much is made of the prevalence of opium and laudanum: Johnny Depp's Inspector Abberline, unlike the character in the original text, relies on opium as a visionary aid to catch the Ripper and eventually dies from an overdose. The appearance of opium admits, in a limited way, the discourse of a racial other and there is a nod, albeit in the stereotype of the opium den owner, to the Chinese population still rooted in the East End and more abstractly to the racial make-up of a metropolitan population. The erasure of Englishness in the movie calls attention to its centrality in the graphic novel and reveals its thwarted potential as a post-imperial text. Arguably, Ripperature's entanglement with ongoing discourses of Englishness contributes to the geopolitical fantasy that Britain's fortress position toward Europe and, in particular, the U.S., ignores the global in favor of the local. However, this turning away from one form of imperialism for what can be construed as another should be viewed as an opportunity to identify new forms of dominance and resistance. As an unconventional form of neo-Victorianism, Ripperature stresses the complications of gathering under the national memory or cohesive potentialities of the Victorian. In addition, the popularity of Ripperature suggests how center-driven retellings of the Victorian can render race, gender and imperialism peripheral again. Without an explicit imperial framework, an illicit and criminal Englishness emerges as a backlash against the memory of empire. In the next chapter, which explores the antipodean history of another criminal named "Jack," I examine the circulation of the Victorian within nationalist discourses in a settler postcolonial context.

Chapter 2

Neo-Victorianism Down Under: Peter Carey's *Jack Maggs*

Like many postcolonial neo-Victorian novels, Peter Carey's second neo-Victorian novel, *Jack Maggs* (1997), deliberately intervenes in a national archive filled with texts and images that have been inherited from Britain. In *Jack Maggs*, Carey revised Charles Dickens' *Great Expectations* and its portrayal of Magwitch, the convict, as England's antipodean Other, defined by Carey as "foul and dark, frightening and murderous" (*Boldtype*, 1998). The novel's intertextuality with its parent text works "to destabilize the very basis of fictional authority – and with its linear, filial lines of influence between metropolis and former colony" (Thieme, 2001, p. 109), a strategy Carey has used before with much success in *Oscar and Lucinda* (1988).[1] Discussing his motivation to write *Jack Maggs*, Carey explains:

> Australians do not like to celebrate this moment when the nation is born, and it has been something of a passion for me to do just that. We carry a great deal of self-hatred, denial, grief, and anger, all unresolved. It took a long time before I could think of exactly how I might use these passions to fuel a novel. Then one day, contemplating the figure of Magwitch, the convict in Charles Dickens's *Great Expectations*, I suddenly thought THIS MAN IS MY ANCESTOR. And then: this is UNFAIR! (*Boldtype*, 1998)

The founding moment of colonial Australia was imprisonment and *Jack Maggs* is Carey's attempt to recover and hence recover *from* the stigma of convict ancestry. Breathing new life into Magwitch is Carey's contribution to the project of "(re)mythologiz[ing] Australia in its own terms" (Hassall, 1997, p. 135) and many of Carey's neo-Victorian heroes and heroines have been instrumental in the recuperation of pieces of history that allow primarily Anglo-Australians to recover (from) their national past while still embracing the foundation of Australia as a settler as well as a penal colony.[2] Coming to terms with convictism, however, seems to facilitate a forgetting of aboriginal dispossession in the past and multiculturalism in the present.

Unfortunately, *Jack Maggs* came at a time when many Australians seemed unsure of what it was exactly they were supposed to be celebrating. The novel was published in 1997 amidst a crisis in Anglo-Australian identity underpinned by two important events. In his famous "Redfern Address," written to launch the International Year for the World's Indigenous People (1992), Australian Prime Minister Paul Keating (1991–6) initiated the process of reconciliation by "recogniz[ing] that the problem starts with us non-Aboriginal Australians" (Keating, 1992) Stopping short of a full apology, the moment was nonetheless the first time an official acknowledged that "[We] took the traditional lands and smashed the traditional way of life. We bought the disasters. The alcohol. We committed the murders. We took the children from their mothers. We practiced discrimination and exclusion" (ibid.). The intent was to heal a fractured nation by unburdening white Australians and succeeding generations from the guilt of the past preventing them from "open[ing] our hearts a bit" (ibid.) and embracing reconciliation and multiculturalism. In 1997, during the first Reconciliation Convention, it was expected that John Howard (1996–2007), Keating's successor, would finally apologize to indigenous groups for the actions of Australia's first white settlers thus completing the process of recovery. However, Howard all but reversed Keating's acknowledgment of guilt by merely "regretting" the experience of the Stolen Generations, and proclaiming that "Australians of this generation should not be required to accept guilt and blame for past actions and policies over which they had no control" (quoted in Davison, 2000, p. 7). In the same year, Pauline Hanson's reactionary One Nation political party swept national elections, running on platform described by critics as a "throwback" to: "zero net immigration . . . an end to multiculturalism and a revival of Australia's Anglo-Celtic cultural tradition which it believes has been devalued; an abolition of native title . . . an end to special Aboriginal funding programs; [and] opposition to Aboriginal reconciliation on the grounds that it creates two nations . . ." (Kelly, 2000, p. 142). Appealing to a sense of unfairness, abandonment, belonging and entitlement, Hanson considers herself a "true" Australian who "draw[s] the line," however, "when told I must pay and continue paying for something that happened over 200 years ago" (Hanson, 1996). Both Howard and Hanson speak to the backlash against state-sponsored multiculturalism that was meant to construct a modern national identity that would undo the White Australia policy of the nineteenth century and describe Australia's indigenous cultures, its English and Irish settler population and the new influx of Asian immigrants.

Carey's decision to establish convictism as a foundational moment seems to be at odds with saying sorry for aboriginal dispossession; Jack Maggs' transportation doesn't seem to address the racial anxieties of Asian immigration; and the novel's celebration of Anglo-Australia seems to problematically oppose Australia's official policy of multiculturalism. Unlike Kate Grenville's Booker Prize-nominated neo-Victorian novel, *The Secret River* (2006), which is dedicated "to the Aboriginal people of Australia: past, present and future" (Grenville, 2006), *Jack Maggs* failed to recognize an indigenous history and presence; nor did it offer a critical exploration of whiteness available, for example, in David Malouf's *Remembering Babylon*, also nominated for the Booker Prize in 1993. The onus of change has fallen on white Australians, now reduced to a series of clumsy terms such as "British-based," "core culture," "Anglo-Saxon," "Anglo-Celtic," and "mainstream" to name a few, and *Jack Maggs*, at first glance, resists this change. Given the cultural-political context of the novel, Carey's privileged position as a two-time Booker Prize winner, valued as someone who could speak for the nation and its multiple traumas of "what it means to be an Australian and what Australia is" (Sexton, 1985, p. 38), seemed threatened. Within this context, Carey's novel could be considered a nostalgic text that, like Pauline Hanson's inflammatory rhetoric, represents a throwback to an ideological construction of Australia as exclusionary and organized around white, male "mateship" – a criticism that this chapter explores.

Carey has discussed Australia's structure of relation to its Victorian past as one of trauma, its symptoms expressed in the present as a profound *unheimlich*. In an interview with Eleanor Wachtel, Carey states that:

> Australia kept on being Victorian long after the British stopped being Victorian. People arriving in Australia many years after the Victorian era well and truly ended would see its vestiges there. In the outposts of the Empire these exiled people were still keeping up the standards, unaware that they were no longer the standards. Things like that happen when people feel they are exiled from where the center is, or from where home is. (Wachtel, 1993, p. 104)

In my reading of *Jack Maggs*, I suggest that the "vestiges" of the Victorian in the Australian present is the so-called "White Australia policy," a legacy of empire enshrined in the Immigration Restriction Act of 1901 whose standards of racial purity continue to traumatize the present.[3] Having abandoned the racialist policies upon which the nation was founded, the discourse of multiculturalism was supposed to articulate a new national direction; a narrative that could tell the new story of vitality, difference, tolerance and affirmation post-Wik and Mabo, and embrace the influx of new immigrants. But multiculturalism, as Ien Ang has argued, "failed to offer white Australians, especially, the discursive means to articulate their experience of the tensions and contradictions associated with the loss of their racial monopoly" (Ang, 2001, p. 107). Evacuated of the rhetoric of race, the supposedly color-blind discourse of multiculturalism left white Australians without a method of narrating the huge cultural, national and personal changes affecting them.[4] White Australians, therefore, are doubly "exiled:" estranged from Britain, they are neither central nor at "home" in the present.[5] Haunted by the legacy of their colonial status and, therefore, not ever being truly British; the "cult of forgetfulness" (Dixson, 1999, p. 107) and embarrassment surrounding the malignant aspects of convictism; and the view of colonial Australians as "unique racial despoilers" (ibid., p. 121); white Australians have been made to feel "ashamed" (ibid., p. 2) of their past and their ancestry leading to an overwhelming sense of self-hatred and guilt. I see this stubborn and debilitating set of legacies manifesting itself in the novel's focus on mesmerism and trauma as Jack Maggs literally falls under the hypnotic spell of mesmerist/popular author Tobias Oates, a parody of Charles Dickens himself. However problematically, I argue in this chapter, one can read Carey's neo-Victorian project as an attempt to change the memory of what the Victorian symbolizes in an Australian context, turning it "down under" to mean instead a renewed civic – rather than racial – identity around which Australia can cohere.[6] As *Jack Maggs* is generational in structure, invested in the relationship between fathers and sons, legacies and inheritances, the neo-Victorian narrative offered by Carey bequeaths a version of "old" Australia to those not able to recognize themselves in the multicultural "new" Australia. And, I will argue, the "old" Australia that Carey hopes to pass on envisions an Australia based on citizenship, membership and mutual recognition.

The House that Jack Built Down Under

Jack Maggs tells the story of the return to London of a transported convict and his search for his adopted English son. In doing so, the novel maps the return of the prodigal father to a homeland that had previously rejected him. Once in London, Maggs is violently disabused of any illusions of

Englishness he harbors; he is required to give up his own "great expectations" both of himself and his son, the homosexual dandy Henry Phipps. Disguised as a footman, Maggs enters service in the disorderly house of a grocer turned gentleman, Percy Buckle, neighbor to the absent Phipps. Pursued by saucy housemaid Mercy, unable to submit to the pecking order of Buckle's household, and prone to debilitating "tic douloureux," (Carey, 1997, p. 29) Maggs is forced to undergo sessions of mesmerism administered by the author Tobias Oates. As Oates wrestles Maggs' life story from the deep recesses of the "criminal mind" (ibid., p. 86) in the hopes of producing his next great novel, Maggs writes his own narrative: a series of letters detailing the Dickensian beginnings of his life as a "Mudlark" (ibid., p. 71) on the banks of the Thames; his brief career as a child criminal under the protection of Mary "Ma" Britten and the tutelage of Silas Smith; and his great love for Sophina, Silas's daughter. Maggs hopes that these letters will explain his convict past, his traumatic transportation and imprisonment, and his sudden return to London to take what he sees as his rightful place as an Englishman and Victorian gentleman beside his chosen son.

As the plot summary suggests, *Jack Maggs* is essentially a domestic novel, concerned with home economics, the relationship between masters and servants and the dynamics of domestic service. The novel offers stories about characters that don't live in their own homes, who clean other people's houses, and look after other people's children. Finding a home, building a home and then feeling at home after the "physical and emotional confrontation with the 'new' land and its ancient and established meanings" (Ashcroft et al., 1989, p. 27) has been the project of the settler and the migrant. Yet the concept of home also insists on binaries of what are not home: inclusion, exclusion, invasion and defense. What we can call the politics of home is best described by Rosemary Marangoly Clooney as a set of "select inclusions:"

> . . . grounded in a learned (or taught) sense of a kinship that is extended to those who are perceived as sharing the same blood, race, class, gender, or religion. Membership is maintained by bonds of love, fear, power, desire, and control. Homes are manifest on geographical, psychological and material levels. They are places that are recognized as such by those within and those without. They are places of violence and nurturing. A place that is flexible, that manifests itself in various forms and yet whose every reinvention seems to follow the basic pattern of inclusions/exclusions. Home is a place to escape to and a place to escape from. Its importance lies in the fact that it is not equally available to all. Home is the

desired place that is fought for and established as the domain of a few. It is not a neutral place. It is community. Communities are not counter-constructions but only extensions of home, providing the same comforts and terrors on a larger scale. (Clooney, 1996, p. 9)

Clooney's catalog of binaries helps identify moments of constructed notions of home in Carey's novel and in contemporary Australian identity politics. Important to Clooney's discussion of postcolonial literature's concern for home is the idea that at different times and situations, home does not necessarily mean "nation" and that "twentieth-century literature in English is not so concerned with drawing allegories of nation as with the search for viable homes for viable selves" (ibid., p. 5).

A contemporary politics of home can be seen in the rhetoric of Pauline Hanson who lamented being "swamped by Asians" (Hanson, 1996) in her maiden speech upon winning her seat as MP of Oxley. Deliberately conflating "home" and "country," Hanson conceded, "of course, I will be called racist but, if I can invite whom I want into my home, then I should have the right to have a say in who comes into my country" (ibid.). Hanson's experience of the uncanny stems from her immersion in a nation post-Mabo and Wik, the heyday of immigration, and greater ties to Asia: to Hanson, Australia looks and feels very different. By positioning herself as a less-than-gracious hostess who has the "right" to "invite" immigrants into her country, Hanson establishes ownership of Australia as her home and while she criticizes immigrants who "form ghettos and do not assimilate" (ibid.), those who can enter nonetheless maintain their subordinate position as her guests. Hanson's rhetoric underscores how these issues of settlement – belonging, accommodation, property and ownership – are not "equally available to all" (Clooney, 1996, p. 9). For the purposes of this chapter, Hanson is a reminder that settlement has been traditionally associated with home-making and women's work and, in her own neo-Victorian move, invokes a return to the White Australia policy and sole British/white control of land and state. *Jack Maggs* responds to a similar set of problems: how to define Australia as home. The novel situates itself in a tradition of colonial and postcolonial fiction that addresses the "great expectations" of the migrant returning "home" to England, but it also fits itself into an increasing trend of Australian postcolonial writers who explore Australia as, if not as home, at least a place to return to. More importantly, *Jack Maggs* explores how convictism – primarily a white, masculine discourse – created a more urgent and sometimes paradoxical relationship to home.

Like Magwitch and his Australian literary counterpart Rufus Dawes, Jack Maggs has been transported "for the term of his natural life."[7] A convict was not allowed to return home or make a new home for himself, unless he was lucky enough like Maggs and Magwitch to make his own fortune in the new land. Moreover, the exile from home was enacted and enforced by England, home itself. Thus, Carey's protagonist is traumatized by "home," so that his "imaginary homeland" (Rushdie, 1992, p. 9) is not the bittersweet nostalgia of Rushdie's migrant but a pathological compulsion to repeat, or in this case to return, to embrace, and identify with the aggressor. Jack stubbornly and irrationally holds on to his English identity even as it is being stolen from him as fast as Toby can write it down and vehemently denied to him by others. Even though he tells Toby that he has a "grand house in Sydney town . . . a street named for me . . . a coach and two footmen" (Carey, 1997, p. 262), for Jack, it is always better "to be a bad smell here than a frigging rose in New South Wales" (ibid., p. 215). Jack's desire to return "home" to England is based on an imaginary so powerful that it becomes what Hassall describes as a "talisman" (Hassall, 1997, p. 131) against the physical torture Jack endured at Moreton Bay. As the "flies might feast on his spattered back' and the vicious "double-cat" shears off his fingers, Jack's mind "crawled forward, always, constructing piece by piece" (Carey, 1997, p. 300) not the squalid home of his childhood but a rich and detailed fantasy of a Kensington home he had once broken into as a child-thief. Seared into Maggs' memory by physical pain, this fantasy, which "he later knew was meant by authors when they wrote of England, and of Englishmen" (ibid.), collapses powerful images of "home" and "country" in the novel and creates a traumatic kernel to which the novel and its characters, Australian and English, compulsively return. This trauma, I will argue later in this chapter, indicates Australia's "imperial turn" (Burton, 2003, p. 2) or rather, its inability to "turn" away from the entwined memory of England, convictism and empire that still haunts the present.

In order to demonstrate an Australian ambivalence toward the concept of home, the action of *Jack Maggs* begins with Jack's apprenticeship as a housebreaker in England, an experience that forms his deep love for English domesticity and a crime for which he is ultimately transported. Upon his secret arrival in London, he invades Percy Buckle's precious house in order to spy on the house next door, the one he has purchased and furnished lovingly from abroad for his son, Henry Phipps. It is in the darkness of Phipps' empty house that Jack does most of his secret writing. Jack is also a spy in Tobias Oates' residence, built from "London brick" and complete with "English smells" (Carey, 1997, p. 46). This middle-class fortress has been paid for by the success of Toby's first novel and completes his "mighty passion to create that safe warm world he had been denied" (ibid., p. 36) as a child. Eventually, Jack leaves behind him a string of broken homes. Buckle's prized inheritance, the "house he worshipped" is turned into a prison as Jack and Toby "quarantine" it against outsiders, driving nails and planks into Buckle's walls and leaving in their place, "jagged wounds, gouges, dents, raw splinters" (ibid., p. 163). And Henry Phipps waits in vain for the title to his own house, receiving unwanted batches of Jack's letters in its place. The house in *Jack Maggs* is a fetishized object but only a particular kind of house: reminiscent of the kind of attention paid to Jane Austen's country estates, the characters of *Jack Maggs* are fixated on, and need to relinquish, the idea that only an English house can be called home.

The houses that represent England in *Jack Maggs* are deeply corrupt yet at the same time, profoundly attractive. They have none of the established order or hereditary privilege of Jane Austen, nor are the novel's households the celebration of order, progress and loyalty to Englishness exemplified in *Upstairs, Downstairs*. If Carey's houses, like those of his nineteenth-century predecessors, are microcosms of England, then his houses are hastily and accidentally appropriated, shoddily run, sites of betrayal and function as metaphors for a nation that Susheila Nasta describes as "fast losing its grip on any sense of coherent national identity" (Nasta, 2002, p. 3). Indicative of this downward turn, Percy Buckle's house in Great Queen St had once been home to a minor aristocracy but the street is now a haven for upwardly mobile commercialists. Buckle's own surprising and unexpected fortune, the house at Number 29 and the Lyceum Theatre, came as a "great shock" to him and with an anxiety about ownership that matches the settler colonialist's, "he tried to follow the dark and slippery lines of blood and law that had led from the body of a deceased stranger to his door in Clerkenwell" (Carey, 1997, p. 11). In addition, Buckle's inheritance consists of a cast of irreverent, uppity and surly servants plus five stray cats. Shortly after his arrival, one footman has committed suicide in the attic in a fit of jealousy over the other footman's relationship with Henry Phipps, and Mercy has taken her place in Buckle's bed as his "Good Companion" (ibid., p. 124). To his troupe of domestic servants, Buckle's house is not a home, but a transient place, a temporary shelter, a place of survival. Like Maggs, they too are "other British," a specific class of mobile people for whom home is a luxury. In Toby's Oates' English brick house the corruption runs even deeper: his affair with his sister-in-law is about to erupt in an ill-concealed pregnancy, like the boil that appears suddenly on his baby's chest. Into this already disordered domestic heart of empire, Jack Maggs will introduce his own chaos. Moreover, Jack's consistent disregard for any physical or class boundaries makes his presence within these English houses an *exposé* of the "the underside . . . of the faltering myth of Empire and its waning fantasy of an invented 'Englishness'" (Nasta, 2002, p. 3). In this Australian novel, empire and Englishness, like domestic and social thresholds or defenses, have become increasingly irrelevant.

The plot to drive Jack out of England (and to drive England out of Jack) involves securing the houses of both Buckle and Phipps against Jack's invasion. An attempt at alliance is made between the two neighbors to murder Jack under the guise of self-defense. Buckle's lawyer, the soft-spoken and ill-named, Makepeace, cites the legal precedent of the "Crown versus Forsythe:" the case of a deposed dowager widow who shot her son, the heir to her property, when he supposedly broke into her cottage with an axe. In what would no doubt be a relief to Pauline Hanson, "the law has always held that reasonable force may be used in defending one's home," Makepeace informs Phipps, "Mrs Forsythe was found not guilty" (Carey, 1997, p. 276). For these scheming characters, house equals nation: something to be defended, not only with axes and pistols but also by law and Crown. Here, law and Crown recall the various immigration laws, visa and passport controls enacted in the overnight jettisoning of the Immigration Restriction Bill underlying the White Australia policy in 1973 and the restrictions on immigration within the Commonwealth to Britain.

If Mercy had not already convinced Jack to return to Australia to be father to his two sons, the confrontation between father and adopted son – Australian and Englishman, convict and gentleman soldier – would have finally and violent disabused Jack of the fantasies of his imaginary homeland. Indeed, Phipps has occupied multiple roles in the novel for Jack: son, gentleman, solder of the 57th Foot Regiment and King, for the portrait that he has been fooling Jack with while he is overseas is, as Toby realizes, that of "George IV dressed as a commoner" (Carey, 1997, p. 244). When Phipps arrives to shoot Maggs it is a shocking reorientation of desire: for Jack, the man in the uniform is not his son but the embodiment of the "Phantom." It is Mercy who stops the fatal bullet meant for Jack and, extending the discourse of legitimacy, loses her wedding-ring finger in the process. Finally, Mercy and Jack are matched in their deformity: both are "castrated" to rewrite the founding topos of Australian identity namely, masculinity and the questions of legitimacy inherent in Mercy's marriage to Jack. Their triumphant escape from England coincides with the distressing death of Toby's sister-in-law and lover and the internal collapse of Buckle's house from flood, rendering it "wet, spongy, beyond repair" (ibid., p. 279). Buckling under the strain of its postcolonial encounter, nothing remains in England worth staying for. Only Mercy, who accompanies Jack back to Australia to "keep house" for his Australian sons (thus tempering some of Hanson's antifeminist recourse to domesticity), receives the comfort of a loving home. As Jack's wife, she supervises the building of her own home, the "grand mansion on Supper Creek Road" (ibid., p. 305); her mansion becomes her revenge against her expulsion from and many years of cleaning Percy Buckle's humbler house. However, the mansion's ostentation is not based on imported English architecture, symbolizing what Cecily Devereux has described as the "idealized past" that the descendents of English settlers do not know but continue to accept as "more valid" and "more relevant" than their own (Devereux, 1994, p. 9). It is Mercy's new and Australian "grand mansion" that manages to banish the "idealized past" from the home that she is to make with Jack: it is her present, not her past as a sexual object and domestic servant that is "more valid" and "more relevant." Leaving England behind, the shame of the convict past is pardoned and redeemed by the feminized closing images of the novel: domestication, family, prosperity and good citizenship.

Charles Dickens, You Bastard

Much of this recovery depends on Mercy's migration to Australia, Carey's most significant rewriting of *Great Expectations* and of the foundational myths of Australia that are based around unsettling questions of legitimacy. According to Hodge and Mishra's analysis of the "dark side" of Australian culture, the "major site of disturbance" (Hodge and Mishra, 1991, p. 22) or trauma at the heart of white Australian identity is the slaughter and dispossession of the aboriginal population. Recovering a history of convictism is problematic in *Jack Maggs* because it shifts the same problems of dispossession and alienation in the (new) land from the body and experience of the aboriginal to those of the incarcerated British and Irish. These traumas – dispossession and convictism – exhibit themselves as recurring questions of legitimacy that need to be constantly reaffirmed. Colonial legitimacy was cultivated by the invention and reinvention of a foundation myth, a "pivotal" moment or event in the past that "unequivocally and irreversibly established the right of the group to transmit its pattern of ownership from generation to generation" (ibid., p. 26). Thus, the importance of dates: the bi-centennial of 1988, according to Hodge and

Mishra, takes its date not from the foundation of the Federation in 1901 but the invasion of the British in 1788. Moreover, foundation myths that are written and rewritten around the difficult experiences and triumphs of early pioneers, settlers and convicts are "not enough" as history – the realities of aboriginal presence or multiculturalism – continually intervenes. So, Hodge and Mishra conclude, "white Australians have had a continuous need to generate new forms of the foundation myth, which exists to annul, defuse, displace and negate the intractable conditions of the foundation event" (ibid., p. 26). This question of legitimacy is linked to the "the bastard complex" (ibid., p. 23) unique to the Anglo-Australian male. In their study of Australian literature, Hodge and Mishra describe the affectionate Australian habit of calling a friend both a "mate" and a "bastard." This is not just an example of the "schizoid quality" of the white, male Australian mind, they argue, but a manifestation of the "bastard complex" or the "secret of the Australian obsession with legitimacy" (ibid., p. 24). Being a bastard is both a question of illegitimacy and of neglect: Jack is also the father of "bastard" sons and it is the novel's and Mercy's agenda to have Jack recognize them, regardless of their belonging to "that race of Australians" (Carey, 1997, p. 292).

Not much critical attention has been paid to the Dickensian details of Jack's childhood other than to point out Carey's remarkable imitation, or bastardization, of Dickens. Reminiscent of Dickens' orphans Little Jo, Oliver Twist and Pip, Jack Maggs is discovered by master criminal Silas Smith in the mudflats of the Thames who pays abortionist Mary Britten to raise him. Ma Britten, or Mother Britain, was "the Queen of England" (Carey, 1997, p. 87) to young Jack who would grow up "often reminded that we were not her children" (ibid., p. 198). Under Silas's guidance, Jack becomes a house burglar and learns the secret language of reading markings on silver to decipher their worth. Jack's "lessons" with Silas begins the intense rivalry with Ma's natural son Tom and sets the stage for Tom's betrayal of Jack and his first love, Silas's daughter, Sophina. The sibling rivalry between Jack and Tom represents a question of legitimacy, of who is the "mud rat" and who is the "son" (ibid., p. 99). Ma Britten is always quick to remind Tom that Jack's place in the family is determined by his "use-ful" (ibid., p. 98) contribution to their welfare: "it is this sooty fellow who is going to take you out of this pit. It was what he was raised to be. It was what you carried home his meat for . . ." (ibid., p. 100). Even before Jack is transported those around him want to read him as Dickens' Magwitch, a nonthreatening character in exile whose job is to provide the legitimate English "parent" and the metropolis with wealth, status and stability. As the "bastard," Jack is to bring home the money but not the "meat."

Jack's childhood may place his narrative in nineteenth-century realist tradition, but his lack of status as an orphan and the novel's recurring incidents of abortion and loss also tap into Anglo-Australian literary tradition: the early Australian settler literature depicting lost children and its more recent branch, stories of abandoned children. In his book, *The Country of Lost Children* (1999), Peter Pierce reads the figure of the lost child in the outback as a collection of anxieties about the "dangers" and "inhospitality" of the new landscape for the colonial settler. Occasionally rediscovered and rescued, the lost child nonetheless reflected distinctly adult anxieties about "the forfeiting of part of the national future, or of an anxiety that Australia will never truly welcome European settlement" (Pierce, 1999, p. 6). The lost child, in Pierce's analysis, also functions as a stand-in for the colonial immigrant and the convict: lost, vulnerable and far from home. In the twentieth century, the metaphor of the lost child has become politically charged as thousands of aboriginal children were forcibly removed from their parents to join white households as what is now known as the "Stolen Generations." In the novel, Ma Britten is a back-street abortionist and her home is a parody of domesticity, with backrooms in which Jack might "find blood in quantities enough to frighten any child" (Carey, 1997, p. 197). The novel also features a cast of absent children: Sophina is forced by Ma Britten to abort Jack's first son; Toby's pregnant sister-in-law is given an overdose of Ma Britten's pills, which results in her horrific death; Jack's sons are abandoned in Australia. According to Pierce, contemporary Australian literature and cultural texts are replete with stories that "describe younger generations, 'stolen,' slain, abandoned, ill-treated, or deliberately not conceived" (Pierce, 1999, p. 96). As an extension of colonial fears about a nation's future, the Australian child – from the girls of *Picnic at Hanging Rock* (Weir, 1975) to the "stolen generations" to the Chamberlain baby – affirms the "rending" (ibid.) rather than the uniting of home and community.[8]

As the condition of legitimacy, recognition becomes the policing agent of what is considered the boundary of home. Drawing upon the rhetoric of race and visibility, Jack believes that his Englishness is perfectly visible and legible in his dress, his manners, his language and his face. He arrives home in London dressed in a conspicuous red waistcoat with a silver-tipped cane, what he imagines an English gentleman would wear, but his size, his missing fingers and his "belligerent quality" (Carey, 1997, p. 3) contrast with the good cut of his clothes. Jack expects the welcome of someone returning home, but characters deny him at every turn; the lack of recognition merely affirming his status as a bastard Englishman, or, his Australianness. By not recognizing Jack as an Englishman, the English characters are obviously protecting their Englishness because recognizing Jack is also an acceptance of things abhorrent: convicts and criminals, but also English guilt, that "God help us . . . Mother England would do such a thing to one of her own" (ibid., p. 84). What is important here, however, is less the English disavowal of Jack than Jack's desire, in the face of his own convict history, to be English. His plans to pass for English, to assimilate to Englishness through Henry Phipps' recognition of him, provides a double commentary on nineteenth-century and contemporary racial and cultural discourse: for Jack to be English while being Australian acknowledges the continued hold of Britain in the national imaginary. However, Jack's vehement denial that he is "of the Australian race" (ibid., p. 292) as if it were ethnically and thus visually verifiable also recognizes that exile from England (and its aftermath in multiculturalism) is a renegotiation of whiteness as a condition of belonging.

"Singing for his Supper:" The National Author in Australia

The trope of recognition extends into the novel's concern over authorship and the authority of Jack's story. Much of the novel revolves around stolen and hidden pieces of writing: as Oates realizes that he has penetrated the secrets of Maggs' convict past through mesmerism, he keeps "as in all crooked businesses" (Carey, 1997, p. 86), two separate transcripts of Jack's mesmerism sessions, withholding the real record as fodder for his eventual masterpiece, *The Death of Maggs*. Oates' traumatic encounter with Jack will provide him with enough material to people fictional worlds for the rest of his life. Equally secret are Jack's letters to his adopted son Henry Phipps; they offer a long explanation of the secret of Phipps' benefactor, Maggs' childhood as a petty criminal, and his reasons for returning to London. Jack labors under elaborate rituals of secrecy: he writes backward with special disappearing ink and his instructions to Phipps are to use mirrors to reverse the writing and then "BURN EVERYTHING" (ibid., p. 70). The precariousness and fragility of Jack's writing, the covert ways in which it is hand-delivered and circulated around London in search of Phipps, indicate the status of colonial and postcolonial writing as marginal and peripheral, at best a supplement to English literature. Moreover, Jack's letters are never read by Phipps, who finds his benefactor's convict past distasteful and terrifying. Unwilling and unable to translate or domesticate Maggs' letters to a narrative of Phipps' own origins, which would fulfill the narrative of *Great Expectations* in which Pip is reconciled to and renewed by his convict surrogate father, Phipps denies the interrelated histories of England and Australia. Phipps too has spent a lifetime writing to his surrogate father who had promised, like Dickens' Magwitch, to "spin him a cocoon of gold and jewels . . . a nest so strong that no one would ever hurt his goodness" (ibid., p. 246). Phipps' letters from "home" offer emotional payment for the very real payments from Jack's colonial enterprises that "top up" (ibid., p. 249) the young man's London accounts each month. Carey writes that Phipps: "had sung to Jack Maggs, sung for his supper . . . without understanding it was a siren song, without ever dreaming that this tortured beast might demand of him that which had been conceived only as a flight of fancy" (ibid., p. 303). Phipps' "siren song," that lures his convict father back to England, recalls parent British texts like *Great Expectations* that haunt other postcolonial novels, and how "English" literature provides the immigrant with fictionalized and powerful accounts of a distant place called "home." And, because Phipps' "siren song" is "sung for his supper," the antipodean nature of the novel is a reminder of the ways in which postcolonial and so-called commonwealth writers are often made to sing for their suppers: to provide a usually Anglo-European audience with tales and images of the exotic. At stake in *Jack Maggs'* self-referential plot is the status and value of the Australian author in the global marketplace and the recovery of the Australian reader: Jack returns to Australia to become a father to his two Australian sons – the appropriate readers for his tale – who are taught to read by Mercy, who is illiterate until she immigrates.

Graeme Turner's article on the "celebrity of Peter Carey" explores the ways in which national and international media attention plays a role in promoting the author's literary and popular reputation at home. According to Turner's research, there are more articles detailing Carey's personal life and biography than there are academic written works written on his novels. Nevertheless, these "extra-literary considerations" (Turner, 1993, p. 135) that make up Carey's public persona as an "ordinary" Australian – growing up while the White Australia policy was still in effect in Bacchus Marsh, going to a grammar school that stressed an Anglicized accent, not reading a book until he was eighteen, his lack of interest in academics and short career in advertising – continue, in Turner's words, to create "a discourse of Australianness with which [Carey] must engage in his role as a national 'voice'" (ibid.). Yet, if "ordinariness" is "Australianness" so too is international fame: Carey's two Booker Prizes, one in 1988 for *Oscar and Lucinda* and another in 2000 for *The True History of the Kelly Gang*, meant that "in Australia, the quickest route to being a national figure is still to make it big *overseas*" (ibid.). This particular public and international attention makes Carey the forerunner for the position or prize of national writer, more so than Thomas Keneally, David Malouf or Frank Moorhouse. Thanks to his double Booker win, Carey has been co-opted into a system of literary prizing that can raise the status of the Australian author in the global marketplace but only, according to Graham Huggan's influential rereading of the politics of the Booker Prize, according to the rules of a corporate (read, British) patronage that has as its effect the continued reference to a [British] center that "still accumulates symbolic capital as a legitimizing cultural force" (Huggan, 2001, p. 117).

Huggan has suggested that the Booker Prize has ambivalent but multiple allegiances to "promoting awareness and legitimization of 'other' literatures, [while] congratulating its own 'British cultural pluralism'" (Huggan, 2001, p. 111) and uses the Commonwealth it awards as commodities for British literary consumers. Carey's double win places him in the difficult position of repackaging "Australianness" as an exoticism available for primarily English consumption. Updating Huggan's argument about the "postcolonial exotic," Karen Lamb argues that Carey's position as a "properly" postcolonial author has been compromised, "images of anti-authoritarianism and the . . . Aussie spirit are revived as essential ingredients of a white Australian colonial heroism, offering little to a contemporary readership concerned to move beyond the clichés of received history and into the less attractive arena of Aboriginal dispossession and suffering" (Lamb, 2005, p. 26).[9] Significantly, *Jack Maggs* was not even long-listed for the Booker in 1997. Housed within *Jack Maggs'* plot about two authors, one English, the other Australian, writing for the supposed munificence of the absurd Percy Buckle, a green-grocer turned patron of the arts (much like the Booker plc's own origins as a food distributor), lies, I believe, a critique of the Man Booker's perceived exploitation of the postcolonial author and the troublesome patronage of Australian literature which perpetuates the myth that Australian literature is "the autonomous reside left over after all alien elements had been subtracted" (Hodge and Mishra, 1991, p. 15).

Jack exerts a lot of his energy in the novel to secure the rights to his own story. More familiar with the business of convict mateship and the surveillance culture of the penal colony, Jack tends to trade in secrets as he explains to his fellow footman Constable, who, recently cast off as Phipps' lover, confesses his own secret homosexuality to Jack. However, convict law and honor does not work in the metropolis; in London, secrets and thoughts are bargained for, bought and sold in the literary market. Securing Jack's secrets and selling Jack's story would make Toby's fortune: weighing the skeletal plot of his novel, Toby becomes "a pawnbroker" (Carey, 1997, p. 185) bargaining unwritten work on the promise of future gain. Realizing that he is being exploited in much the same way as the characters of Toby's comic puff pieces for the newspapers are, Jack destroys several versions of the beginnings of the book based on his life in a vain attempt to stem the flow of "thoughts" that Toby has bought with his "pennies" (ibid., p. 217). On the one hand, Maggs is accusing Toby of exploiting his private and personal memories, all he has left of his childhood that is sacred and untouched by the later trauma of transportation and torture. On the other, Maggs is desperately trying to staunch the unequal flow of consumption: Toby has been, ever since the first bargain was struck, slowly consuming Maggs' past for his own fiction. And while Toby wholeheartedly believes that he is the "first cartographer" of the "Criminal Mind" (ibid., p. 167), his enthusiasm also marks the recognition of an unplumbed literary field for a voracious British reading audience. At the same time, Toby's meticulous documenting of Jack's life, the pages devoted to hands, hair, eyes, scars and pelicans are cataloged and filed in the individual pigeon holes of his desk, also recalls the fetishistic value of the exotic and the authentic. Via the struggle between Toby and Jack over authorship, the novel offers a commentary on how Carey's status as an "Australian national author," as a token "postcolonial writer," and as a "multicultural writer" affects the mainstream circulation of his books within "a powerful discourse of desire" for exoticism (Huggan, 2001, p. 154).

Surprisingly, the figure of Percy Buckle, the reader rather than author, best characterizes the novel's writerly concerns, its portrayal of national literatures and Carey's relationship with the Booker Prize. In Percy's ridiculous figure, one can trace the Australian novel's relationship to this new kind of patronage. Percy Buckle is Jack's temporary master as he seeks refuge as a footman in Buckle's house next door to Henry Phipps. A "seller of fried fish" in Limehouse turned "humble grocer in Clerkenwell" (Carey, 1997, p. 10), Buckle's upward mobility narrative accelerates when his labors are rewarded by an unforeseen inheritance. His newfound and sudden wealth allows him a luxury he had never before contemplated: *"I can read all day"* (ibid., p. 11). While Buckle is an *avid* reader, Carey intimates that he may not necessarily be a *good* reader or judge of literature: Buckle's involvement with middlebrow cultural institutions like the "lending library" and the "Workingman's Institute" (ibid.) only serves to link Buckle with (and reduce his beloved *Ivanhoe* to) middlebrow literature. Buckle's sudden wealth also leaves him a sham, a pretender to his respectability and property, and Jack's employment as his footman only serves to overemphasize the roles that they are playing rather poorly, their daily interactions registering a "hundred little clues, perceived by the brain but not so easily named, to the counterfeit they were so earnestly enacting" (ibid., p. 74). Jack's first chore in Buckle's employment is to serve dinner for a "Grand Occasion" (ibid., p. 15), the arrival at Great Queen St of seven gentlemen, among them Henry Hawthorne the actor and Tobias Oates the best-selling writer. Buckle's discomfort and eagerness to please, despite his love of books, marks him as an accidental patron – yet, he plays a pivotal role in the novel as a harborer of writers and of criminals.

As Toby begins to realize Jack's usefulness as the content of his next great novel, several more bargains are struck, some of them writerly: Buckle will keep Jack's secret as long as Jack leaves England quietly without implicating those who sheltered him; in exchange for Jack's memories, Toby will provide him with an appointment with Partridge the Thief Taker who will help Jack track down his son; in exchange for the trouble that Jack has caused Buckle, namely imprisoning his servants within his precious house, Toby promises a distraught Buckle a book dedication that would read, "*To my friend Percy Buckle, a Man of Letters and a Patron of the Arts, without whom this book could not have been written*" (Carey, 1997, p. 132). Essentially, Carey turns a writer's supposed loyalty to the patron into a relationship built on bribery, coercion and (unfair) economic transactions thereby firmly situating himself and his writer characters into the flows and modes of the imperial/global marketplace. Carey anticipates the kind of corporate sponsorship of literature that the Man Group's taking over of the Booker Prize represents. If patronage used to come in the guise of money and encouragement of the protection offered by the patron's good name then Jack, Buckle and Toby are all in the patronage game together. Buckle's "patronage" of Toby rivals Jack's "patronage" of Henry Phipps. Percy, in his own devious plotting against Jack, acts as the means by which Toby will become the gentleman writer he has dreamed of being; Henry Phipps, through Jack's money, will be the "better class of son" (ibid., p. 297), the English gentleman that Jack himself had dreamed of becoming; and Jack eventually uses his convict wealth to help Toby pay off his debtors and remain the respectable gentleman author. Like Edmund Spenser's *The Faerie Queene*, dedicated to patron Sir Walter Raleigh, Jack and Percy only hope that they will be able to "fashion a gentleman of noble person in virtuous and gentle discipline" (Spenser, 1590, p. 544).

Despite its availability in Australia, the Maggs clan never reads "That Book," *The Death of Maggs*, eventually completed by Toby, during Jack's life.

Mercy makes up for this loss by compulsively reading and amassing a small library of the different editions and volumes of the sensational novel Toby has written in revenge against her husband. But Mercy has been reading for future generations because it will only be in the present that the English and Australian narratives are finally archived together. Mercy's collection is secured "(together with Jack Maggs' letters to Henry Phipps) in the collection of the Mitchell Library in Sydney" (Carey, 1997, p. 306).[10] On first read, it would seem that initial suspicions have been confirmed: archived in a library in metropolitan Sydney, housed in parentheses in the text, are Jack Maggs' letters to Henry Phipps, a mere supplement to the seven volumes of the parent text. It would seem that Australia cannot produce the kind of fiction that, as a nation, it so desires: the Australian novel and the Australian novelist. Instead of a celebration of the possibilities of intertextuality with a parent text, like *Jack Maggs* itself is, Jack's letters are a shameful reminder of the impoverished nature of a national archive. This would be the case if Mercy's final revenge was not the "v. rough excision," carefully noted by the Mitchell's librarian on index cards in Mercy's collection, of the dedication page:

Affectionately Inscribed
 To
PERCIVAL CLARENCE BUCKLE
A Man of Letters, a Patron of the Arts (Carey, 1997, p. 306)

Mercy's unfortunate castration of Percy from the text of her husband's life as payment for his treatment of her, marks Carey's awareness of his feminized position within the new (corporate) patronage that the Booker Prize awards. At the same time, the excision of Percy Buckle's name from the novel restores Jack's letters to visibility in the act of archiving. Without Percy, Australian literature can recuperate some sense of identity or even coexistence with the nineteenth-century texts that formed its origins. And more importantly, these various texts, including Carey's own, become inheritances that can continue but also break the transmission of traumatic narratives.

Mesmerism and Trauma

The novel's extended use of mesmerism establishes intertextuality or, the incorporation of one narrative by another, as a trauma. More simply,

Carey also establishes the trauma of colonialism as a kind of hypnotic or mesmerizing experience. Jack's goal and his recovery from trauma will be to remaster his own text – to cease being the "medium or object of someone else's speech . . . to being the subject of one's own" (Brison, 1999, p. 48). An epigraph from the Marquis de Puysegur, a pioneer of animal magnetism in the early nineteenth century, forms the epigraph to the novel. In dialogue form, the epigraph describes the most effective mental and physical positioning of the mesmerist to his patient. Once the mesmerist has begun to think of himself "as a magnet" with his outstretched arms and hands forming "two poles" (Carey, 1997, p. 1) magnetic fluid should then begin circulating between the poles of the mesmerist's hands and the passive patient. Above all, mesmerism was about control, the "act of . . . will" (ibid.) that the mesmerist asserts over the patient to heighten or deaden the sensibility of the nerves of the individual. If, however, the patient threatens to break out of the somnambulistic state, the mesmerist should concentrate on the eyes: "in order to connect your idea to its object, you might lightly rub his eyes, while willing that he open them; and the effect never fails to occur" (ibid.). In a novel so concerned with national and personal identity as refracted through literary texts and acts of writing, the focus on vision draws attention to the hijacking of one person's point of view by another.

However, the two poles of the mesmerist's hands also function as a description for the antipodean geography of the novel: the affectionate naming of Australia as the land "down under" reflects the commonly held view that England and Australia were literally at opposite ends of the globe. What Ien Ang calls an Australian "spatial consciousness" stems from this geographical separation from the "mother country," which was "so far away and yet so emotionally overpowering" that early white settlers had a "particularly antipodean sense of place, a spatial consciousness of self" (Ang, 2001, p. 128). This "spatial consciousness of self," *Jack Maggs* suggests, exists as self-contradiction and the (in) voluntary suspension of will and judgment in the face of violation, control, invasion and theft in order to effect a bond. The indescribable and contradictory pull or tie that Jack feels for England and for the grown son he has never met can be understood in terms of his surrender and susceptibility to Toby Oates' hypnotic control. The extended use of mesmerism as a metaphor for the "unhealthy incorporation" (Winter, 1998, p. 342) underlying such social cohesion allows Carey to frame the impetus for Jack's return in terms of an antipodean psychogeography – of a mind and a country dominated by the magnetic "will" and influence of England.

Hypnosis and mesmerism (as well as spiritualism and trance) are fields not easily separated and often tread the same fine line between genuine scientific or medical use and exploitative charlatanism and performance. Regardless of scientific merit, these discourses offered radically new forms of explicit, spectatorial control, sexuality and communication. Explaining the Victorian fascination with Du Maurier's Jewish conductor, Svengali, with his "Evil Eye" and hypnotic enslavement of the beautiful Trilby, Daniel Pick argues that hypnosis "profoundly reinforced doubts about mental 'singularity;' it complicated Victorian ideas about the nature of the self, the subliminal aspects of all relationships, the indeterminate border between covert command and creative collaboration, inspiration and interference, partnership and possession" (Pick, 2000, p. 64). The slippage between "covert command . . . creative collaboration, inspiration and interference, partnership and possession" can be found throughout *Jack Maggs* and underscores the bargain struck between the dueling writers, the "two sets of books" (Carey, 1997, p. 86) that Oates keeps to hide the results of Maggs' hypnosis session and the two novels eventually written: *The Death of Maggs* published late in Toby's life and *Jack Maggs* itself. What begins as an "equal but opposite enthusiasm" (ibid., p. 47) soon grows out of control as Jack realizes that his thoughts and his history are no longer his own; the scales have tipped, and Jack knows that "he had become the captive of someone whose powers were greater than he had the wit to ever understand" (ibid., p. 138).

The most experimental subjects of spiritualist and psychic sessions were usually charity patients; they were easy to mesmerize and easier to control because they were more like "animals" or "machine-like" (Winter, 1998, p. 62). Doctors like Elliotson (1843) disliked mesmerizing their peers because "middle-class patients" would have brought with them an "undesirable obtrusion of their own sense of identity, freedom of action, and speech into the experimental setting" (ibid.). The Irish, the poor, the disenfranchised and women – and to this list, we can add Australians – were the ideal subjects supposedly because they were seen to be convenient voids. Mesmerism involved the exploitation of supposedly conflicted or confused subjects with no clear sense of identity. Therefore, Jack"s uncertain identity makes him the perfect subject for Toby's foray into the "Criminal Mind." His already fractured self is further emptied during the hysteria-like attacks of his *tic douloureux*. It was one of these sudden attacks during a dinner at which Toby, author and "secret Magnetist" (Carey, 1997, p. 28), is guest of honor that puts Jack literally under Toby's spell. The pain knocks Jack out of himself, filling him "with a horror so profound" (ibid., p. 29) that he becomes temporarily without an identity or a sense of place or time. Thus alienated and disempowered, Jack "for once, did exactly as he was told" (ibid.) and falls victim to Oates' mesmeric power. After the first session, the tic is pronounced by Oates to be a result of "Phantoms," and "hobgoblins inside your head" (ibid., p. 46). For Jack, these demons represent the deep traumas of transportation: flogging, punishment, imprisonment, loss and betrayal all mixed up with images of England.

The novel returns to this muddy moment in psychoanalysis in the nineteenth century specifically to conceptualize a traumatized, and, I would argue, an Australian, self: one in which a victim returns willingly to his abuser. In the early 1840s, a sitting with the mesmerist would probably look like this; Winter describes how:

> [m]esmerist and subject would stare into each others' eyes as he made "magnetic passes" over her (or him . . .) After a period ranging from a few minutes to over an hour, the subject would sink into a state known as the mesmeric "trance" or "coma." She appeared to sleep, though her eyes might stay open for a short time . . . Her senses of smell and touch disappeared, as did all awareness of her surroundings. She also lost her speech and hearing, unless the mesmerist addressed her. *A strange communion would develop between them: she would speak his thoughts, taste the food in his mouth, move her limbs in a physical echo of his* . . . Finally, after a spell of time lasting up to several hours, a different set of "passes" would rouse her from the magnetic sleep. (Winter, 1998, p. 3, italics mine)

What is being described in italics is what Ruth Leys calls a radical act of "mimesis," or "the problem of hypnotic imitation" (Leys, 2000, p. 170) a set of theoretical and practical difficulties that arise around the use of hypnosis in the treatment of trauma. In her study of the genealogy of trauma, Leys privileges certain continuities and repetitions of themes and ideas that take her beyond the politics that surround trauma's medical, legal and literary uses. She returns to hypnosis in the early nineteenth century as a starting point for the solidification of current concepts of trauma because hypnosis, which reached its height in the nineteenth century, was "not just an instrument of research and treatment but played a major theoretical role in the conceptualization of trauma" (ibid., p. 8). Leys' argument revolves around the mimesis/antimimesis debate which emerges from the relationship between hypnosis and trauma. "Trauma," she claims, "was defined as a situation of dissociation or '"absence'" from the self in which the victim unconsciously imitated, or identified with, the aggressor or traumatic scene in a condition that was likened to a state of heightened suggestibility or hypnotic trance" (ibid.). Under hypnosis, the subject, usually female, became so immersed and "unbound" within the reenactment of the traumatic scene that she becomes "open" to hypnotic suggestion of, and identification with, the "aggressor" (ibid., p. 9) or hypnotist. Any so-called multiple personalities that surfaced from the session were merely signs of the subject's openness to the hypnotist's suggestions. In other words, hypnosis is likened to a repeated birthing of a subject but one that is only a "blind" (ibid., p. 36) imitation of the Other. In the context of *Jack Maggs*, this filling of one psyche by another lies at the heart of the traumatic vacancy left by Victorian imperialism.

Tracing the work of early psychoanalytic theorists like Freud and Charcot, Leys remarks on the ways in which the reoccurrence of hypnotic suggestibility, or the complete identification of hypnotized to hypnotizer, was subsequently perceived to be not suggestibility but the subject's own desire. The mimetic paradigm needed to be simultaneously accepted in the field, because it explained and accentuated the victim's vulnerability to "suggestibility and abjection," and vigilantly disavowed, so as to retain "an ideal of individual autonomy and responsibility" (Leys, 2000, p. 9). Thus, Freud will eventually attribute any mimetic behavior on the part of his patient as the subject's own sexual desire. Furthermore, the narrative that ensues from the hypnotic session is not a product of mimesis but a "diegesis" in which the patient "recounts and recollects the traumatic scene in full consciousness" (ibid., p. 37). In recent work, the antimimetic turn is evoked to avoid the thorny ground of False Memory Syndrome while the mimetic has appealed to feminists because it makes it possible to "acknowledge the hideous ways in which the victim can come to psychically collude in the scene of violence through fantasmic identifications with the scene of aggression" (ibid., p. 38). Because the Australian psyche can be seen to participate in the same mimetic activity as the female "victim" and is therefore feminized, there has been an overemphasis on masculinity and a lack of stories, perhaps a repression, about female transportation and immigration, a story line rescued by Carey in the aptly-named character, Mercy.

If it can be argued that *Jack Maggs* is centered around the mimesis/antimimesis debate, the novel also empties Homi Bhabha's concept of mimicry of much, if not all, of its subversive potential. In *Jack Maggs*, hypnosis raises other concerns and provides a set of theoretical language to describe the attitude of ambivalence in Bhabha's phrase "almost the same, but not quite" (Bhabha, 1994, p. 86). The disruptive effect of mimicry, according to Bhabha lies in this ambivalence, its performance and "proliferation of inappropriate objects that ensure its strategic failure, so that mimicry is at once resemblance and menace" (ibid.). Mimicry is a "double articulation," an act of appropriation of the Other through "reform, regulation and discipline" but also the "sign of the inappropriate" (ibid.) as the mimic forces allowances to be made for him or her within the authoritative discourse thereby undermining it. Bhabha's analysis and examples consist of words like, "trompe-l'oeil" (ibid., p. 85) and "camouflage" (ibid., p. 91) that suggest agency in imitation. But hypnosis, which is also about imitation, is passive: a radical emptying of the self to be filled with the attributes, even thoughts, of the dominant party. In *Jack Maggs*, hypnosis and imitation contain distinctly textual elements as well: in what ways is Australian literature merely a "copy" of metropolitan literature? In what ways is it too "almost the same, but not quite?"

Thus, in place of colonial mimicry, the novel substitutes the dialectic of mesmeric mimesis/antimimesis. Leys writes that in the mimetic model, "hypnosis threatened to dissolve the distinction between self and other to such a degree that the hypnotized subject came to occupy the place of the 'other' in an unconscious identification so profound that the other was not apprehended as other" (Leys, 2000, p. 46). During the attacks of his *tic douloureux*, Toby projects his own improvisations and literary phantoms, substitutions like "Behemoth and Dabareiel, Azazel and Samsaweel" (Carey, 1997, p. 86), into Jack's head as Jack repeats or "quotes" those projections in the first-person. Jack's already fractured identity, the novel suggests, allows for such "unconscious imitation or mimesis that connotes an abyssal openness to all identification" (Leys, 2000, p. 32). Even if Jack suspects that the Phantom was "planted" inside him and that he was "not there before" (Carey, 1997, p. 248), his submission to mesmerism reveals the strength of the desire to be English: to be placed under Toby's subjection is to become a British subject again. The specular game of mimesis climaxes when Jack reads Toby's first chapter of *The Death of Maggs* and "knew that his life and death were not his own" (ibid., p. 255). As "real" Jack confronts fictional Jack, the process of mimesis is stalled. Jack refuses to separate himself from the "character who bears [his] name" (ibid., p. 262) and after destroying Toby's notebook, Jack issues another string of other commands: "You will not use your magnets. You will not write my name in your book. You will not write the Phantom's name." And, in direct contrast to Toby's plans for the fiery death of the fictional Jack, he hurls the notebook into the river where, "its pages opened like a pair of wings" (ibid., p. 263).

Jack's method of recovery is very different from the way in which Toby had hoped to cure Jack's *tic douloureux* and the trauma that haunts him.

Toby's half thought out method is some sort of exorcism: at the end of the hypnosis sessions, Toby and Jack will burn the transcripts together, casting the Phantom symbolically into the fire. The transcript would be another one of Jack's narratives that will be destroyed by fire, anticipating the death by fire that Toby has planned for his fictional convict. This method would be sound except that Toby discovers Jack's stubborn refusal to be cured, possibly because Jack has initiated his own cure by writing his narrative down as a series of letters to be bequeathed to his adopted son, Henry Phipps. In one of their final and most violent sessions, Toby is summoned to quiet a pain-crazed Jack. For the first time, Toby is unable to control his subject who writhes against and fights the "magnetic chains" (Carey, 1997, p. 189). Toby has forged to hold him. Frightened, Toby worries that "he had done something against the natural order, had unleashed demons he had no understanding of" (ibid.). A distressed Jack confesses to Toby that the Phantom has captured his "babe;" believing this to be the long sought-after breakthrough, Toby commands Jack to take back the infant and "repair" (ibid., p. 191) the wound. "When his wound is healed, yours will be too," Toby argues, "it is the same wound." Surprisingly, Jack violently rejects Toby's logic of rehabilitation and, exhausted, reveals, "I want it, fool. It is all I have left of him" (ibid.). This powerful episode marks the paradox and the politics of trauma: to heal the wound, as Toby wants, is to rob Jack of the only memory of his aborted son. The novel appeared in the same year that the Human Rights and Equal Opportunity Commission officially presented *Bringing Them Home* (1997), its report on behalf of the "Stolen Generations" to the government. Using Jack's troubled memory, Carey addresses the very rhetoric that underlies the discourse of healing the nation circulated by politicians, commentators, cultural critics and historians. In terms of reconciliation with and reparations to indigenous groups the novel poses a dilemma: to recover a convict ancestry or to heal aboriginal trauma can be considered sacrilegious, a forgetting of dispossession and genocide as the very events that call for the need for multiculturalism in the present.

In the end, the novel rests the question on the "listener" or audience of Jack's narrative. Toby draws back from the position of sympathetic listener in what seems to be a revenge of imitation. Once his manuscript is discovered by Jack, Toby is marched back to London as the convict's prisoner; he is forced to burn all the notes he has ever taken on Jack Maggs; following Jack's advice, he administers Ma Britten's pills to his trusting, pregnant lover, Lizzie, and as a final insult is forced to take Jack's money: "it was the Criminal Mind which now controlled Tobias" (Carey, 1997, p. 283). Lizzie's death from her induced abortion makes the two writers equal at last in their tragedies. By the end of the novel, both men have lost the women that they loved and have seen the death of their children not even born. The two narratives of the novel have been less integrated with each other than infected by each other. Toby has become, according to Dori Laub's observations on the dangers of "bearing witness" to trauma, a "participant and a co-owner of the traumatic event: through his very listening, he comes to partially experience trauma in himself" (Laub, 1992, p. 57). Ideally, the listener to trauma remains a "separate human being" despite the potential for contagion: "while overlapping, to a degree, with the experience of the victim, he nonetheless does not become the victim – he preserves his own separate place . . ." (ibid., p. 58) But, because of the mesmeric bond that the two writers share in the novel, the process of blame is set in motion, Toby believes without a doubt that "[i]t was Jack Maggs who had done this" and, "in his grief," begins to construct the Jack Maggs that "the world would later know" (Carey, 1997, p. 304). Through writing, rather than mesmerism, Oates asserts his ultimate power over Jack, reducing Jack Maggs to Abel Magwitch, and transforming Australian into convict.

Citizenship

While Oates (and Dickens) is largely responsible for cementing the Australian as convict in English literature, Carey attempts to supplant that memory with Mercy Larkins, a character Toby fails to imagine in his convict's future. In his best-selling novel, there is "no young woman to help the convict recognize the claims of Richard and John to have a father to kiss them good night" (Carey, 1997, p. 305). Mercy returns down under with Jack and takes up her roles as a "disciplinarian," mother and wife, transplanting the young family from the "bad influence of Sydney" and settling it in "Wingham" where "she not only civilized these first two children but very quickly gave birth to five further members of 'That Race'" (ibid.). The end of the novel emphasizes parenthood and citizenship: Jack Maggs becomes a benign and prosperous patriarch and at the end of his life had been "twice president of the shire" (ibid.). The novel's solution to the problems of national and personal identity that I outlined at the start of this chapter is citizenship, a term that can transcend nation but can also encompass the many singularities of what it means to be Australian. At the same time, it can be stretched to include nationalist and internationalist contexts. In other words, citizenship should be as Wayne Hudson explains, "site specific" and "multiple" in membership and in form (Hudson, 2000,

p. 16). Citizenship can also help shift the debate from essentialist notions of Australianness, the basis of anti-Aboriginal feeling and the core of Jack's crisis in the novel, to "capacities for citizenship" rather than "rights" (Rowse, 2000, p. 86) to increase the education, environmental and civil capabilities for those disenfranchised to be able to exercise and participate in what it means to be a "citizen."

The limits to citizenship are many: it reduces collectivity and communality to a social contract for example, and in many cases, "citizenship" is merely a stamp in a passport that allows countries to regulate and control their population. And finally, quite simply, there may also not be enough kinds of citizenship to go around to allow for the kind of specificity and heterogeneity that Hudson calls for. For example, the conclusion of the novel stresses heteronormativity: it leaves unquestioned Mercy's reproductive role in the civilizing mission of nation-building and it creates no room for the immigration of Constable, the novel's other homosexual character. Yet, Carey ends his novel with the image of a family that has gained a sense of responsibility to a community that they may not have felt much love for at the start: "The Maggs family were known to be both clannish and hospitable, at once civic-minded and capable of acts of picturesque irresponsibility and it is only natural that they have left many stories scattered in their wake" (Carey, 1997, p. 305). And even if these are "many stories" of prosperity, not hardship, which makes "being a citizen" easier, and even if the contradictions between "hospitable" and "clannish" are glossed over, these "stories" are worthy to be left to the "succeeding generations of Maggs who still live on those fertile, river flats" (ibid.). The "many stories" of "old" Australia collected by the Maggs clan becomes a legacy bequeathed to those not able to recognized themselves in the "new" Australia that official multiculturalism supports. "Old" Australia is reimagined as healthy and more importantly, as uninfected by its traumatic encounter with England.

Chapter 3

Neo-Victorianism South of Nowhere: Margaret Atwood's *Alias Grace*

Neo-Victorianism, Whiteness, and Multiculturalism

Published a year before *Jack Maggs*, Margaret Atwood's novel, *Alias Grace* (1996), also makes use of a criminal character to depict the psyche of an ex-settler colony and returns to the moment of Canada's unification as a nation in the nineteenth century. The novel is a fictionalization of the history of Irish servant girl Grace Marks, "one of the most notorious Canadian women of the 1840s" (Atwood, 1996, p. 461), imprisoned for murdering her English master, Thomas Kinnear, and his mistress, another servant named Nancy Montgomery. Forced to live out her life sentence in service to a colony of "Britishers" (ibid., p. 84), Grace Marks, the "celebrated murderess" (ibid., p. 23), appears to be the appropriate figure for exploring "the lure of the unmentionable ... the mysterious, the buried, the forgotten, the discarded, the taboo" (Atwood, 1998, p. 1509) in early Canadian history. Atwood's recipe of criminality, femininity and settlement in a distinctly Canadian landscape has paved the way for other neo-Victorian projects like Stef Penney's murder mystery *The Tenderness of Wolves* (2006), but it is Atwood's status as a national author and indeed, a national industry, that makes her brand of neo-Victorianism so unique and compelling.

Describing her own distinctly Canadian neo-Victorian project, Atwood claims that by "taking a long hard look backwards, we can place ourselves" (Atwood, 1998, p. 1512). By looking backwards to the Victorian, she can answer the questions, "where did we come from, how did we get from there to here, where are we going, who are we now?" (ibid.). But, who is this "we" in Atwood's statements? What is the "unmentionable" and the "taboo" in *Alias Grace*, especially since the novel does not adhere to the postcolonial neo-Victorian agenda of restoring or recovering the lost voices and stories of those "who inhabited this space before white Europeans arrived?" (ibid., p. 1509). In this chapter, I argue that the Victorian is deployed in *Alias Grace* to make visible the origins of the "we" or, the hegemonic view of Canada as an "unmarked" nation, to play on Grace's surname, "imagined as naturally white, male, Christian, middle and upper class, English-speaking, British, and more recently, Northern European in cultural heritage . . ." (Lee and Cardinal, 1998, p. 218). These characteristics are now "more or less synonymous with the idea of 'Canadianness'" (ibid.). Reading Grace's Irishness, class and gender, her problematic status as both a victim and a perpetrator, we can measure the "marks" or contradictory projections of Anglo-Canadian identity: Anglo-Canada is both a colonizing force over Native and French Canada; a subaltern formerly to Britain and now to the U.S.; and a dominant settler colony whose system of law, education and culture have contributed to a recognizable Canadian national identity. Neo-Victorianism can elucidate this "unmentionable" entanglement of postcolonial and post-imperial engagements by establishing a new memory for Canada. Specifically, I argue that *Alias Grace* rewrites the foundational story of the Dominion of Canada in 1867 as the moment when Englishness and white Europeanness became the unquestioned, natural, inevitable outcome.

In his influential book, *White* (1997), Richard Dyer argues for the paradoxical invisibility of whiteness as a racial position. According to Dyer, white power reproduces itself because it appears and is upheld as "normal." Only when whiteness is particularized and racialized, or, "made strange" (Dyer, 1997, p. 10) in Dyer's terms, does it become visible and open for analysis. Refining Dyer's work, Sneja Gunew points out that even this "myth of the white monolith" (Gunew, 2004, p. 48) requires historicization, especially in former settler colonies. "Too often in postcolonial critiques," Gunew stresses, "European immigrant groups are homogenized and made synonymous with a naturalized 'whiteness' or with various imperialisms," with little regard for the "very different histories relating to colonialism and imperialism" (ibid.). *Alias Grace*, I suggest, explicitly participates in this project of making whiteness "strange" in the description of nineteenth-century Toronto. Grace observes that the streets are populated by a panoply of whitenesses, "many Scots and some Irish, and of course the English, and many Americans and a few French . . . and some Germans" (Atwood, 1996, p. 124). Overwhelmed by the linguistic variations, Grace describes the city as "just like the Tower of Babel" (ibid.) and, marveling at the "skins of all hues" (ibid.) around her, begins to disrupt the hegemonic and invisible block of whiteness articulated by Dyer. At this point in Toronto's history, however, there is not yet a common whiteness defined against the "Red Indians" (ibid.) that Grace also encounters. Instead, the novel offers a racialized whiteness, one that is still in formation or, in the process of becoming "invisible," with its own border politics of inclusion and exclusion, internal hierarchies, and privileges that can be accessed and defended. In its original nineteenth-century context, phrases like "Tower of Babel" were used to lament Canada's non-British, therefore nonwhite, immigration policy: "[t]his policy of building a nation on the lines of the Tower of Babel," complained *The Calgary Herald* in 1899, "where the Lord confounded language so that the people might not understand one another's speech, is hardly applicable to the present century . . ." (Cameron, 2004, p. 19). Drawing attention to whiteness as the prehistory of official multiculturalism has huge ramifications for a postcolonial neo-Victorian project: in a Canadian context, the Victorian is deployed to confront whiteness historically but in a way that does not reaffirm its normativity.[1]

Alias Grace was written in 1996, at the height of yet another potentially devastating Quebec Referendum. On 30 October, 1995, with a record turnout of 96%, Quebec voters rejected by the slimmest of margins (50.6% to 49.4%), the government's proposal of Quebecois succession (Mackey, 2002, p. 14). Regardless of the results of the Referendum, it brought the issues of Quebec's separatism, national identity and the "breakup" of Canada to the fore. Already weakened by the so-called "Oka crisis" in 1990 and the defeat of the Meech Lake (1990) and Charlottetown (1992) Accords, the second Referendum raised new doubts over the ability of Canada's official multiculturalism policy to hold First Nations, ethnic groups and French and Anglo-Canada together.[2] As one of the most outspoken critics of Canada's official multiculturalism policy, Himani Bannerji's work best represents the debate over the continued dominance of whiteness in the management of Canadian diversity. She echoes Dyer's argument when she states that a "truly multicultural state" may be impossible to achieve "when all the power relations and the signifiers of Anglo-French white supremacy are barely concealed behind a straining liberal democratic façade" (Bannerji, 2000, p. 106). Whiteness misrepresents itself as "just another cultural self floating non-relationally in a socio-historical vacuum" rather than admitting that it functions as an immovable core and departure point against which plurality is defined. So-called "visible minorities" are inserted into an ongoing rivalry between Anglo and French Canada with no say in the construction of an "imagined" Canada, reduced to scrabbling over cultural issues rather than wielding any real political control or resistance. In such categories as "visible minority" and indeed in the very term "multiculture" itself, Bannerji finds "a thinly veiled, older colonial discourse of civilization and savagery" and that "implied in these cultural constructions is a literal denigration, extending into a valorized expression of European racist-patriarchy coded as white" (ibid., p. 107). Official multiculturalism falls under neo-Victorianism's purview because it emerges as one of the most important and ongoing experiments dealing with race relations in the aftermath of colonialism. Neo-Victorianism helps reveal the remnants of nineteenth-century racialist policies in the present's multicultural legislation and thus, *Alias Grace* is situated, I argue, within the very important and urgent project of contesting the invisibility of whiteness within Canadian multiculturalism.

Alias Grace equates the Victorian with Anglo-Canadian whiteness and, as I will explain later, explores Victorian domesticity as a "white cultural practice" (Frankenberg, 1993, p. 191) that generated a pedagogy of lived and ideological practices which became an extension of the imperial project. Through the Victorian "cult of domesticity," white women settlers inculcated the standards of normative whiteness and masculinity within the familial unit. Women in particular were to reconstruct British civility in the Canadian colonies, stabilizing a white predominantly male population and preventing intermarriage with indigenous women.[3] Atwood's obsession with the concrete materialities of Victorian domesticity stresses the ideology of colonial settlement as an English, specifically white, civilizing project. Domestic details often overwhelm any markers of Canadianness in the novel and tend to mask its commentary on a specifically Anglo-Canadian national consciousness; this effect is also indicative of the powerful normalizing effect of whiteness. In a Canadian context, domesticity is also an expression of the act of settlement, as Justin D. Edwards argues "to settle the nation, to carve out a sense of homeliness on foreign terrain, has been part of the Canadian imperial enterprise of eradicating unsettledness and settling down at the cost of other cultures and nations" (Edwards, 2005, p. xx). Atwood thus feminizes the neo-Victorian project and, like Peter Carey, forces the reader to pay attention to the domestic work and the exclusionary *and* inclusionary practices that underlie Anglo-Canadian settlement.

Grace's demonized and racialized Irishness draws attention to how migrants are positioned differently within British imperialism and how whiteness can confer certain privileges like belonging to those whose skin color represents sameness. Grace's Irishness, along with James McDermott's, was consistently recalled as the racial grounds of her criminality: "*both of the accused were from Ireland by their own admission.* That made it sound like a crime, and I don't know that being from Ireland is a crime;

although I have often seen it treated as such" (Atwood, 1996, p. 103). Seen as nonwhite, denigrated as "white negroes" and "smoked Irish" (Ignatiev, 2008, p. 41), often depicted in racist cartoons as ape-like and simian but also granted at times the privilege of whiteness against Native Americans, slaves, Asians and other European migrants, the case of the Irish demonstrates whiteness as a "coalition" (Dyer, 1997, p. 51) with its own internal borders and hierarchies. In this novel, the plight of white Irish women can be used to interrogate nation and address what Gunew has identified as the "natural façade of racialization" (Gunew, 2004, p. 23) that continues to construct relations in Canada in the strict binary of black versus white, a binary which underlies such categories as "visible minorities" and "women of color." Recovering the Victorian as a history of Irish migration to Canada and as a counter-memory to white Europeanness contributes to thinking through the conditions and experiences of hybridity, cooperation and complicity within whiteness and how settlers experience, understand and enact their roles as colonizers in their relationships with an indigenous population.

However, the limitations and dangers of Atwood's neo-Victorianism are quite clear: to what extent can the reimagination of Grace's traumatic passage from Ireland to Canada speak to the experience of recent migrants? In the context of multiculturalism, does deconstructing whiteness through an Irish genealogy sanction the privilege of ethnicity at the expense of a more complex understanding of race? A serious probing of Grace's liminal position as an Irish immigrant, servant and prisoner reveals a critique, I believe, of Canada's continued romanticization of itself as a "victim." Even after recognizing oneself as an oppressor, Diana Brydon argues, it is easy "to cast oneself as the victim of one's identity as an oppressor and to use that new identity as an excuse for continued inaction and even self-congratulation for one's inaction" (Brydon, 2004, p. 171). Such self-recriminating guilt can paralyze further analysis of ongoing complicity in systemic forms of discrimination and domination. Neo-Victorianism's deployment in this context represents a serious attempt to explore Canada's settler postcolonialism: the return to the Victorian emphasizes that decolonization in Canada has not yet been realized thus troubling the subversive qualities so lauded in postcolonial criticism. Eventually Grace herself "settles," both into a house of her own and a practical marriage in upstate New York; at the same time, the reader "settles" for the disappearance of Grace into history. Canada, and perhaps Canadian postcolonialism, it seems, cannot accommodate her.

From Susanna Moodie to Grace Marks

Atwood's obsession with the nineteenth century as a particularly compelling moment to theorize about Canadian identity culminates in *Alias Grace*. She has returned to the nineteenth century before in her groundbreaking volume of poetry, *The Journals of Susanna Moodie* (1970), a fictionalization of the experiences of an English pioneer who settled in the harsh Canadian wilderness.[4] In different configurations throughout her career, Atwood told and retold the story in which Moodie meets Grace Marks in a Toronto lunatic asylum. Susanna Moodie wrote several autobiographical volumes: *Roughing It In the Bush* (1852), which chronicled her life in the wilderness battling wild animals, disease, disappointment and death; and *Life in the Clearings* (1853), written when the Moodies began their new life in the growing city of Toronto. Structured in three parts or "journals," Atwood's poems depict Canada's transformation from bush to clearing and the Canadian settler's transition from immigrant to settler (Foster, 1977, p. 7). Prized for their illumination of the settler mindset, the poems draw on the familiar tropes of the Canadian wilderness: survival, alienation, isolation and violence which make up the characteristics of a Canadian literary canon outlined in Atwood's influential (and now much derided) book *Survival: A Thematic Guide to Canadian Literature* (1972).[5] The story of settlement that Atwood tells in the *Journals* begins the project of identifying a version of feminism, heavily rooted in the domestic, complicit in the hegemony of Anglo-Canadian identity. In many ways, *The Journals of Susanna Moodie* is about accommodating feminine whiteness to the wilderness.

Journal III ends with Moodie's death and features her curious afterlife as a ghostly figure haunting the urban landscape of contemporary Toronto and the literary terrain of "Can Lit.". Michael Redhill will take up this idea of the remnants of the Victorian buried in a landfilled harbor underneath twenty-first century Toronto in his Booker-nominated novel, *Consolation* (2007), about, among other things, "forensic geology" (Redhill, 2007, p. 11). As success alleviates the difficulty of settlement in the poem "Thoughts from Underground," Mrs Moodie reaches an epiphany, admitting her love for Canada causes a schism, "and my mind," she says, "saw double" (Atwood, 1970, p. 54). Critics have often read this doubling in terms of the "violent duality" that Atwood outlines in the Afterword: "[t]his country is something that must be chosen – it is so easy to leave – and if we do choose it we are still choosing a violent duality" (ibid., p. 62). In *The Journals*, the doubleness that divides Mrs Moodie remains an expression of the ambivalent tension between losing her Englishness and gaining a sense of Canadianness. Atwood writes that Moodie "claims to be an ardent Canadian patriot while all the time she is standing back from the country and criticizing it as though she were a detached observer, a stranger" (ibid.). This pathological sense of belonging, Atwood continues, is "perhaps . . . the way we still live;" and she suggests that the postcolonial Anglo-Canadian experience is the "paranoid schizophrenia" which comes from the belief that "we are all immigrants to this place even if we were born here" (ibid.).

As "hostile cities replace[d] hostile forests" (Atwood, 1972, p. 149) in the Canadian imaginary, Atwood began to turn toward an episode in *Life in the Clearings* in which Moodie documented her visit to the Toronto prison and lunatic asylum where she viewed, rather than visited, the "celebrated murderess" (Atwood, 1996, p. 23) Grace Marks. Something about Grace's story enticed Atwood away from Moodie as a symbol for Anglo-Canada's cultural past. This meeting was to obsess Atwood for almost thirty years as she wrote and rewrote the episode first in a television play, *Grace Marks*, later screened by CBC as *The Servant Girl* (1974) and next, in an abandoned drama, simply entitled *Grace* (1979).[6] In the 1990s, Atwood had a vision of Grace Marks in Thomas Kinnear's cellar and set down her first draft of *Alias Grace*.[7] With each successive rewriting, Moodie begins to fade out of the picture: while *The Servant Girl* was a straightforward account of Moodie's version of the Kinnear–Montgomery murders, the drama, *Grace*, begins to take a more skeptical approach to Moodie's veracity. By the time Atwood writes *Alias Grace* in 1996, Moodie has all but faded into the background, remaining only as an intertext, described by Grace as a "literary lady" inclined to "embroider" her texts with melodrama (ibid., p. 191) and later, as a "beetle . . . round and fat and dressed in black" (ibid., p. 358). The dates of Atwood's rewritings are significant: *The Journals of Susanna Moodie*, published in 1970, was sandwiched between the centennial celebrations in 1967, the findings of the Royal Commission on Bilingualism and Biculturalism (1961–9), and the "Multiculturalism within a Bilingual Framework" policy announced by Prime Minister Trudeau in 1971.[8] Struggling between Moodie and Grace Marks in the two plays, both sign-posts on the way toward official multiculturalism, Atwood gave up until her vision of Grace in Kinnear's cellar occurred in the 1990s, a few years after the passing of the New Multiculturalism Act in 1988. At each crisis point in Canadian identitarian politics, Atwood, like Peter Carey in Australia, returned to the nineteenth century. Each version of Moodie and each retelling of the Kinnear–Montgomery murders, I would like to argue, significantly revises the definition of Canadian identity in the one before.

Moreover, *Alias Grace* interacts with and revises the "victim positions" that Atwood laid out in the opening chapter of *Survival*. In this guide to Canadian literature, Atwood identified the theme of "survival" as the "central symbol for Canada" (Atwood, 1972, p. 32): not only is "survival" the cornerstone of a distinct Canadian literary canon but it also forms an imagined community, for it "holds the country together and helps the people in it to co-operate for common ends" (ibid., p. 31). Having identified survival as the Canadian "neurosis," Atwood developed the claim that Canada "*as a whole* is a victim, or an 'oppressed minority,' or 'exploited' by the 'mother country'" (ibid., p. 35, italics mine). "If Canada is a collective victim," Atwood states, then attention needs to be paid to what she defined as the four "Basic Victim Positions." "The positions," she argues, "are the same whether you are a victimized country, a victimized minority group or a victimized individual" (ibid., p. 36). Interestingly, the four positions lead to what can be imagined as Canada's coming into "wholeness" or, a progressive recovery from being a helpless victim in denial (Position 1) to a "creative non-victim" (Position 4) (bid., p. 38). Redhill's novel, which relies on more conventional understandings of past recovery, advances the idea that, in the postmillennium, Canadian identity, having survived, might now require "consoling." Atwood tantalizingly suggests that by a slight but important pronoun change, "if you were to substitute 'we' or 'our class' or 'our country' for 'I' . . . a more complicated analysis of Canadian colonialism" (ibid., p. 40) would appear. However, it is clear that Atwood's pronouns refer only to European/settler Canadians like Susanna Moodie, "the land *was* hard," Atwood insists, but "we have been (and are) an exploited colony; our literature is rooted in those facts" (ibid., p. 41). By the time Atwood writes *Alias Grace* in 1996, these "victim positions" have come under heavy fire and places the reader in a critically uncomfortable situation: should we measure the settler's trauma of arrival against the trauma of First Nation dispossession? Or, against the imprisonment of Japanese-Canadians during WWII? Without belittling her experiences as a poor, immigrant woman to nineteenth-century Canada, can we critically address the ways in which Grace is considered to be "the traumatized survivor of a notorious double murder" (Darroch, 2004, p. 103)? More importantly, why would Canada still insist on victimization in order to demonstrate its coherence as a "whole?"

According to Marita Sturken, the recovered memory debate reifies wholeness and how it can be achieved through the act of remembering. Remembering, she argues, "becomes a process of achieving close proximity to wholeness, of erasing forgetting" (Sturken, 1999, p. 243). To remember means to reach some kind of explanation, for abuse, for lack, for a feeling of unhappiness in the present. Forgetting, on the other hand, is demonized as a "threat to subjectivity," as loss and absence. Yet, Sturken reminds us, forgetting is also "strategic" and is "a primary means through which subjectivity is shaped and produced" (ibid.). With this in mind, Atwood's turn from Susanna Moodie to Grace Marks – essentially also tracing the development of neo-Victorianism's recovery work over time – indicates the larger problem of Canada's continued desire for what Sturken has described as "victim/survivor status," a powerful position imbued with "moral authority" and "the weight of cultural value" (ibid., p. 241). Sturken's discussion takes place in the context of the recovered/false memory debate and its consequences for a feminism equated with victimization. In such a context, it is hard, Sturken admits, to address the popular "romanticization of victimhood and survivor status" (ibid., p. 242) and its attractive benefits of sympathy, legitimacy, solidarity and attention in the public sphere. As Atwood moves closer toward Grace's story, her portrayal of Susanna Moodie becomes increasingly unflattering: having survived, Mrs Moodie becomes a smug, moralistic, even repressive figure and her survival and victimization over the years has become highly problematic, even irrelevant. As Atwood writes in *Survival*, later immigrants arriving in Canada find themselves victimized by precisely what Moodie represents, "the place of the feared, unfriendly and treacherous natives has been taken by – of course – those earlier immigrants, the WASPS and the French" (Atwood, 1972, p. 149).

It is easy to see why Grace Marks captivated Atwood: rather than the labels of "criminal," or "mad woman," or even "celebrated murderess" attributed to her by Mrs Moodie, Grace is an "alias" (Atwood, 1996, p. 23), a chimera constructed out of gossip, speculation, official newspaper reports, witness testimony, the expertise of the medical community, the legal system and public opinion. Grace muses: "how can I be all of these things at once?" (ibid.). These deliberately ambiguous versions of Grace, however, form part of Atwood's neo-Victorian strategy; as she records in her lecture, "In Search of *Alias Grace*," "I did what neither Susanna Moodie nor I had done before: I went back to the past" (Atwood, 1998, p. 1513). Going "back to the past," Atwood self-consciously rejects Moodie's chronological version of the murders and embraces the essential fictiveness of history itself. But, going "back to the past" is also a specifically Canadian neo-Victorian project: as Linda Hutcheon claims in *The Canadian Postmodern*, postmodernism's "ex-centric" properties and concerns are particularly well-suited to "settler/colony history and its marginal place in international terms but also because Canada has no centralized core" (Hutcheon, 1988b, p. 3). By shifting the focus from Moodie to Grace Marks, the novel moves away from categorization and containment in order to question the very means by which those categories are made and enforced. Moving from Moodie's experience of a "violent duality" to Grace's amnesia and multiple personality disorder challenges the construction of a bounded national space and moves closer toward exploring the implications and ramifications of official multiculturalism. By making Grace the Canadian subject rather than Moodie, Atwood can explore not just the "unmentionable – the mysterious, the buried, the forgotten, the discarded, the taboo" (Atwood, 1998, p. 1509), but all the exclusionary practices that make up Anglo-Canadian primacy while also maintaining the necessary elusiveness and incompletion of Canadian identity.

White Men Need Not Apply

Because of Canada's proximity to the U.S., neo-Victorianism can shift to address neo-colonial North/South relationships. In *Alias Grace*, the use of the Victorian becomes twofold: to explore Canada's emergence from British imperialism and to help it maneuver against the imperialism of the U.S. Interestingly, the "other" history to *Alias Grace's* interest in Canada's union in 1867 is the beginning of the U.S.'s own border politics, the start of the Civil War, in which Simon Jordan ironically loses his own memory. In his introduction to *White Civility*, Daniel Coleman describes the racial taxonomy of Canada's early immigration policy, which descended "in preference from British, Americans, Scandinavians, Germans, and French to southeastern Europeans, Austria-Hungarians, Balkans, Hebrews, and Italians" (Coleman, 2006, p. 22). Groups and ethnicities beyond the "White borders of Europe" were considered "incompatible with the national project of building a British-based civility" (ibid.). Eva Mackey refers to this immigration policy as "icy white nationalism" or, a "racialized 'Canadianness' [which] was mobilized to create links between Canada and Britain and other north and 'civilized' nations, to differentiate Northern and Southern people (races), and to distinguish Canada from the USA" (Mackey, 2002, p. 30). By portraying the U.S. as degenerate and plagued by racial problems, violent, and without ties to the British crown, Canadian identity was produced as white in all its attributes and ideals by groups such as the Canada First movement.[9] This history of European immigration to Canada and the border politics of whiteness are dramatized in *Alias Grace* by the courtship of Grace by men who represent various ethnicities in the hierarchy of Britishness. At the same time, the use of the

Victorian taps into contemporary concerns about multiculturalism by exploring the different modes of belonging and assimilation that these men can offer Grace.

In a game played with Mary Whitney on Halloween night, the girls peel apples they think will foretell their husbands' identities: Grace's peel extends into the letter "J" and so Atwood loads the dice against Thomas Kinnear and in favor of the other men in the novel who all have the letter "J" in their names. Atwood notes in the Author's Afterword to *Alias Grace* that Kinnear came from a "lowland Scots family from Kinloch, near Cupar, in Fife, and to have been the younger half-brother of the heir to the estate" (Atwood, 1996, p. 463). Astutely, Grace guesses that he had been "packed off to the Colonies to get him out of the way" (ibid., p. 229). Kinnear is reminiscent of what Coleman has defined as the allegorical figure of the "enterprising Scottish orphan" who encompasses the view that the Scots were "the primary inventors of English Canada through their leading roles in business . . . politics . . . religion . . . [and] education . . . but also because Scots, historically, were the primary inventors and promoters of the category of Britishness that is the conceptual foundation of the Canadian idea of civility" (Coleman, 2006, p. 6). Unlike *The Servant Girl* and *Grace*, the novel omits any reference to Grace's feelings for Kinnear in an attempt to downplay an attraction toward the elements of Britishness and an iconic whiteness that he represents. Kinnear appears, paradoxically, forgettable: "he has faded; he's been fading year by year, like a dress washed over and over, and now what is left of him? A faint pattern. A button or two. Sometimes a voice; but no eyes, no mouth" (Atwood, 1996, p. 296). So normative does Britishness become as its value rises that Kinnear and his Scottishness disappears from the text.

Instead, Grace's romantic interests are limited to American and Irish men: in Simon Jordan and Jeremiah, the peddler, both from Massachusetts, Atwood emphasizes the influence of the U.S. in the Canadian imaginary. And, in James McDermott and Jamie Walsh, the fictional Grace's eventual husband, both from Ireland, we are shown the fissures within a hegemonic English-Canada. Irishness, I will argue, works to unpick a hegemonic and paradoxically unremarkable whiteness. Stephanie Lovelady has read the emphasis on "Irish nationality" in *Alias Grace* as one of the many public discourses that construct Grace. Distancing herself from her Irishness, Lovelady argues, allows Grace the possibility of passing, "both in terms of ethnic passing, assimilation and in hiding her identity" (Lovelady, 1999, pp. 48–9). However, Lovelady's identification of "passing" and "ethnic assimilation" must be thought of in terms of the (in)visibility of whiteness;

and Grace's immigration and her Irishness must be treated in terms of the novel's neo-Victorian project of confronting whiteness.

Grace's first suitor in the novel is the traveling peddler Jeremiah. Like Simon, Jeremiah is an American, but ethnically mixed, "he looked like a Jew or a gypsy . . . he was a Yankee with an Italian father who'd come over to work in the mills in Massachusetts; and his last name was Pontelli, but he was well-liked . . ." (Atwood, 1996, p. 154). Italians, Ukrainians and Jews, like the Irish, were indicative of the "instability of white as skin colour" (Dyer, 1997, p.57), capable of being included or excluded within the boundaries of whiteness at will. Throughout the novel, we learn of Jeremiah's many aliases as Jerome Dupont, the "neuro-hypnotist;" "Signor Geraldo Ponti, Master of Neuro-Hypnotism, Ventriloquist, and Mind-Reader Extraordinaire" (Atwood, 1996, p. 425) and finally, Gerald Bridges. The variation in his last name, "Ponti" and "Bridges," cements his position as a character who crosses borders and can assist Grace in similar acts of passage and passing. Jeremiah, however, as Lovelady has argued, can offer Grace the capability of "passing" that McDermott cannot. Jeremiah describes border crossing as "like passing through air, you wouldn't know it when you'd done it" (ibid., p. 266). As a peddler, "paying the Customs duties on my goods would be an inconvenience to me" and, as the laws "were not made by me or mine, but by the powers that be, and for their own profit," Jeremiah's resistance to state apparatus, to his mind, are "harming no one" (ibid.). As a peddler, Jeremiah prefigures the role of economics and financial exchange like NAFTA, that form a "bridge" between the U.S. and Canada. He also represents the transnational character that must, by his nature, resist any form of nationalism or essentialism and thus, he can be an allegorical figure for a North Americanness that forms part of Canada's process of self-identification.

If Grace runs away with Jeremiah, she too will be "homeless, and a wanderer, like the peddlers and those who worked in fairs" (Atwood, 1996, p. 155); Jeremiah will offer Grace a "French name" and have her embark on a career as a "medical clairvoyant" (ibid., p. 268). By accepting Jeremiah's offer, Lovelady suggests, Grace can be "assimilated into society under a new name, no longer bound by her identity as a celebrated murderess, her childhood poverty, or her Irishness" (Lovelady, 1999, p. 45). However, this may be too celebratory: Grace rejects Jeremiah's offer because, without the protection of marriage, Grace might be left "in the lurch, by myself in a strange place" (Atwood, 1996, p. 268). Grace's thoughts of survival here are important: Jeremiah's offer of transnationality and limitless borders threaten Grace's dreams of a secure "home" and a secure sense of Canadian identity. As an essentially nomadic character traversing a pan-American space, Jeremiah voices the fear of a loss of Canadian distinctiveness.

On the other hand, Simon Jordan offers Grace a very different potential for "passing." Readings of Simon are often negative, perhaps as they should be. He is incapable of reading Grace although she leaves him ample clues to be read. He cannot draw any connections between his desire for Grace and his desire for his landlady, Rachel, nor is he capable of understanding the sado-masochistic economy that underlies his relationship with both women. A man of his time, he is chauvinistic, idealistic and loath to break from the mold of medical discourse. He fantasizes about Grace as "terra incognita" (Atwood, 1996, p. 389), a geography to be explored and mapped. Before she was a "celebrated murderess" and amnesiac, she was merely a "flat landscape" (Atwood, 1996, p. 389) with nothing to attract him. As his observation of and involvement with Grace grows, Simon's own narratives, seen in his incomplete letters home, become more and more erratic and incoherent: "he has been traveling blindly," he realizes, ". . . like those who have searched fruitlessly for the source of the Nile . . . The maps are wrong . . ." (ibid., p. 293). Simon's fantasies are often from high Romance; he sees Grace as the "nun in the cloister, a maiden in a towered dungeon, awaiting the next day's burning at the stake" (ibid., p. 59) Grace is also, "the cornered woman" and the hysteric. All these versions of Grace are "as it should be" (ibid.). As Grace's story-telling begins to entrance Simon, he comes to the sudden realization that "Grace Marks is the only woman he's ever met that he would wish to marry" (ibid., p. 388).

As an American, Simon serves as a reminder of the contradictory sentiments that Canada has toward the U.S. As Mackey's study of Anglo-Canadian identity reveals, it remains important to demonize the U.S. as an external other in the project of creating national unity through difference and it remains popular to define Canada in opposition to the neo-colonialism of America. Nonetheless, there exists a surprising admiration for the U.S. with its strong sense of patriotism and sense of a "secure identity" (Mackey, 2002, p. 145). In addition, Mackey's study revealed that many so-called "Canadian-Canadians" found that "a more American pluralist model was desirous as a solution to the problem of Canada's fragmented and even non-existent identity" (ibid.). The assimilationist "melting pot" model in the U.S. is perceived to be capable of managing internal diversity and differentiation in the service of a core culture whether or not (or especially because) that core culture is perceived as "unmarked," white and "authentic" (ibid., p. 153). As an *American* love interest, Simon can offer Grace the opportunity to disappear into this white core. For example, when Grace and James McDermott, tried and executed as her accomplice and "paramour," cross the border to the U.S., Grace dreams of ghostly disappearance:

> ... the waves kept moving, with the white wake of the ship traced in them for an instant, and then smoothed over by the water. And it was as if my own footsteps were being erased behind me, the footsteps I'd made as a child on the beaches and pathways of the land I'd left, and the footsteps I'd made on this side of the ocean, since coming here; all the traces of me, smoothed over and rubbed away as if they had never been, like polishing the black tarnish from the silver, or drawing your hand across dry sand.
> On the edge of sleep I thought: It's as if I never existed, because no trace of me remains, I have left no marks. And that way I cannot be followed.
> It is almost the same as being innocent. (Atwood, 1996, p. 342)

In light of Dyer's argument, this moment is Grace's passing into "whiteness" by shedding the "marks" (ibid.) and "black tarnish" (ibid.) of her Irishness. Immigration to Canada, the "pathways of the land I'd left," and her temporary border crossing into the U.S., are the acquisition of further "marks" of whiteness, which paradoxically, must be disappearance, "all the traces of me, smoothed over and rubbed away as if they had never been" (ibid.). Insofar as Simon can be said to stand in for America, he has the opportunity to offer Grace the kind of erasure and disappearance that she equates with "innocence."

Lovelady observes that James McDermott and Jamie Walsh are "two distinct kinds of Irish identity," with James representing the "criminal, rebellious, Irishman" and Jamie, his diminutive, a "considerably less threatening version of the Irish-Canadian" (Lovelady, 1999, p. 48). Like Grace, McDermott was also from Ireland, but he had "joined the army in England" until he had "deserted, and stowed away on a ship bound for America; and when discovered, he's worked out the rest of his passage; but had landed in Canada East rather than the United States" (Atwood, 1996, p. 226). Beginning with this accident of arrival, McDermott worked the border "on the boats that plied up and down the St. Lawrence River" (ibid.). Like many of the other immigrant characters in the novel, McDermott finds it hard to accommodate his expectations and work for an English "gentleman." According to the novel, "his family was respectable enough, being from Waterford in the south of Ireland, and his father had been a steward" (ibid.), but the narrative of his immigration is of a fall from civility, the experience of being "raced" is only emphasized upon his landing in Canada. McDermott's initiative and participation in the murders reveals a desire to exterminate Kinnear's symbolic Englishness, but also to inhabit or emulate it, as the episode of exchanging Kinnear's shirt with McDermott's own demonstrates. Consistently described as a "liar and a braggart" (ibid., p. 227), a violent drunk, a potential rapist and eventually, a murderer, McDermott's execution would seem to conveniently excise the negative aspects of his ethnicity from the foundational core of Anglo-Canadian identity. McDermott functions in the novel as a "scapegrace" (ibid., p. 226), literally the one who will allow Grace to escape punishment, but also as what I want to argue is the novel's version of "white trash." As John Hartigan argues, "white trash is used to name those bodies that exceed the class and racial etiquettes required of whites if they are to preserve the powers and privileges that accrue to them as members of the dominant racial order . . ." (Hartigan, 2005, p. 115). Thus, the demonization of McDermott evokes a category crisis within Anglo-Canada's symbolic order revealing its fragility by threatening its civility and "icy white" purity.

Historical Grace Marks was reported to have been released from prison to "a home provided" (Atwood, 1996, p. 439) and history stops narrating there. Instead, Atwood decides to restore Jamie Walsh to the narrative: he reappears suddenly at the end of the novel as a parody of the romantic hero, ready to marry the rehabilitated Grace and to be forgiven for his role in her imprisonment. Their marriage is arranged instantaneously and Grace writes, "I made a show of hanging back, though the reality of it was that I did not have many other choices, and it would have been most ungrateful of me to have said no, as so much trouble had been taken" (ibid., p. 452). Through Jamie's love, undiminished supposedly over the 30 years that Grace has spent in prison, she eventually fulfills her dreams of a house, quilts of her own, and even potentially, children. The couple retires to Ithaca, New York, to an "ordinary farmhouse, white in colour, and with shutters painted green" (ibid., p. 454). They have a cat named "Tabby" who "is the colour you might expect and a good mouser, and our dog is named Rex . . ." (ibid., p. 455). "These are not very original names," Grace tells Simon (now rendered the ideal audience by his own amnesiac silence) in a final letter, "but we don't wish to get a reputation in the neighborhood for being too original" (ibid.). With only his physical characteristics to mark him as ethnically other, Lovelady claims that Jamie Walsh is the best romantic choice for Grace because he allows her to "pass." If Kinnear's whiteness is made remarkable paradoxically by its very lack of characteristics,

Jamie Walsh's Irishness is similarly unremarkable. Walsh poses no threat to the stable symbolic order of Anglo-Canadian identity because he has been granted access to respectability and thus, "white" unremarkability.

Historically, Walsh took the stand against Grace Marks' at her trial, claiming that he saw her on the day of the murders, acting strangely, wearing Nancy Montgomery's clothing. In the context of whiteness, we can read Walsh's Irishness as complicit, one that colludes in the policing of boundaries and the law and refuses to draw attention to itself by service to the state. Walsh is rewarded for his betrayal of Grace with membership in the category of "white," erasing his difference as Irish; he is given a job in Toronto after making "such a good impression as a bright up and coming lad, at the trial" (Atwood, 1996, p. 451). By marrying Grace, Jamie confers upon her an "honorary whiteness" (Hartigan, 2005, p. 194) in which membership or dominance is enacted through domestic practice. The degree of assimilation that Jamie exhibits and can eventually offer Grace depends on his success and affluence and his immigration to the U.S., "as he was of the opinion that there was more opportunity for becoming a self-made man down there" (Atwood, 1996, p. 451). Despite being set in the nineteenth century, Atwood enters into the debates raging in the early 1990s in Canada over whether or not it was appropriate to import the melting pot model of multiculturalism from the U.S.[10] Both Jamie and Grace's Irishness have been assimilated by the U.S.'s "melting pot" version of multiculturalism, which stresses that, "you were what you had, not where you'd come from, and few questions asked" (ibid.). Ultimately, the "mosaic" of Canada would only emphasize the couple's "originality," their difference and Grace's status as a "celebrated murderess." Significantly, Grace writes, "I would not wish any here to learn my true name" (ibid., p. 456), thus losing any further "marks" of difference and signaling her "survival" as boredom or, the successful assimilation to the dominant ideology. Grace's exile, which can also be read as expulsion, to the U.S. in what is essentially a Canadian novel asks the question that is behind much criticism of multiculturalism: is there a point where diversity, or being an Irish "celebrated murderess," begins to threaten social cohesion and the myth of Canada, that has its origins in the nineteenth century, as civilized, tolerant and peaceful?

Quilting: Multiculturalism and Feminism "Made Strange"

The novel's emphases on daily woman-centered activities like cleaning, sewing, collecting, scrap-booking and especially quilting exploits and tests neo-Victorianism's ability to narrate multiple versions of nation opposed to dominant forms of historical record. The affluent, normal, almost perversely domestic scenes at the end of the novel also stress the "unmarked," apparently neutral institutional and social arrangements that constitute white privilege. The litany of domestic living can be termed "white cultural practices" (Frankenberg, 2003, p. 191): Grace's daily chores, her sewing, her cleaning, her decorating, the mundane fact that she will "always wear gloves to town" (Atwood, 1996, p. 456) index "practices" that maintain the invisibility of dominance. Read this way, Grace becomes a neo-Victorian avatar of the domestic imperial project, at once a critical observer and an embodiment of the Victorian ideals of civilization and of progress. Throughout the novel, Grace has demonstrated a certain understandable prickliness toward her domestic work; she becomes quite peeved, for example, when Simon "pesters" her about using and cleaning the "slop pail" (ibid., p. 216). Coleman's term "wry civility" or critical civility may be useful here in understanding the novel's scrutiny of domesticity. In his study of how a "normative concept of (English) Canadianness came to be established" (Coleman, 2006, p. 5), Coleman identifies an "English Canadian whiteness" organized around a "specific form of civility modeled upon the gentlemanly code of Britishness" (ibid., p. 10). Calling this "white civility," Coleman identifies various Canadian male literary figures (Kinnear's reprisal of the enterprising Scottish orphan, for example) that demonstrate how "the Canadian nation mediated and gradually reified the privileged, normative status of British whiteness in Canada" (ibid., p. 6). Coleman is not interested in critiquing the effort to establish a civil society in Canada especially if it creates structures and ideals of justice and equality. Instead, Coleman takes as his project, the difficult task of analyzing "the White supremacy embedded in a real project of civility" (ibid., p. 9). "Wry civility," according to Coleman, "remains aware that civil ideals have been partially and unevenly pursued in the past and that we in the present are as likely to be blind to similar exclusions and unevennesses as were past Canadians" (ibid., p. 239). Grace's "wry civility," her unyielding attention to domestic work and details, calls whiteness into question using a feminine "code," at the same time providing commentary, via the Victorian, on contemporary Canadian feminism, its desire to speak for equality on the behalf of all women and its historical origins in nation.

In *Alias Grace*, the Penitentiary Governor's wife's scrapbook offers a model of civility and plurality that the novel rejects because it functions in service of the kind of Anglo-conformity that the Governor's wife represents. The scrapbook is a macabre collection of newspaper cuttings of "all the famous criminals" (Atwood, 1996, p. 26) who have been imprisoned or executed at the Penitentiary. Grace's recognition that "repentance" (ibid.) functions as a form of assimilation and coercive belonging illustrates how some models of cultural pluralism work only to absorb difference by making it comply with dominant, here British, cultural values and norms. Grace's criminality as a form of difference is held up against the Governor's wife's adherence to Victorian gender conventions, as her title "Governor's wife" indicates, which guarantees her membership to Anglo-Canadian society and thus, citizenship. The Governor's wife titillates her guests and manages the boundaries of her own civility through the domestic, yet imperialistic, hobby of collecting. Her scrapbook sits in the parlor, covered with a silk shawl "sent from India by her eldest daughter who is married to a missionary" (ibid., p. 24). Heavily decorated with ornate images of flora and fauna versus the simplicity of Grace's quilt-blocking, the silk shawl is a casual reminder of the Governor's wife's complicity in the imperial project which equates missionary work with her own patronage of Grace: both conversion and repentance become technologies of assimilation.

On the same table as the Governor's wife's scrapbook can be found an American import, the Godey's Ladies' Book, "with the fashions that come up from the States" (Atwood, 1996, p. 24), and also the keepsake albums of the Governor's two daughters, Lydia and Marianne. Godey's Ladies' Book appears several times in the novel as a marker of trade and cultural influence from the U.S. but, in a rather unsubtle critique of such commerce and exchange, Grace describes to a curious Simon the customs of the "privy," where "what was in there for wiping was an old copy of the Godey's Ladies' Book" (ibid., p. 216). Instead, the keepsake albums serve as a second model of collectivity and memory; primarily collections of girlish memorabilia, fashion items, literary tidbits and travel, the albums are governed by feminine sentimentality. On discovering a keepsake from a girl who drowned in the lake who shares the same name as Nancy Montgomery, Grace scoffs: "I don't know why they are all so eager to be remembered. What good will it do them? There are some things that should be forgotten by everyone, and never spoken of again" (ibid., p. 26). Grace seems critical of this feminine kind of history, dismissing the girls' memorabilia as trivial with no sense of what counts as recorded history. Later, in prison, Grace muses about what she would put in her own keepsake album, whether it should be "only the good things" or "all of the things?" And, whether she would be "truthful to [her] own life?" (ibid., p. 382). If history, or a narrative of nation, is constructed out of fragments, an ethical choice must be made that the girls' keepsake albums do not follow. Grace criticizes them for "cheating," for creating memories out of "scenes and events they have never witnessed" (ibid.) and for being neither specific nor future-oriented in their collections. Yet, her greatest condemnation lies in their editing of the albums to reflect only the "good things" that do not threaten the sanctity of home or nation. In order to maintain the myth of civility in the present, Coleman argues that there is a "different kind of cherishing of evil memories, an elegiac discourse by which Canadians demonstrate their civil sensibilities through mourning the traumatic, but supposedly necessary, losses that were inevitable along the path of progress" (Coleman, 2006, p. 29). The discourses of memory implied and rejected in the scrapbook and keepsake albums provide a gloss on neo-Victorianism's ability to manage national memory.

The quilting metaphor has garnered the most attention in *Alias Grace* with readings that range from deconstructive narrative strategies to explorations of alternate feminist modes of expression, narration and experience. Each chapter of the novel is named after a particular Canadian quilt pattern emphasizing Atwood's interest in a female collectivity crafting a national past. In Atwood's neo-Victorian project, quilting best "makes strange" the discourses of multiculturalism and feminism: displacing them back to the Victorian reveals new forms of imperialism, new ways of oppression or obfuscations that might undermine what the partnership between multiculturalism and feminism hopes to achieve. The richness of the quilting metaphor for the "mosaic" model of contemporary multicultural Canadian identity becomes apparent as, according to Fleras and Elliot:

> the Canadian mosaic, sometimes referred to also as a quilt, consists of an arrangement of individual tiles with distinctive shapes, colours, and textures. These tiles are aligned in a unified and coherent pattern whose overall image is one of unity and coherence. The overall effect transcends the individual tiles, although all continue to retain their integrity and distinctiveness" (Fleras and Elliot, 2002, p. 65).

Though attractive, this model has its flaws: some have argued for its status as merely a romantic metaphor rather than expressing any real understanding of how to manage diversity. Others have argued that in reality, the model is a "vertical mosaic" in which the tiles are often uneven in shape and height, "reflecting their differential status and unequal contribution to society" (ibid., p. 66).[11] Grace herself offers these critiques in her silences and in her relationship to quilting as labor. While Grace describes in detail the various quilt patterns women should have at various stages in their lives for Mary Whitney and the reader, she deems this information too "ordinary" (Atwood,

1996, p. 162) to share with Simon, thus withholding from him an important key to her own memories and also to quilting as a pedagogy of nation. Transformed into a metonym for "home" and "hearth" (ibid., p. 98), the "Log Cabin" (ibid.) quilt Grace sews is, significantly, not for herself but as part of one of the Governor's daughter's trousseau. The story of nation being told by this particular quilt is deceptive: Grace's sewing skills produce prison work such as mailbags and uniforms, but the Governor's wife also exploits her "fine work" (ibid.) to reproduce quilt blocks. Thus, Grace labors to maintain the appearance of stability and fixedness within the state and a home that are not hers. Grace experiences belonging or settlement as a series of rough displacements and negotiations and her home "work" is in service to ease the belonging of others.

Atwood makes explicit the connection between quilting and nationalist discourse when Grace describes laundering the multicolored quilts with Mary Whitney, "when we'd hung a half-dozen of them up on the line, all in a row, I thought that they looked like flags, hung out by an army as it goes to war" (Atwood, 1996, p. 161). In another oft-quoted passage, Grace connects the quilt-as-flag motif to women, sexual danger, and the domestic sphere as she reflects on "why is it that women have chosen to sew such flags, and then to lay them on the tops of beds?" (ibid.). Jennifer Murray's reading of this passage highlights both the dangers of everyday life that women faced in the mid-nineteenth century and also the nationalist connotations of the quilt as "flag." For Murray, the flag pulls together various images of belonging, "to a group (national or team flags) or of claiming territorial rights" (Murray, 2004, p. 73), for example. Murray continues that, for Grace, this speech is "a moment of stock-taking, where the meaning of the quilt becomes that of communal experience, under the 'banner of Woman . . . it is a 'warning' flag, presumably to let other women (future generations) know what dangers they may be exposed to" (ibid.). However, while the quilt holds multiple meanings in its patchwork, the flag tends to fix meaning, privileging unity over plurality. Grace's conflation of the quilt as flag and Murray's extension of the patchwork as an allegory for women and/in Canada itself seems problematic as the parallel between contemporary multiculturalism and Victorian domestic discourse makes for an uneasy fit. In what ways can Grace's quilt be a "banner" of solidarity for "Woman," or rather, which "Women" can Grace's quilt be a banner for? When are quilts "flags" for war, as when visible minorities fight for resources or supposedly threaten the unity of Canada, and when do quilts become the blanket that knits together diverse and disparate experiences? And, if the party-line toward multiculturalism insists that it "be seen as a great national bandage to bind over all of the divisions" and that it "provides a language with which to talk about problems which are seen as *threatening* to the national fabric" (quoted in Mackey, 2002, p. 68), then is the quilt metaphor to be juxtaposed against that other scrap of fabric, the handkerchief or "bandage" (Atwood, 1996, p. 6) with which Grace allegedly strangles Nancy Montgomery? Both feminism and multiculturalism are revealed to be internally fraught and, it seems, have the potential to be dangerous disruptions to the romance of Canadian civility and unity.

That feminism and multiculturalism share the same problematic rhetoric becomes evident in the final scene of the novel in which Grace describes her variation on the "Tree of Paradise" pattern that is not based on the "approved reading" (Atwood, 1996, p. 459). Grace's quilt will have a "border of snakes entwined" as "without a snake or two, the main part of the story would be missing" (ibid., p. 460). Each panel will consist of scraps of fabric taken from the clothes of the various women in Grace's life – Mary Whitney's petticoat, a prison nightdress, a dress from Nancy – and finally, Grace makes one tree out of triangles rather than a collection of trees. Embroidering or framing each triangle, she will "blend them" them into the pattern, and "so," she concludes, "we will all be together" (ibid.). Grace's quilt affirms the domestic as a necessary component in the creation of a national life and manages to incorporate her memories of three Canadian women. While fulfilling the neo-Victorian agenda to recover and include "the mysterious, the buried, the forgotten, the discarded, the taboo" (Atwood, 1998, p. 1509) of the past in the present, the border of snakes and the keepsakes of the clothes worn by servants also record the gendered process of writing and nation-making that dominates the end of the novel. Readings of the last lines of *Alias Grace* have been primarily celebratory, "and so we will all be together," Murray claims, leaves us with "the effect of a unified, patterned whole" (Murray, 2004, p. 81) that draws on the metaphor of flag, quilt/mosaic, and even, as Murray suggests, rewrites the notion of the Trinity. However, this final image of domestic security and coherence also emphasizes the unwieldiness of utilizing the discourse of unity and multiculturalism to discuss the project of Anglo-Canadian identity. In the phrase, "and so we will all be together," Atwood can be criticized for attempting to unify all women under a single Anglo-Canadian quilt or "flag," what Lee and Cardinal have called a "hegemonic nationalism" or "universal model" that is invoked "as a means of promoting unity in feminist politics" (Lee and Cardinal, 1998, p. 225). Unfortunately, they claim, even liberal feminism appears haunted by what can be conceived as a Victorian imperialism that maintains the centrality of the experiences of white,

European women, "while articulating a political strategy that claims to achieve the opposite" (ibid.).

While the novel recuperates the voices of nineteenth-century European, immigrant, working-class women on whose backs middle-class narratives of belonging are made, the absence of any voices of those who do not belong is palpable. In fact, the novel's only ethnic characters are a "part Red Indian" (Atwood, 1996, p. 31) female inmate of the lunatic asylum; Clarrie, "the regular laundress . . . who is part coloured and used to be a slave once, before they did away with it here" (ibid., p. 64); and Mary Whitney, Grace's friend and fellow servant, who claims that "her grandmother had been a Red Indian" (ibid., p. 150). Ien Ang has argued that feminism itself is defined by border politics: conceived of as an ever-expanding "political home which would ideally represent all women," difference is recast as an "overall politics of inclusion" (Ang, 2001, p. 191). A "politics of inclusion," in which "we will all be together," can elide practices of exclusion and maintain white, European women as the norm. The novel's Victorian setting prohibits the imagination of women of color and Canada's other visible minorities and immigrants, for example. However, their absence in Atwood's reconstructed past points to Canadian feminism's role in support of a hegemonic understanding of nationalism.

"Je me souviens:" Neo-Victorian Memoro-Politics

In order to emphasize how the mechanics of memory in the present are fluid and contingent, postcolonial neo-Victorian novels such as *Jack Maggs* and *Alias Grace* return to a moment in the nineteenth century when the borders of psychoanalysis as a discipline were fluid and fragile. More often than not, early psychoanalytic practices were tinged with the suspicion of charlatanry and thus open to attack, manipulation and ridicule on all sides. At this time, spiritism or spirit-tapping sat comfortably alongside trance, mesmerism, neuro-hypnosis, animal magnetism and early versions of Freud's "talking cure." When Simon Jordan arrives in Toronto, he finds himself embroiled in the heavily politicized context surrounding Grace's release from prison, a world of "Committees" and "Petitions" (Atwood, 1996, p. 77) that he had not been prepared for. Because Grace claims that she suffers from traumatic amnesia, unable to recall and thus account for her participation in the murders, various, predominantly male, authoritarian figures have been summoned to aid in her recovery. Simon, a proto-Freudian who studies the relationship between "association and suggestion" (ibid., p. 140), must contend with Reverend Verringer, whose domain is Grace's soul; Mrs Quennell, "the celebrated Spiritualist and advocate of an enlarged sphere for women" (ibid., p. 82); and Jeremiah, disguised as Dr Dupont, a "trained Neuro-hypnotist, of the school of James Braid" (ibid., p. 83). Simon is also challenged at every turn by Grace herself who prefers to omit information about her past as much as she embroiders it for him out of pity, "as I suspected that not all was going well with him," says a charitable Grace, "I did not say that I could not remember. Instead I said that I had indeed had a dream" (ibid., p. 242). The gathering of these early discourses of memory and their fictional representatives at the session define what Ian Hacking has called various "claims to knowledge" (Hacking, 1998, p. 211) that can be selected or rejected in defense of Grace. By conflating personal memory with collective, national memory, the novel can express the ways in which discourses of memory are politicized and harnessed in response to preferred ways of being a "self." The status of Grace's memory becomes the moral terrain upon which others set the terms of their personal and collective selfhoods.

In his discussion of "memoro-politics," Hacking describes the ways in which political movements are legitimated by the politicization of memory.[12] Hacking writes, "memoro-politics is above all a politics of the secret, of the forgotten event that can be turned, if only by strange flashbacks, into something monumental. It is a forgotten event that, when it is brought to light, can be memorialized into a narrative of pain" (Hacking, 1998, p. 214). Putting to use the concept of something that has been forgotten but that can be retrieved and thus restoring a narrative of wholeness to the present is central to memoro-politics and indeed, to neo-Victorianism itself. In Hacking's understanding, recovery is not simply a cure, rather, it will be the discovery or invention of the event narrativized as "pain" which will grant the privileged status of victim or survivor to an individual or group. As a neo-Victorian novel, *Alias Grace* reframes this "narrative of pain" by foregrounding the fictions, including the novel's emphasis on story-telling, amnesia and other diagnoses of pathological memory, that need to be told in order to divert attention away from Grace's problematic status as a victim *and* a perpetrator.

The novel's interrogation of the discourses of memory culminates in a highly charged scene of hypnotic trance instigated by Jeremiah. Disguised as the enigmatic Dr Dupont, Jeremiah suggests that, in the interests of science, he will put Grace into a "deliberate relaxation and realignment of the nerves, so that a neuro-hypnotic sleep is induced," an experience similar to a "fish, when stroked along the dorsal fin" (Atwood, 1996, p. 296). At the sitting, attended by the respectable "Britishers" (ibid., p. 84), Jeremiah veils Grace and slowly, through suggestion, puts her to sleep. When Grace's eyes remain open, Jeremiah comfortably explains that this is merely a "peculiarity of the nervous organization" (ibid., p. 397). But Simon has his doubts: Dr Dupont's performance is "too theatrical, too tawdry . . . it reeks of the small-town lecture halls of fifteen years ago" (ibid.). Supposedly under hypnosis, Grace dramatically reveals a hidden but dominant second personality, her "alias," the outspoken and daring, Mary Whitney. A highly sexual and knowledgeable "Mary," very different from the girl remembered and described by Grace to Simon, reveals to a shocked audience that *she* was protecting Grace, that it was "Mary" who seduced McDermott into murdering Kinnear, and "Mary" who strangled Nancy. For the reader, questions of Grace's "guilt" are suspended, as it is never clear whether or not she colludes with her old friend Jeremiah in order to absolve herself of responsibility for the murders.

After hypnosis, Dupont urges Simon to accept a diagnosis of "double consciousness" when "two distinct personalities . . . coexist in the same body and yet have different sets of memories altogether" and remain, "for all practical purposes, two separate individuals (Atwood, 1996, p. 405)." While Dupont argues that the "self" is "what we remember," Simon muses that we are, conversely, "what we forget" (ibid., p. 406). With a diagnosis of "double consciousness," the nineteenth-century prototype for contemporary multiple personality disorder, proclaimed, Grace cannot be held accountable for her own actions. This episode has been analyzed by multiple critics, Heidi Darroch, for example, argues for a correlation between Dupont's diagnosis and contemporary trauma theory, in particular, the "troubling proliferation of diagnoses of multiple personality disorder in the late 1980s and early 1990s, a phenomenon widely criticized in both the therapeutic community and the wider society as proof of the dangerously leading role played by some trauma therapists" (Darroch, 2004, p. 116). Darroch's argument helpfully addresses *Alias Grace's* intervention in contemporary debates surrounding memory (specifically the Recovered Memory Movement and its twin, False Memory Syndrome) and feminism, but what is less clear, perhaps, is what the diagnosis of "double consciousness" means when adopted for Canada's structure of relation to its nineteenth-century past.

Applying "double consciousness" to contemporary Canada can be read as a revisionary, perhaps even corrective, move on Atwood's part especially given that if a Canadian mentality or national psyche can be identified at all, as William Kilbourn claims, it is "schizophrenic" (Kilbourn, 1989, p. 1). "The Canadian identity," according to Kilbourn, can be considered "both a chimera and an oxymoron . . . full of odd conjunctions, split visions, and unresolved tensions" (ibid.). A similar diagnosis is echoed in Atwood's Afterword to *The Journals of Susanna Moodie*: "if the mental illness of the United States is megalomania," Atwood quips, "that of Canada is paranoid schizophrenia" (Atwood, 1970, p. 62). However, as Hacking explains in his genealogy of multiple personality and the sciences of memory, "multiple means more than two. Neither double consciousness nor dédoublement was multiple personality" (Hacking, 1998, p. 171). "Double consciousness," rather than "schizophrenia" can be viewed as a deliberate diagnostic choice related again to the shifts and debates between biculturalism and multiculturalism. As neo-Victorianism also offers a bifurcated vision in its awareness of the past in tension and in tandem with the present, it becomes a fitting strategy with which to address the complicated contours of Canadian identity politics.

The peculiar insistence on schizophrenia as the national disease describes an Anglo-Canadian identity perceived to be under threat by multiculturalism. As Grace tells us about her time in the lunatic asylum, "running mad" suggests "mad is a different house you could step into, or a separate country entirely" (Atwood, 1996, p. 33). But, she continues, "when you go mad you don't go any other place, you stay where you are. And somebody else comes in" (ibid.). Here, the discourse of invasion and entrapment, nation and madness, strongly suggests the fiction of an Anglo-Canadian identity under threat by the "somebody else" coming in, hence schizophrenia. In their introduction to *Tense Past*, Paul Antze and Michael Lambek draw an explicit comparison between multiple personality disorder, how the term is used to describe the presence of "two or more distinct personalities . . ." (Antze and Lambek, 1996, p. xxiii) within a self and is used interchangeably with schizophrenia, with Benedict Anderson's concept of an "imagined community" (Anderson, 1991, p. 23). A nation usually imagines itself as a bounded, unified, healthy whole. Yet, the experiences of mass migration, transnational subjectivities and the realities of globalization often mean that a pathology such as multiple personality disorder serves as the most appropriate metaphor for understanding or expressing contemporary collective experience. As Canadian academics, Antze and Lambek seem particularly attuned to this "unhealthy" mapping of a personal disorder on to national terrain. In their formulation, alter personalities emerge as "bounded sub-individuals" (Antze and Lambek, 1996, p. xxii) that threaten the unity of the whole. Multiple personality disorder admits the concept of an endangered whole but it nonetheless supports multiple *bounded* individuals "of the same order" which is preferable to "the idea of an amorphous or poorly bounded whole" (ibid., p. xxiii). Thus, multiple personality disorder, they argue, "is comparable to a state with several reified ethnic groups envisaged in permanent conflict with one another or with the state itself" (ibid.). We are left with the bizarrely simple formula that a schizophrenic nation is better than a "poorly bounded" alternative: as Reverend Verringer extorts, "we cannot be mere patchworks! It is a horrifying thought . . ." (Atwood, 1996, p. 406).

If, as I argued earlier in this chapter, "violent duality" emerged in Atwood's early work in response to the Royal Commission on Bilingualism and Biculturalism (1968), can we read its pathologization in *Alias Grace* as a critique of the way in which French and English Canada continue to dominate and manage the differences between Canada's multiple cultures? In other words, like *Jack Maggs*, *Alias Grace* takes advantage of the slippages between schizophrenia, multiple personality disorder and "double consciousness" in the past in order to stage a discussion about managing diversity in the postcolonial present: is the goal to be the unity-within-diversity model which stresses multicultural plurality or biculturalism which could stress "asymmetrical federalism between unequal sectors" (Fleras and Elliot, 2002, p. 168)?

This makes the emergence of "Mary Whitney," Grace's supposed alter personality, during her hypnosis particularly suggestive. Readings of Mary Whitney as Grace's "alias" have been diverse: according to Holly Blackford, "Mary's" appearance represents the "angry resistance to colonization, deeply repressed in the Canadian character" (Blackford, 2006, p. 23); critics taking a more psychoanalytic approach, such as Rose Lucas, suggest that "Mary" is evidence of Grace's dissociation from trauma and that "Mary" is an "aspect of Grace's identity which contains the violent rage, grieving and sense of victimization which has proved utterly incompatible with her other self" (Lucas, 2003, p. 185). But, in a novel that is populated by European immigrants, and that features Mary Whitney as the only "native-born Canadian" (Atwood, 1996, p. 150), what is at stake when the novel suggests a "native-born" voice to be either repressed or cast in the figure of the protector? Can "Mary" also be read as the suppressed (rather than repressed) desire within English Canada that still wants to pursue its "native-born" identity? During the hypnosis, "Mary's" voice is described as so deviant that it can only be heard at the Asylum: "I liked it there at first," "Mary" tells her stunned audience, "I could talk out loud there. I could laugh. I could tell what happened. But no one listened to me . . . I was not heard" (ibid., p. 403). Gerald Kernerman has argued that English Canada has always been capable of asserting itself as a nation rather than insisting on a Pan-Canadian identity that could include the ever-problematic Quebec. "Given the need to accommodate Quebec in order to keep it in Canada," he argues, "English Canadians have always had to refrain from pursuing their own national vision, making it weak and apologetic" (Kernerman, 2006, p. 62). Could the "alias" Mary Whitney contain a critique of Anglo-Canadian identity and its nationalist impulse? As Grace comments, "without her it would have been a different story entirely" (Atwood, 1996, p. 102).

The novel introduces doubt into the hypnosis event and a powerful polyvocality in Grace that helps identify the basis for new forms of racism within Canada's settler postcolonialism. Although it does not address the multiple ethnic positions available in Canada, the appearance of "Mary" dismantles a national rhetoric that stresses a sovereign, autonomous self as "normal" or "healthy" with identifiable characteristics different from anyone else's. Read in terms of the vernacular of official multiculturalism, "Mary" within Grace illustrates how adopting Grace as an allegory for a victimized, feminized Canada evinces a powerful fantasy that can, as Mackey has described, "create national innocence" by "locating oppressors safely outside the body politic of the nation" (Mackey, 2002, p. 12). "Mary's" appearance presents an alternate, much more uncomfortable model of Canada, one that suggests a "differentiated and non-unified body laden with internal oppressors and victims" (ibid.).

". . . A White Lie Such as the Angels Tell"

In both *Jack Maggs* and *Alias Grace*, hypnosis signals an anxiety in the novel over identity. In Chapter 2, I argued that for the recovery of an Australian psyche, the mesmeric, potentially mimetic relationship between hypnotizer and hypnotized (an allegory for Britain and Australia) must be broken if desire for Englishness is no longer to inform Australian autonomy. No such narrative of recovery is available in *Alias Grace* as the psychotherapeutic relationship between Simon and Grace fails primarily because the supposed therapy is more about confirming the borders of *his* identity than seeking any sort of cure for Grace. The more Grace tells Simon, the greater the difficulty he has in maintaining the line between doctor and patient. Simon comes to the disheartening realization that "it's as if she's drawing his energy out of him – using his own mental forces to materialize the figures in her story, as the mediums are said to do during their trances" (Atwood, 1996, p. 291). In order to avoid "his own mental forces" (ibid., p. 132) being hijacked, Simon maintains the stubborn belief that Grace's memory can be fully restored and that there lies an accurate, unblemished record somewhere in Grace's mind, "below the threshold of her consciousness" (ibid.) that can be accessed and retrieved. To admit mimesis, that "his own mental forces" shape Grace's narrative, would be to confirm all of Simon's fears as a therapist, but it would also dissolve the strategic identification of cultural distinctions and national borders between the U.S. and Canada. This anxiety is mirrored in Grace's escape across the border to the U.S. with McDermott. Once there, Grace observes wistfully that, "the scenery of the U.S. was much the same as that of the countryside we had just come from, but it was indeed a different place, as the flags were different" (ibid., p. 341). Grace's disappointment in the similarities between the two nations, in the very insubstantiality of the border to mark anything, gives her very little relief at the thought of her escape. Even the landmark gash, the geological wound of Niagara Falls that separates the U.S. and Canada, cannot be relied upon as any significant delineation because Grace's entry point into the U.S. is "nowhere near the Falls" (ibid., p. 340). Here, Grace voices concerns over one of the largest threats to Canadian national identity: so undifferentiated is the landscape of Canada to its neighbor that it is defined only by its flag and an overwhelming sense of sameness, not even lack. More importantly, this episode admits the uncomfortable fact that "Canada" must necessarily include the U.S. in its construction, often in uneven, always circulating, relationships of power.

Throughout the novel, Simon has been attempting to enact the process of associative memory, a "method based on suggestion, and the association of ideas" whereby he will "reestablish the chain of thought, which was broken" and restore the "shock of the violent events" (Atwood, 1996, p. 85) into a coherent narrative. But, the novel also wants to debunk a notion of recovery that is often, as Ruth Leys has argued, a "powerfully entrenched, if undertheorized, commitment to the redemptive authority of history – even if that commitment is tempered by an awareness of the difficulty of historical reconstruction" (Leys, 2000, p. 109). Thus, the novel champions Simon's failure or, the "*not to know*" (Atwood, 1996, p. 424), the "snatch[ing] at hints and portents, at intimations, at tantalizing whispers" that drives Simon "close to nervous exhaustion" (ibid.) and back to Massachusetts. Feminist critics have often argued that Grace's storytelling and the protective mantel of amnesia are her only forms of control, that Grace exhibits not amnesia but rather "embodied resistance" and a "refusal to be trapped in ... linguistic matrices of power" (Stanley, 2003, p. 379) and the "multiple colonizing systems" (ibid., p. 382) that control her. While overwhelming Simon with her ability to offer a recovery *of* minute detail, "every item of laundry she ever washed . . . and such things as the boat race that preceded her own flight across the Lake" (Atwood, 1996, p. 372), Grace deliberately frustrates her readers in her withholding of a recovery *from* trauma, loss and amnesia. The novel is simply not interested in offering a model of recovery, preferring instead a bewildering proliferation of stories. So, if the novel isn't interested in recovery, what is its postcolonial neo-Victorian project?

At the end of the novel, Grace writes a final letter to Simon Jordan and disrupts the relationship between the "listener" and victim and the possibility for the integrative purposes of witnessing. Dori Laub stresses that to become a responsible witness the listener "partakes of the struggle of the victim with the memories and residues of his or her traumatic past. The listener has to feel the victim's victories, defeats and silences, know them from within, so that they can assume the form of testimony" (Laub, 1992, p. 58). In order for the listener to become an "enabler of the testimony," a listener must "preserve his own separate place, position and perspective" (ibid.) lest s/he too be overcome or paralyzed by the telling of the traumatic event. In *Jack Maggs*, the trauma of convictism was infectious, overwhelming Toby in his desire to witness Jack's transportation. In *Alias Grace*, however, the relationship between story-teller/listener, analyst/analysand constantly shifts: the novel seems more invested in exploring the qualities of victimization rather than offering any viable mode of recovery. Atwood deploys the vocabulary of victimhood to describe Grace's married life to Jamie Walsh. Treating Simon as a feminized confidante, Grace muses on the continued importance of storytelling in her marriage. Although she would prefer to "forget about that portion of my life, rather than dwelling on it in such a mournful way," Jamie pushes her to retell and embellish the more titillating aspects of her imprisonment: her descriptions of physical discomfort, "improper behaviour," "cold baths naked and wrapped in a sheet" and the terror of being sexually pursued by Kinnear send Jamie into "raptures" and "ecstasies" (Atwood, 1996, p. 457). After hearing the exaggerated details of Grace's experiences as a captive, Jamie begs Grace for "forgiveness" (ibid.). Grace realizes that the "forgiveness" that she has the power to dispense is – like her testimony during the trial, her sessions with Simon, and possibly during her hypnosis – a "white lie such as the angels tell [which] is a small price to pay for peace and quiet" (ibid., p. 458).

"Peace and quiet" appears to refer to the domestic tranquility, normality and privacy that the couple eventually cultivates in their marriage. The couple's insistence on anonymity and Grace's eventual fade into the domestic can be read as a re-evaluation of the ordinary, everyday of women and the gendered, under-represented process of nation as home-making.

However, despite the end of the novel being set in New York, Atwood's choice of words here is reminiscent of Canada's self-portrayal as a "peaceable kingdom." In the Bronfen lecture, Atwood describes how her fellow writers in "Angloland" focused on the contemporary rather than the past as "history for us, either didn't exist, or it had happened elsewhere, or if ours it was boring" (Atwood, 1998, p. 1508). "Boredom" and domesticity, foregrounded in the novel as unmarked, normative and thus as invisible attributes of whiteness, are tied up with the debunked myth of *terra nullius* and what Mackey calls a "heritage of tolerance" (Mackey, 2002, p. 2) in Canada which misremembers its legacy of conquest and dispossession as uniquely "tolerant" and peaceful while remembering the U.S.'s treatment of its native Indians as brutal and violent.

Jamie's insistence on being forgiven because "he can't seem to go on comfortably without it" (Atwood, 1996, p. 458) speaks strongly to a misplaced sense of guilt. After telling a "few stories of torment and misery," Jamie's sexual desire is stirred and Grace tells of how "he clasps me in his arms and strokes my hair, and begins to unbutton my nightgown" all while asking "will you ever forgive me?" (ibid., p. 457). This resonates with what Dyer has called the "exquisite agony" (Dyer, 1997, p. 206) of white guilt. As Grace says, it would be more appropriate for Jamie to forgive *her* rather than "wanting to have it the wrong way around" (Atwood, 1996, p. 458). Capable of descending into stagnant self-reflexivity and self-flagellation, white guilt, "at its most performative has the additional effect of diverting attention from the facts of white racism and oppression to how badly the Enlightened White Liberal feels about it" (López, 2005, p. 23). Once Grace has performed the act of forgiveness, "I turn my eyes up and look solemn, and then kiss him and cry a little," Jamie returns to "playing on his flute as if he's a boy again . . . and we are out in the orchard making daisy chains at Mr. Kinnear's" (Atwood, 1996, p. 458). This return to an idyllic time prior to the murders is a form of forgetting, perhaps even a version of the settler's "genesis amnesia" (Lawson, 2004, p. 154) that is even more insidious than doubt over Grace's loss of memory. If Grace grants "forgiveness" in order to maintain the "peace and quiet," she emphatically tells a "white lie" that appropriates but does not enact the language of official reparations and apology. In Grace's analysis of "the truth about forgiveness" (Atwood, 1996, p. 457), she sheds new light on the discourse of victimization:

> It is not the culprits who need to be forgiven; rather it is the victims because they are the ones who cause all the trouble. If they were only less weak and careless, and more foresightful, and if they would keep from

blundering into difficulties think of all the sorrow in the world that would be spared. (ibid.)

The "victim" in this passage is the novel's closest articulation of a white Canadian identity that adopts a subject position by appropriating the very strategies of victimization used by those previously oppressed. Grace's wistful and strange accusations, that these particular "victims" be "less weak and careless," "more foresightful" so as to avoid "blundering into difficulties" can be identified as Atwood's criticism against white backlash. White backlash presents itself as a prevailing sense of being "disadvantaged" by minorities who have benefited from government policies such as multiculturalism in Australia and Canada, or Affirmative Action in the U.S. According to Roger Hewitt, white backlash forms "part of a socially disparate set of responses to equalities discourses as they unfolded from the 1960s to the present" (Hewitt, 2005, p. 4). Under these circumstances, neo-Victorianism's recovery work is used to illustrate the larger historical context of a racial phenomenon perceived to be entirely of the present.

Deploying the Victorian, the novel constructs a version of settler postcolonialism dangerously close to lapsing into white guilt and continuing to articulate a narrative of victimhood even within the context of contemporary multiculturalism. These are issues that Atwood cheekily displaces too onto the U.S. by writing the marriage of Grace Marks and Jamie Walsh in Ithaca, New York. While the study of whiteness can lead to dangerous grounds of white nationalism (for example, Pauline Hanson's One Nation party which both sullies and informs the context for *Jack Maggs*), it can also aid in thinking critically about the status of ex-settler colonies within the field of postcolonialism. The reluctance to admit the category of a postcolonial whiteness into the canon of what is "properly" postcolonial dismisses "a number of post-empire, post-mastery whitenesses attempting to examine themselves in relation to histories of oppression and hegemony" (López, 2005, p. 6). As a neo-Victorian novel that has as its agenda the critical act of "taking a hard look backward" (Atwood, 1998, p. 1512), *Alias Grace* identifies a key historical moment in the nineteenth century when whiteness was consolidated or its presence made felt. The novel speaks urgently to multiculturalism in the present, which, in its more celebratory moments, can be an injunction to forget the colonial past. "Canada" is famously depicted as being haunted by no ghosts, with a sense of national ennui from carrying no baggage associated with its colonial past.[13] However, it may be the return to the Victorian that materializes the ghost of whiteness that haunts multiculturalism.

Chapter 4

"Far-Flung" Neo-Victorianism: Hong Kong and Jackie Chan's Neo-Victorian Films

Another "Island Story"

In this chapter, I address neo-Victorianism's curious presence in the imagination and memorial practices of Hong Kong, a city born out of the first Opium War (1839–42) fought between Britain and China, and that has been shaped by both British and Chinese imperial discourses. The last significant "outpost" in the collapse of the British Empire and part of China's re-establishment of its own imperial boundaries, Hong Kong's improper postcolonialism offers new terrain on which to explore neo-Victorianism's global potential. After more than a decade of traumatic events – the signing of the Sino-British Joint Declaration in 1984, negotiated by Thatcher without consulting Hong Kong, and the Tiananmen Square massacre in 1989, which rocked Hong Kong's faith in China to keep her obligations to the territory – Hong Kong was reunified with China in 1997. Overnight, Hong Kong "disappeared" (Abbas, 1997a, p. 25) and became a postcolonial anomaly, a territory neither decolonized nor emancipated by the exiting colonial power but simply "handed over" to another imperial entity.[1] For Hong Kong, neo-Victorianism would be a particularly effective way to express what Abbas has described as "the displaced chronologies or achronicities" (Abbas, 1997b, p. 6) that accompanied the perceived end of Hong Kong's coloniality. After all, "one country, two systems," the premise underlying Hong Kong's governing document, the Basic Law, also expresses the situation of "one country, two temporalities" as reversion to Chinese rule is both a return and, for Hong Kong, the threat of an overwhelming sense of cultural backwardness. However, since Hong Kong has no claims to nation it rarely looks backward, unlike Australia, to its own foundational moment to tell a progressive story of its own rise. And since it does not have a significant precolonial history, it does not readily seek the Victorian to stage a pivotal moment or originary trauma of colonial dispossession that requires redress in the present. It does not tend to generate nostalgic memories around the nineteenth century, as it does around other more recent moments in its history, because Hong Kong does not adhere to a standard narrative of decolonization. Instead, neo-Victorianism has been displaced by other technologies and strategies of representation. There exist, however, a small cluster of neo-Victorian texts about Hong Kong, and more importantly *from* Hong Kong, that puts the circulation of the Victorian into a global context that does not reproduce the geography of empire as mapped by representatives from London and Beijing. This chapter focuses primarily on the neo-Victorian movies of Jackie Chan – *Project A* (1983), *Shanghai Noon* (2000) and *Shanghai Knights* (2003) – that investigate the kinds of self-writing available in the neo-Victorian for Hong Kong. Jackie Chan's cult of personality and the new demographics reached by the global popularity of these films change the dynamics of neo-Victorianism's often strict ties to nation and decolonization and offer new ways of thinking about Hong Kong's nineteenth-century past and its present as always already determined by the framework of transnationalism.

For China, reunification was a moment of national healing and recovery from the outcome of the Opium Wars and centuries of humiliation at the hands of the British: quoted in the *South China Morning Post*, President Jiang Zemin claimed, "the Chinese people have never recognized the unequal treaties imposed on them, never forgotten for a single day the humiliating state of Hong Kong under occupation and never stopped their indomitable struggle for state sovereignty and national emancipation" (Jiang, 1997, p. 8). Such protestation over China's structure of relation with the past as wounded and victimized occludes the act of reunification as the fulfillment of an imperial mission. For Britain, 1997 became a post-imperial spectacle: the ceremonies of leave-taking in collusion with the worst rainstorms of that summer were a fitting end to what Ackbar Abbas has termed the "long good-bye" (Abbas, 1997a, p. 3) to the empire's most prosperous possession. Hoping to showcase Hong Kong as its most graceful imperial exit, and to preserve the memory of British colonial rule as nothing less than the firm establishment of liberalism, free speech and the rule of law, any deviation from the official narrative of the Opium War as a "trade war" remains dangerous. These Chinese and British narratives tend to generate stubborn memories about the Opium War that maintain imperial and orientalist structures and East/West binaries. Such commemorative strategies continue to reduce the complexities of Hong Kong's (post)colonialism to stock narratives and images of contact between imperial China and Britain and subsequently deny the globalizing forces that Hong Kong represents.

Recalling the Victorian in the context of Hong Kong has made the territory synonymous with opium, the master signifier of British aggression and of Chinese weakness and decline. The imposition of opium onto the Chinese market was Britain's attempt to redress the trade imbalance between itself and China; there was simply no market for British goods in the Chinese market until opium. What followed was centuries of "gunboat diplomacy" (Hanes and Sanello, 2002, p. 157) in which larger and larger concessions were demanded from the Chinese who found themselves consistently and deliberately provoked and subsequently under attack. After lengthy hostilities, the first Opium War was ended by the signing of the Treaty of Nanking, the first in a series of what Chinese officials referred to as "unequal treaties," which granted trade access to the British and ceded the island of Hong Kong "in perpetuity" to Britain.[2] China clings to the memory of the Opium Wars, for example, by restaging imperial drug commissioner Lin Zexu's burning of over 20,000 baskets of British opium in 1839 by igniting 150 kilograms of heroin and "ice" at the Opium War Museum in Humen, Dongguan in 1997.[3] But, Hong Kong's emergence from the first Opium War is a fact that Western powers and media habitually repress, preferring instead to emphasize China's cultural and political backwardness and liken reunification to handing the "pearl of the Orient" back to a grubby peasant child.[4] Rey Chow has termed these narratives the "King Kong syndrome" or, "cross cultural, cross racial representation aimed at producing 'China' as a spectacular primitive monster whose despotism necessitates the salvation of its people by outsiders" (Chow, 1998b, p. 94). The "syndrome" masks the recurring condition of "extraterritoriality," one of the provisions afforded by the Treaty of Nanking in 1843, which Chow defines as the "double standard that allowed the West to act in China without being subject to Chinese jurisdiction *but not vice versa* . . . that is, the privilege of being (judged) outside China even when they were acting in China" (ibid., p. 98). The last governor, Chris Patten's (1992–7), final attempts to introduce the germs of democracy in the colony were perceived by Chinese authorities as yet another Western affront to Chinese sovereignty: the West (democracy) continues to "act" in China even after Britain's departure and is thus regarded as yet another episode of the Opium War.

However, if one traces the production, circulation and trading routes of opium the story of Hong Kong becomes transformed into one of global dimensions. Opium was "deeply integrated into global colonial trade" (Chouvy, 2010, p. 6) along with tea, sugar and cotton, and the profits of its production and trade facilitated the economies of the British Empire. The first Opium War marks a crisis point in nineteenth-century global capitalism when the opium trade redefined concepts of the market and the understanding of terms like commodity and exchange (Wickberg, 1999, p. 35). It was a crisis, arguably, that Qing officials failed to read correctly in their interpretation of the problem of opium as one of addiction rather than consumption (Karl, 2001, p. 237). Turning away from Britain and China, the opium system created an international network of migrant laborers and immigrants, a story recovered by Amitav Ghosh in *Sea of Poppies* (2009) and the subject of the final chapter of *Neo-Victorianism and the Memory of Empire*, that undergirds the nineteenth-century globe. The foundation of Hong Kong begins as the official story of British and Chinese imperial posturing but also tells a more illicit geopolitical history of trade and migrancy that affects India, the Americas, the Golden Triangle of Southeast Asia, the Golden Crescent (Afghanistan, Iran and Pakistan) as well as other European imperial powers such as France (Chouvy, 2010, p.7). More importantly, opium is a gateway drug that restores the centrality of Hong Kong as a gateway, the crucial "transition between nation and diaspora" (Ho, 2009, p. 6). Via Hong Kong, neo-Victorianism becomes less a temporal understanding of the present's relationship to the past and more a spatial one. Since its foundation as a treaty port in the nineteenth century, Hong Kong has been a "classic immigrant city," both a "departure point and a destination" (Pan, 1990, p. 363). My discussion of Jackie Chan's neo-Victorian movies recovers this history of immigration and diaspora and revises the memory of the Victorian in the present as one of transit, movement and expansion rather than a specifically imperial history rooted in geography and sovereignty.

Smoke and Mirrors: The Opium War in Hong Kong Texts

Britain and China have been actively producing neo-Victorian fictions and revisionary histories about Hong Kong as part of their own continuing discourses of colonialism and imperialism. Novels such as James Clavell's international bestseller, *Tai Pan* (1966), Timothy Mo's *An Insular Possession* (1986), and the mainland Chinese movie, *The Opium War* (1997), have evoked the Victorian and replay the Opium War as commentary and critique at key moments in contemporary Hong Kong history. However, these texts often subjugate Hong Kong to an imperial story and emphasize its disappearance precisely when the nineteenth century is recalled. All three texts rehearse the standard narrative of the Opium War as a trade war and an ideological battle over the principles of free trade. As examples of a more conventional neo-Victorianism, these texts tend to elide this other history of opium, denying the global scope of the Victorian and revealing a suspicion of the politics of hybridity and an anxiety about modernization that recovering such a history would represent.

Tai-Pan, for example, depicts the story of the colony as a capitalist adventure: one man's dream of domination to which the founding of Hong Kong is subordinated. If it were not for the enigmatic and heroic Dirk Struan, *the* Tai-Pan of the Noble House, one of the character's notes, "there'd be no damned Hong Kong" (Clavell, 1966, p. 23). The reassuring mission of British annexation, according to the novel's Western characters is, "not just to get rich on trade and leave" but "to use riches and power to open up China to the world and particularly to British culture and British law so that each could learn from the other and grow to the benefit of both" (ibid., p. 69). Written in 1966, the novel predates the pro-Communist riots in 1967 and 1968 when dissatisfied Hong Kong workers, inspired by the Cultural Revolution on the mainland, joined in with left-wing extremists to protest against British colonial rule. The violence brought the city to a standstill. After the riots, Britain was forced to enter fully into the governance of the colony and began to introduce local Hong Kong people in its decision-making processes. Responding to Hong Kong's needs, the British government created a Westernized, modern and successful city that forever lessened the appeal of reunification with the mainland.[5] Read in this context, *Tai-Pan's* pro-British stance reveals a reassuring fantasy for Western readers: a Scotsman can understand the mysticism of the East, negotiate with inscrutable mandarins, adopt Asian values (especially cleanliness) and children, and can ultimately sacrifice himself to the ideals of free trade that Hong Kong offers.

But *Tai-Pan* has also been criticized as having one of those "thick and spectacular plots that glamourize the working of capital" and therefore "cannot take the risk of addressing the ordinary and banal" that make up the local of Hong Kong's identity politics (Abbas, 1997a, p. 112). Indeed, the "local" voices in *Tai-Pan* are reduced to the thousands of immigrants from China streaming into the newly established British ports, the "swarms of junks and sampans were leaving and arriving" and the "thousands of tiny hovels [that] had sprung up like obscene mushrooms on the slopes of one of the hills" (Clavell, 1966, p. 251) to shock Struan's sense of aesthetics. Incapable of imagining Hong Kong's locals as anything more than "swarms" and hoards of Chinese, the novel focuses instead on Struan's Eurasian son and comprador of the Noble House, Gorden Chen. As the head of the underground criminal organization of Triads or *tongs*, Chen begins his own governance of the Chinese immigrants streaming into Hong Kong. As Straun's comprador, Chen negotiates the complications of business between imperial officials, Chinese traders and British *hongs*. As the head of a secret, Chinese anti-imperialist society seeking haven on the island under "barbarian control" (Clavell, 1966, p. 44), Chen is also intimately involved in the early Chinese diaspora to Hong Kong. For better or for worse, triads have throughout the centuries been involved in such illegitimate forms of diaspora as illegal smuggling and human trafficking; but, they are also, like Chen, a curiously hybrid organization, at once intensely local but also having ties to anti-imperialist sentiment and influences in China (Snow, 2003, p. 38). As a representative of some proto-local identity, Chen is reviled by those around him as the "Tai-Pan's bastard by a Chinese whore" and is pitied by the English as "of neither one world nor the other. Desperately trying to be English wearing Chinese robes and a queue" (Clavell, 1966, p. 25). Chen dies in the same typhoon that conveniently kills off Struan before he can take his Chinese mistress back to Scotland, thus denying Hong Kong (and Britain) a hybridized voice as a means of expression. To give value to Chen would be to admit an underworld of criminals, anarchists, drug dealers and a black market rather than the "benefits" of a free market championed by the British above. Admitting such an unappealing and alternate form of modernization would emphasize a failure in the British rule of law and certain stereotypes of Chineseness not glossed over by reunification rhetoric.

While *Tai-Pan,* one of the most well-known novels about Hong Kong, can be generally dismissed as an Orientalist romance, Timothy Mo's *An Insular Possession*, short-listed for the 1986 Booker Prize, garners more academic attention. An immense pastiche of a Victorian realist novel, *An Insular Possession* consists almost entirely of fictionalized letters, official documents and competing reports from pro-British newspapers, all of which construct, through their acts of description and inscription, the "insular possession" that will be Hong Kong. The plot follows American expatriates Gideon Chase and Walter Eastman from their *hong* in Canton to the expatriate haven of Macau, and documents their work setting up the *Lin Tin Bulletin and River Bee,* the newspaper the pair publish to counter the hegemonic voice of the British biased *Canton Monitor.* Set primarily in Canton and Macau, not Hong Kong, the novel participates in the discourse of absence that surrounds representations of the colony. The casting of American characters sits uneasily with the novel's postcolonial agenda to find some third space from which to decenter the overwhelming imperial narratives that structure Hong Kong, especially during a time when the retrieval and assertion of a nativist Hong Kong voice was so central. Written in 1986, only two years after the signing of the Joint Declaration, the novel holds the present and its nineteenth-century counterpart in tension: both are moments when history should be a "narrative of cross-cultural contact" but were, in fact, "two discrete histories, each enclosed within itself, unable to articulate itself to the other" (Ho, 2000, p. 73). Throughout the novel, contact between expatriate and Chinese is reduced to gestures, guttural expressions, pidgin English and inaccurate acts of translation. In an early hunting scene involving the Canton *hong's* American and British characters, for example, the Chinese gang that they stumble upon is described as "the rascalliest, dirtiest, most heavily armed and sinewy Chinese ruffians ... ever seen" (Mo, 1986, p. 91). Chase, the novel's bilingual scholar, is rendered speechless, "no saliva left at all," and wonders whether or not they will "simply cut our throats or well they mutilate us first as well?" (ibid.). As the novel's hybrid character, Chase's anxious silence mimics the novel's 1980s present when China and Britain debated the territory's future without consulting its residents. Ultimately, Hong Kong's noticeable absence in the novel underscores that its official history, past and present, can only be the voice and record of its imperial owners.

Despite the *Lin Tin Bulletin* and Chase's heroic efforts to enter the world historical stage as a translator for Captain Charles Elliot, the unpopular and uncommemorated "founder" of Hong Kong, the myths of race and empire are not easily dismantled.[6] Stripping away the imperial representations of Hong Kong, Mo suggests, reveals nothing. Without the Western gaze turned upon it, as critics have argued, Hong Kong disappears.[7] Chase's carefully worded and researched articles in the *Lin Tin Bulletin* on Cantonese life disappear when Eastman decides to end its publication; Chase's long career as "early Sinologue and writer," his status as "a bridge between the first generation of the 'pioneer' scholars of the Chinese language ... and the second" and his "considerable prestige with the Chinese Government" (Mo, 1986, p. 654) are catalogued as a footnote at the end of the novel with a reminder that "the increasing wildness of his non-academic views ... should not be allowed to obscure his contribution to China studies in the middle and late years of the last century" (ibid.). An excerpt from Chase's "unfinished and unpublished autobiography" (ibid., p. 663) appears in the second appendix of the novel: expelled to the margins and private spaces of the text, Chase's voice, like Hong Kong's, according to Eastman, will "simply cease to be, vanish, be remarkable only for its absence" (ibid., p. 649). Constructed entirely out of Western discursive practices, the novel reveals unspoken anxieties about the racial integrity of the imperial center: can Western elements, represented in *An Insular Possession* as intellectual and linguistic contamination, be forcibly excluded from the hegemony of Englishness *qua* whiteness?

The difficulties of disappearance and hybridity extend beyond the novel to Mo as an author: his book biographies always include that he was born in Hong Kong to an English mother and a Cantonese father yet he insists repeatedly in interviews on his "British" identity. Unfortunately for those like myself wishing to claim Mo as a privileged insider to Hong Kong culture, Mo has always considered himself first and foremost British: "I know nothing about Chinese culture," he has declared in interviews, "[i]t is hard for me to write about things Chinese as it must have been for Paul Scott or J. G. Farrell to write about India. I'm a Brit" (quoted in Ho, 2000, p. 13). For Elaine Y. L. Ho, the epithet, "I'm a Brit" is an unfortunate denial of his Hong Kong upbringing and a negative valuation of the other binary term "Chinese." At best, Ho argues, Mo's articulation of hybridity belies an adherence to strict boundaries rather than as a prized subject position. Such gestures of refusal, Ho claims, demonstrate that 'Mo is patently uninterested in the nativist fictions of identity or projects of postcolonial cultural reconstruction and retrieval" (ibid., p. 84). However, the fact that Mo has chosen to return to the nineteenth century with all its racialist and imperialist undertones at this specific moment in the 1980s must be important. The greatest critique that *An Insular Possession* offers of itself as a *British* novel is that such a perfect ventriloquism of nineteenth-century imperial discourses should still be relevant in the supposedly postcolonial present. Furthermore, for an Anglo-Asian author from Hong Kong to declare himself a "Brit" during Thatcher's denial of the right of abode to Hong Kong subjects, many of whom had a similar upbringing and sense of belonging as Mo, forms a deceptively powerful and political act.

Hong Kong's disappearance occurs again in Chinese director Xie Jin's movie, *The Opium War*, in which the colony's foundation forms a mere episode in the clash between two great empires: the establishment of "Hong Kong British Territory" is announced by a close-up of a hand-written wooden sign. Then described as the most expensive mainland film ever made, set in both Britain and China, Xie spectacularly recreated the events of the first Opium War. The film is dominated by two central scenes: Lin Zexu's burning of more than 22,000 chests of opium and the British Parliament's vote of 271 – 262 in favor of sending naval forces to secure Britain's trading rights in China. In just over two hours, Xie covers the corruption and downfall of the Qing dynasty; Britain's establishment of free trade at the expense of Chinese addicts; and the "shameful" ceding of Hong Kong to

Britain. Released in 1997 across Asia, *The Opium War* was commonly dismissed by Western critics as Chinese propaganda, although Xie maintained that the film was not propaganda but a "special gift for the motherland and the people . . . to ensure we and our descendents forever remember the humiliation the nation once suffered" (quoted in *Digital China/Harvard*, n.d.). The events surrounding the release of the film were symbolically farcical: Chris Patten, the colony's last governor, was not invited to the Hong Kong premiere and neither was the head of the Jardine Matheson Group. A representative to Jardine's great rival, Swire, however, did show up at the opening claiming that since the company had nothing to do with opium he could be present at the event with a "clear conscience" (quoted in Higgins, 1997).[8] Such scandals surrounding the release of the film, Gina Marchetti notes, "seems to be another episode in the saga of the Opium War, with Hong Kong still serving as booty to be lost or won, a token of China's lost national integrity" (Marchetti, 2000, p. 297).

Drawing on this concept of the prized token, Xie creates a spectacle of commodification through the use of coded objects, a strategy that Jackie Chan's movies also employ. Lin Zexu, the incorruptible and heroic mandarin sent by the weak-willed emperor to purge opium from China and thus "cure" (Xie, 1997) the empire, becomes the voice piece for the film's ideas about China's place in the new world order. Throughout the film, Lin is forced to revise his beliefs in Chinese superiority over the British aided in part by the bilingual character, Shanzi, the son of a corrupt *hong* owner arrested by Lin. Having served aboard the ship owned by the mercenary British trader, Denton, Shanzi's usefulness lies in his ability to supply Lin with the essence of Western knowledge. The China portions of the film appear oppressive to the viewer as Xie relies on shadowy interior shots within the Forbidden Palace, courtrooms and opium dens, to emphasize Lin's inability to navigate through China's crisis of modernity. As Chinese forts and militia are destroyed rapidly by British technology and troops, Lin is shown looking puzzled at the difference in size between the two nations on the model of the globe and sounds out the words "England" and "China" in unfamiliar English. While the countries' names are illuminated by light from the window, shadows cast ominous bars over the globe. Unable to reconcile opium's status as a shifting cultural and economic signifier with the globe in his hands, Lin fails to guide China through this new phase of global capitalism.

By contrast, Queen Victoria and the British merchants are expert readers of the new global system and the scenes in Britain tend to be vast exterior shots flooded with light. Capable of delivering lengthy speeches on free trade, "whoever opens up China will have the entire East, the nineteenth century!" (Xie, 1997), and deftly manipulating her aged, male politicians, the young and vivacious Victoria stands for modernity itself: a mixture of feminism, technology and power. In one scene, Victoria is shown approving a postage stamp with her profile while an official flatters her on the global reach of her influence. In stark contrast to Lin's static globe, the stamp underscores Victoria's (and the Victorian's) global scope and a new understanding of imperial circulation and trade that is at odds with the Chinese reliance on enforcing its imperial boundaries. In another significant British scene, Denton convinces Parliament to vote in favor of force by showing his audience Chinese cultural objects as evidence of China's weakness and arrogance. Displaying a jade vase and a bronze urn that represent high points in Chinese civilization and self-sufficiency, Denton also presents his audience with a richly decorated Qing dynasty porcelain vase that might appear "plump and proud" but is nonetheless fragile and "filled with nothing but self importance" (ibid.). Denton demonstrates Britain's symbolic might by smashing the Qing vase to the floor. A fitting reminder of the battle over commodified signifiers like opium and essentialized forms of Chineseness that are lost in the events of the film, the camera zooms in on the broken shards.

Unlike Queen Victoria's robust youthfulness, Emperor Daoguang appears sickly, ill-informed and over-reliant on his courtiers. The final scenes of the film depict him weeping with shame while kowtowing to portraits of his ancestors, each one labeled and dated by subtitles to emphasize continuity and history. The emperor's sons are shown in a line behind him performing the same rituals of atonement. The audience is left with this line of filial and fixed signification rather than the globe that Lin has sent to the emperor before his exile along with the message that the Qing dynasty can no longer isolate itself from the rest of the world. What Lin has learned about the new world order or, the "essence of Western knowledge," sits uneasily with the line of imperial descent which shifts abruptly to a close-up of a stone lion whose eyes glow menacingly red and the message of recovery superimposed over this final image of the film announcing that "on July 1, 1997 the Chinese government recovered sovereignty over Hong Kong" (Xie, 1997).

This ambivalence toward China's embrace of Western knowledge, the result of which is the foundation of Hong Kong, can more clearly be seen in the treatment of Shanzi. Like Gideon Chase, Shanzi is denied the privileged position of the hybrid despite his role of interpreter; like Hong

Kong, Shanzi is present at many meetings between Chinese and English officials but only capable of repeating the words of both sides by translation. Forced into self-interest and thus history itself by Lin's arrest of his father, Shanzi becomes involved in the plan to derail the English by convincing the prostitute Rong'er to seduce and then kill, Captain Elliot. Distrusted by both sides and equally swayed by both sides, Shanzi is ultimately executed for betraying both. To return to the film's use of coded objects, Shanzi wears a hat to which is attached a fake queue: in learning Western ways, he has cut off his queue which symbolically makes him Chinese, a crime that is punishable in China by death. Under the gaze of not one but two nation-states, hybridity becomes an enforced cleaving to borders: assenting to hybridity is less a fluidity of nationality and cultures and more likely singular adoptions, like Shanzi's hat, of one or the other. In being a hybrid, one ultimately runs the risk of being accused, as Hong Kong has many times, of being not Chinese enough or its opposite, "tainted" by colonialism. Hybridity, as Bhabha suggests, has the potential to "split" the dominant discourse's ability to be "representative [and] authoritative" and represents "that ambivalent 'turn' of the discriminated subject into the terrifying, exorbitant object of paranoid classification – a disturbing questioning of the images and presences of authority" (Bhabha, 1994, p. 113). This definition helps recast the question of Hong Kong's disappearance as a strategy enacted by its imperial owners for managing hybridity, constraining its influence, and even to evacuate it of its political efficacy. Not only does the film question whether or not Westerners can live with Chinese but also, can Chinese live with other Chinese without enforcing exclusions based on authenticity. The negative treatment of bilingual, go-between characters like Shanzi and Chase reveals an intense distrust of the translator or hybrid as the forerunner of those who live in Hong Kong, and it complicates hybridity as a model for Hong Kong's future, what Ien Ang has called a "cultural prohibition of de-sinicization" (Ang, 2001, p. 292). Those Chinese living in Hong Kong are not to be viewed as cosmopolitans or cultural hybrids but as unfortunate Chinese who have forgotten the ways of home. Yet, they are not to be allowed into that other British "home" which has, through decolonization, decided to retrench its boundaries. Can Hong Kong tell its own story through a neo-Victorian lens that would not involve such multiple losses? What alternative spaces open up when the binaries of hybridity are ditched in favor of establishing a more integrative identity that would not involve being "merely" Chinese or "shamefully" colonial British?

Neo-Victorianism and Jackie Chan I: "Born in Hong Kong"

I would like to turn now to Jackie Chan, Hong Kong's most well-known actor and director, who literally embodies the cultural codes and memory of Hong Kong in spite of the changes in his career that have "disembedded" (Fore, 1997, p. 130) him from the specifics of Hong Kong's cultural space and propelled him to the forefront of global cinema. Born to a poor family who fled the Cultural Revolution to Hong Kong in the 1950s, Chan was indentured at an early age to an acrobatic Peking Opera school. He began his career as a stuntman in early Bruce Lee films; after Lee's death, Chan's unique brand of slapstick comedy, beautifully choreographed fight scenes and on-screen persona of the likeable, good-hearted local boy soon eclipsed Lee's hypermasculinity and allegiance to a mythical China.[9] Across the board, critics have read Chan's success and his films as indicative of Hong Kong's own history of identity politics: from local icon to Asian star to a global product, "made in Hong Kong," for international audiences.[10] Abbas attributes Chan's rise to fame in movies such as *Drunken Master* (1978) and the *Project A* series to the optimistic and prosperous 1970s, before Thatcher's visit to China, when there was "a sense of how it was local ingenuity and professionalism more than imported talent that had brought about the city's great success" (Abbas, 1997a, p. 30). Steve Fore, and others like Gina Marchetti, have identified *Rumble in the Bronx* (1995) as Chan's emergence into the global market, opting for a transnationalism that reflects Hong Kong's identity as a world city. Marchetti extends this insight by tracing, in the double mapping of the Bronx onto the actual set location of Toronto, the entwined histories and kinships of both the Chinese and the black diaspora taken to their logical, ludic conclusions in the *Rush Hour* series, Chan's most successful movies to date (2001, pp. 151–2). For Rob Wilson, Chan has developed into an "agent of global/local skills who can mime and de-mint the global codes of action cinema into a reverse-commodity and counter-flow" (Wilson, 2005, p. 266), capable of wielding his uncanny "Hong Kong localism" to destabilize the "white mythologies" and "image-empires" (ibid., p. 265) entrenched by globalization's reach. Despite these influential readings of Chan's career, the significant presence o the Victorian in Chan's work has remained unstudied and I want to claim his films as a powerful vehicle for moving neo-Victorianism in new, more global directions. In what follows, I turn to *Project A*, *Shanghai Noon* and its sequel, *Shanghai Knights* (I will treat *Around the World in Eighty Days*, a "steampunk" revision of the Jules Verne novel separately in the next chapter) and provide an analysis of Chan's biopoetics and his films' ability to restore history to the discourse of Hong Kong's disappearance that do not recapitulate the standard narratives of the Opium War.

More so than British heritage films, *Project A* and the *Shanghai* series comedically, and sometimes violently, show the workings of neo-Victorianism, making visible its attributes of temporal anachronism, inauthenticity, incompletion and escapism, to name a few, and making them available for global consumption. In lieu of the desire-fulfilling machinations of conventional heritage film, Chan's films hijack memories of the Victorian that have long been conscripted for versions of Englishness and in doing so tell and insert memories of different stories. Working with Freud's definition of "screen memories," memories that "screen" or hide difficult childhood memories from recall and interpretation, Marita Sturken argues for the fluidity between memory and "historical" images especially in the formation of national myths and cultural memory. Since there are no "original" memories, only those that have been transformed and reformed, she makes a case for the power of a photographic or cinematic image to create or become a substitute for "real memory" (Sturken, 1997, p.8). Using the popular memory of what constitutes the Victorian, Chan's neo-Victorian films visually compensate for the loss of a version of nineteenth century history that is accountable to Asian, specifically Hong Kong's, experience.

In 1983, Chan starred in and directed *Project A*; set in Hong Kong around the late nineteenth century, the movie's heroics center around the plan to secure the colony against piracy in the South China Sea. Chan plays Sergeant "Dragon" Ma of the Water Police who is demoted to a policeman when his unit is disbanded after the sabotage of its resources and its inability to catch pirates who are kidnapping, ransoming and killing local residents traveling between Hong Kong and China. Despite its heavily staged atmosphere and almost garish costuming, *Project A* depicts a healthy, Westernized, colonial Hong Kong at ease with its Cantonese values and culture (Chu, 2003, p. 82). The film appears bi-leveled: on the surface lie the authoritative structures of colonial power and wealth represented by the police station and the VIP club, while stairs and hills lower the viewer down to more local scenery, street businesses, dessert stands, warrens of traditional housing and teahouses. The representation of the territory in *Project A* articulates a strong sense of local identity emerging within colonial, British symbols. The early fight scenes in the film exude a pleasurable nostalgia as Chan and his enemies interact all over the local map of Hong Kong using, in typical Jackie Chan fashion, all objects of daily life from bicycles to ladders to chamber pots. In addition to the fast-paced action, the audience is treated to a fetishistic orgy of local places and things where the larger conflict between the colonial past and the impending postcolonial future is temporarily solved by the competing bodies in the film. Comic, improvised and presented as natural, *Project A's* fight scenes emphasize, rather than dismantle, the sense of security in the territory.

The responsibility for maintaining this colonial harmony falls on the British colonial government, the Hong Kong Police and the Water Police, who must battle a series of internal and external enemies such as Chou, the wealthy tycoon and gunrunner, his henchmen who run the black market and Pirate Lo, who terrorizes the outlying islands and harbor. As an officer on sea and on land, Ma mixes justice, selflessness and honor with the protection of the body politic: in this neo-Victorian context, however, the disciplinary nature of *Project A* raises no Foucauldian red flags. Chan reprises the police officer role in many films, but *Project A* recovers the history of the Water Police, a body, Karen Fang identifies as a "truly local police force" (Fang, 2003, p. 295), formed by the British Royal Navy in the 1840s. Utilizing Hong Kong's limited number of heritage sites, the film is shot on location at the former Marine Police headquarters in Kowloon. Innovative in its policing techniques and recruiting process, the Royal Navy drew from a local pool of applicants for Water Police hires. The survival of the Hong Kong Police and the Marine Police, "archetypes of the British colonial administration," Fang notes, is a "strange persistence of imperial structures in the period after colonial sovereignty" (ibid., p. 293) and is one of the more unremarked upon successes of "one country, two systems." Significantly, the presence of Sikh officers haunts the film's definition of the local; appearing in the background or limited to silent gestures they underscore the racial phobia underlying both colonial policy and Hong Kong's identity agenda. Anticipating the plight of Hong Kong residents of South Asian descent who essentially became stateless after 1997 the film nonetheless remains a celebration of the rule of law.

The film dramatizes the rule of law through rivalry between the Water and Hong Kong Police and conflicts with the British administration. The British colonel in the film does speak Cantonese and is at least capable, if unwilling, to communicate with his officers. Filmed in 1983, only a year before the Joint Declaration was hammered out, the film suggests that British officials can still enter into dialogue with the territory it governs by learning and sharing linguistic and communal codes. Yet, the film punishes an effeminate Chinese manager of the VIP club who speaks English for violating codes of solidarity. While the film denies an embrace of expatriatism for its establishment of localness, it does insist on difference between Hong Kong and mainland Chinese. In an early scene set in a Westernized tavern frequented by both police units, the two groups joke about the colony's security: the police loudly proclaim that it would be foolish to take a boat from Hong Kong back to one's ancestral home in Canton because the Water Police are so inept at patrolling the waters. The Water Police respond by acting out a skit in which a blind uncle of one of the men arrives in Hong Kong from the mainland: one man asks how the uncle can find his way to Hong Kong because he is blind; the other man answers that he can navigate using the familiar smells of various neighborhood foods and, "if he can hear the sound of whistles, he must be in Hong Kong!" (Chan, 1983). The joke forms around the useless blowing of whistles by police who cannot catch their criminals. A rousing fight occurs between the two groups involving chairs, beer bottles and large plates of spaghetti. The friendly, if violent, slap-stick sparring between the two units denotes a sense of enjoyment and play in contrast to the intense raid that the police make on Chou's VIP club later in the film that is viciously dismantled in the altercation. In the bar, Ma attempts to keep the peace by insisting that they are "all the same people," all "law enforcers" (Chan, 1983) and that they should not fight. Drawn into the action, however, Ma's fighting style is no different from those of his colleagues and the camera rarely focuses on Chan, opting instead for wide shots of general, comedic mayhem. The collective action scenes establish the sameness of the two groups and emphasize the cultural difference between them and the mainland.

The objective of both exchanges lies in defining "home." On the one hand, the anecdote of the blind uncle's journey from China to Hong Kong suggests that there are already identifiable and familiar sounds and smells of home linked with the abundance of food. On the other hand, the fight scene implies that the lawlessness of Hong Kong might be in danger of being the same lawlessness in China, a threat underscored by Chou's deals with mainland gangsters and corruption within the police force. What will define Hong Kong as home will be the principles of law and order, a colonial import that the boys must learn to unite under. Even if the enunciation of the colony as home is problematized by the evocation of privileged sites such as ancestral homes or other ties of kinship to China, there remains no doubt in the fight scene that, despite their animosity to each other, the Water and land police are all "local boys."

Defined by law and masculinity, the film's writing of the local also seeks to incorporate Sammo Hung's more corporeal character, "Fei," a childhood friend of Ma's and an honorable thief whose trickery, pragmatism and bravery offers an alternative identity. After Ma tires of bureaucratic corruption and leaves the police force, Fei jokes that Ma should join him as a thief, one of four professions guaranteeing profit. Significantly, as Fei makes this speech, the duo descends into the more local street scenery of colonial Hong Kong. Here, "thief" is projected as a Hong Kong stereotype of the unscrupulous businessman (versus the violent trafficking in weapons that the villain Chou represents) whose entrepreneurial spirit is to be celebrated. For Fei, colonialism facilitates a lucrative way of making a living and forms the basis of economic survival and potential prosperity. Fei's character reminds the viewer that coloniality can be read as a choice for the majority of immigrants and refugees to Hong Kong in the nineteenth century and beyond, of escaping one kind of colonialism for the opportunities and benefits available in another. Unlike Ma, who requires multiple warrants and badges in order to move legitimately around Hong Kong's spaces, Fei passes easily between the twinned worlds of the gambling den and the Westernized VIP club, and later, even enters Pirate Lo's lair disguised as a pirate. Fei addresses Hong Kong's position as a postcolonial anomaly moving beyond even the mimicry described by Homi Bhabha and toward a willingness to colonialism that can be critically uncomfortable. Fei may be temporarily distracted by the principles of "making a living" when he brokers deals with both villains and heroes but, he ultimately knows right from wrong when, in the final fight against Lo, Fei gives up his stolen booty and returns to his lair to rescue Ma. Unproblematically reincorporated into the story of community that *Project A* tells, Fei finally accedes to the values of community that Ma represents and helps to preserve.

The movie's final confrontation takes places when Ma frees the British hostages and defeats Pirate Lo, who is unmistakably Chinese but so covered in tattoos and facial hair that he is immediately aligned with barbarity and ex-territoriality. Sitting on a throne made out of bones and displaying superhuman strength, Lo exhibits a monstrous kind of cultural Chineseness, another version of the "foreign barbarian." Lo's distance from the sophistication and order of the colony is so extreme that it expresses itself in Darwinian excess. Wearing the captured Rear Admiral's decorative coat during the hostage negotiations, Lo questions Ma about this strange entity, the Hong Kong government, a question which stems more from ignorance of civilized order than a refusal to recognize the British administration's legitimacy, which China continued to do up until 1997. The film's final conflict shifts significantly from colonial discontent and internal scrabbling to battling Lo's unacceptable Chineseness: after a lengthy and violent fight scene, Ma, Fei, Inspector of Police, Tin-Tsu and another Water Police sidekick, wrap Lo in a carpet and blow him up with British hand grenades.

Unlike the anxiety exhibited in *The Opium War* about Chinese culture in conflict with European modernity, the closing scenes of *Project A* depict Ma and his cohorts interacting with Western technology with pragmatic glee. However, in its replay of the kind of hybridity I located in other neo-Victorian narratives about Hong Kong, it takes four men with a combination of martial arts, swordplay and modern firepower to overcome Lo. To successfully prevent a backslide into backwardness, the film suggests, requires a healthy appropriation of Western materials, but without sacrificing the characteristics of Hong Kong that the movie ultimately celebrates and that can be catalogued and fetishized as injury on Chan's body.

Chan's films almost always end with out-takes that showcase his athleticism as well as the mistakes and injuries that occur when stunts go wrong. In *Project A*, Chan's escape from a reconstruction of the Kowloon–Canton Railway clock tower goes horribly wrong and he drops several storeys, hitting his head on the ground. In the film, the fall is shown twice, regardless of continuity, first with Chan injured, and again, as a flawless execution. This creates a neo-Victorian effect, a dramatic hiccup in time that allows the viewer to dwell in slow-motion on the memory of one of the few remaining examples of Hong Kong's colonial architecture and then incorporate it seamlessly into progressive time. Shown again in the final out-takes of the film, footage of the fall affirms Chan's DIY mastery, daredevil antics and ingenuity – all desirable local attributes. This extra-textual material posits a kind of "real" or authentic moment not just for Chan who suffers the abuse but also for the viewer who is now interpellated into constructing the "fantasy" of the film by accepting the "reality" of the out-takes that come after it.

Sandwiched between Lo's violent death and the out-takes of the film is the real ending of the movie which shows Ma, Fei and the remaining Water Police paddling at sea on a makeshift raft, pirates in tow. Law and order remain triumphant but the sailors turn the raft one way and then another, testing the wind in vain for the direction back to Hong Kong. One can read this image as emblematic of Hong Kong's identity crisis in the years leading up to 1997, but the image can equally be one of a voyage away from home toward an imagination of the local not as disappearance nor as a stable and bounded nation-state but as an expression of fluidity and flexibility heralding a new era in the Chinese diaspora. While the physical act of sitting through the credits to wait for the out-takes suggests that "Hong Kong" can only be achieved by staying and refining a position through which the continuing love affair with place can be maintained, the raft evokes Hong Kong's history as a port city: transitional, provisional and constantly in motion. Reconstructing Hong Kong as a port, as various historians and cultural critics like Rey Chow have done, expands the Hong Kong story beyond that which has been "fixed" by imperial centers. Indispensable to the center, the port occupies, according to Chow, the position of the "debased" (Chow, 1998a, p. 177) but:

> Etymologically, the word "port" illuminates all the aspects of Hong Kong's "origins" that are suppressed in the eventual interpretations of the city. "Port" refers, of course, to Hong Kong's status as an *entrepôt*, an entrance point or *port*al to China and Asia. It also refers to Hong Kong's amazing economic development – to Hong Kong's status as a vast em*por*ium with a plentitude of ex*ports* and im*ports*. More significantly, though, it alludes to the trans*port*ing function that is part and parcel of Hong Kong's intended role as a carrier of valuables and values between cultures. In performing this function to its utmost capacity, Hong Kong has fully established itself as a land of op*port*unities. If Hong Kong remains in the avant-garde of world city culture, it is because it makes *port*ability, including the portability of postmodern cultural identities, a fact of life. (ibid., p.176).

Chow's delightful highlighting of the im*port*ance of the "port" concept in thinking Hong Kong allows for the re-evaluation of the "port" itself as a place of infectious contact, contamination and disease and offers new ways of thinking about hybridity. An *entrepôt* clears space for an alternate history that can forge continuities between Hong Kong's past, present and future and that goes beyond the boundaries of colonialism and the compulsion of recalling the Opium Wars. The return to the Victorian in Chan's later films, however, represents a continued need to question the portability of the term *entrepôt* itself lest privileging the periphery of Hong Kong also condones a neo-imperialist approach to diaspora where hegemonic notions of China and Britain (alternately, Chineseness and whiteness) still haunt the alternative networks of identity and belonging. I turn now to this interrogative project in *Shanghai Noon* and *Shanghai Knights*.

Neo-Victorianism and Jackie Chan II: *Shanghai Noon, Shanghai Knights*, and the Chinese Diaspora

In 2000 and 2003, Jackie Chan produced and starred in two neo-Victorian movies with Owen Wilson, *Shanghai Noon* and *Shanghai Knights*, the former set in the American West and its sequel, set in Victorian England during the aftermath of the Opium Wars. In both movies, Chan plays Chon Wang, a Chinese imperial guard (a variation on the police officer of *Project A*), who becomes a lawman in the West and an immigrant, two roles that speak strongly to Hong Kong, the larger Chinese diaspora and support the stereotype of the "model minority." Both *Shanghai* movies, I argue, perform the double duty of recalling the nineteenth century as the first wave of mass migration from China (Pan, 1990, p. 43), and the 1980s and 1990s, when leaving Hong Kong became a politicized act of refusing Chineseness. Britain's denial of the right of abode to Hong Kong residents in 1981 made it clear that Britishness, and subsequently whiteness, would also be unattainable. Thus stranded, it is possible to diagnose the psyche of Asian immigrants, as David Eng and Shinhee Han do, as laboring under "racial melancholia," the condition of being caught in constant personal and political conflict between mourning *and* melancholia, or more accurately, between assimilation and exclusion (Eng and Han, 2003, p. 363). Drawing on Freud, Eng and Han attempt to depathologize racial melancholia by refining rather than separating the relationship between recovery and sustained damage. Adopting mourning and melancholia as a sustained spectrum of possible relationships, they believe that the "communal appropriation of melancholia [and] its refunctioning of everyday life" would help "annul[s] the multitude of losses continually demanded by an unforgiving social world" (ibid., p. 366). Reading Chan's martial arts as a staging of such a conflict and the *Shanghai* series within such a politics of memory signals a departure from both the local politics of *Project A* and marks a significant re-evaluation of the relationship between East and West traced by the Opium War narrative.

While not strictly neo-Victorian because it does not depict nineteenth-century Britain, I choose to include *Shanghai Noon* in this chapter because the history of immigration that I trace illustrates that "Hong Kong" affects not only China and Britain but also those that accept its immigrants such as the U.S. Furthermore, the turn toward the American West in *Shanghai Noon* recovers a history of Chinese labor in America's imperial expansion westward that opens neo-Victorianism up to addressing neo-imperialism beyond its usual boundaries, in this instance, within the term "diaspora" itself. *Shanghai Noon*'s revision of the Victorian emerges when multiculturalism in the U.S. appeared increasingly under stress and when China's position as an economic and cultural power became undeniable. The film opens in a similar fashion to Xie's *The Opium War* with scenes of the Forbidden City, the seat and symbol of Chinese imperial power. Influenced by ideas of (Western) freedom in the fairy tale of the Frog Prince, Princess Pei-Pei, played by Lucy Liu, runs away with her English tutor to America in order to escape an arranged marriage to the emperor's favorite nephew. The first English phrases that Chon Wang learns as he guards the princess are "America" and "happily ever after." As news of the princess's disappearance spreads through the Forbidden City, Chon joins the three bravest imperial guards of the Palace as a lackey on the mission to retrieve Pei-Pei. However, the year is 1881, one year prior to the passing of the Chinese Exclusion Act in the U.S. and the height of China's concessions to foreign power: by 1881, Beijing had been occupied by both the French and the British, its Treaty Ports opened for forty years, and its frontiers and territories ceded to Japan and Russia.[11] The movie begins by troubling the conventional "logic of the wound" (Chow, 2000, p. 4) of China's victimization by the West by locating "happily ever after" in the U.S. while also evoking the racism and exclusions institutionalized at the point of destination.

Shanghai Noon dramatizes this double estrangement from both locations and recovers two intertwined histories of nineteenth-century imperialism, usually rendered ghostly, for recovery in the present. Lured by the villain Lo Fang's false reputation as a philanthropist who aids new Chinese immigrants fallen on hard times, Pei-Pei is betrayed by her tutor and imprisoned in a labor camp outside Carson City, Nevada. A former imperial guard described as a traitor who has "run away from the Forbidden City" (Dey, 2000), Lo Fang's plan involves stealing Pei-Pei's ransom money to provide the Chinese slave labor necessary to build the trans-continental railway, one of the greatest technological feats of the nineteenth century that enabled America's westward expansion. While the central Pacific Railway Company, which built the eastward track of the Grand Pacific Railroad, hired between 12,000 to 14,000 Chinese coolies during this time, the workers' legitimacy in the nation's foundation was called into question by the Chinese Exclusion Acts (Pan, 1990, p. 43). The zoom shot of Chon's arrival in Nevada narrows down to show him as a Chinese man in imperial robes riding a train through the desert having taught himself to read and speak English from the same book of fairy tales abandoned by the princess. This focus reveals how inhabiting the role of the "model minority" provides necessary visibility in U.S. history (Eng and Han, 2003, p. 351). But the ensuing fight scene in which Chon attempts to avenge the death of his uncle at the hands of O'Bannon's mutinous bandits while incidentally dismantling the train they're riding on also illustrates the conflict between mourning and melancholia indicated by Eng and Han. Chon's failed attempt to mourn his murdered father figure through fighting is entangled with the technological supremacy of the West he is simultaneously shut out of.

Chon and (more problematically) Pei-Pei participate in the migratory patterns of the nineteenth century that were dominated by the movement of Chinese men enticed by wages and work in places as far away as Havana, Peru, Hawaii and San Francisco. *Shanghai Noon* claims the essentially nineteenth-century term of "sojourner" as relevant to the present. The term sojourner usually used to refer to single, male, indentured workers constrained by what they could earn with monetary ties and obligations to their ancestral villages and extended families in China, to which they would eventually return. Sojourner also functions, as critics have noted, as an ideological term circumscribing all overseas Chinese people regardless of differences in experience and reifying potentially debilitating definitions of Chineseness as universal.[12] Contemporary sojourners such as "returnees" and "astronauts," distinctly Hong Kong slang for the mobile populations returning to and moving between Hong Kong and other host countries (Skeldon, 1994, p. 10), exceed questions of assimilation, hybridity, alienation and origins that structure diasporic texts, in much the same way that "Hong Kong," "Asian-American," and "Overseas Chinese" exceed China's (and by extension, the U.S. and Britain's) boundaries and definitions of itself as a nation. By holding the nineteenth-century sojourner past up against the immigrant in the present, *Shanghai Noon* moves beyond simple comparison and illustrates how diaspora is a sedimented experience.

As he pursues the princess, Chon finds his masculinity and Chineseness revised, to much comedic effect, by his reluctant partnership with Owen Wilson's character, Roy O'Bannon (later revealed to be Wyatt Earp), and Chon's alliances with other diasporic and dispossessed groups in the West. Encumbered by multiple histories, names and costumes, many of the fight scenes in the film depict Chon physically solving the contradictions of cross-cultural contact: through action, he sheds his Chineseness and gains enough of the desired attributes of whiteness to become a respected sheriff. In *Shanghai Noon*, as in many of Chan's movies, this act of recovery occurs through the use of coded objects. Unlike the discourse of commodification that dominates the use of objects in *The Opium War*, *Shanghai Noon* offers a system of investment based on the economics of mourning. *Shanghai Noon* enacts Freud's theory in "Mourning and Melancholia" that recovery from loss is achieved through the successful transference of the libido to new objects of value (Freud, 1917, p. 311). As in *The Opium War*, much is made of Chon's queue as a symbol of Chineseness: it has been both a hindrance and a weapon for Chon throughout the film until Lo Fang cuts it off to demonstrate Chon's "slavishness" (Dey, 2000) to imperial China. Significantly bald, given Chon's attachment to his queue, Lo Fang is presented as a figure of anxiety, utterly devoid of any ties to his home country and willing to exploit his countrymen. This portrayal of Lo Fang valorizes – and moralizes – the hybridity that Chon represents. Thus castrated, Chon's role as immigrant is solidified: he can never, as Lo Fang states, return to China. Only through Lo's action, however, does Chon relinquish his sojourner status and its melancholic structures of return for the permanence of the immigrant. Through Roy's gentle cajoling, Chon learns to recast the loss of the queue as empty vanity rather than allegiance to his Chinese lineage. In the final standoff over Pei-Pei and the ransom money, Chon must protect the princess against Lo Fang and the demonized imperial guards who are, like Chon, "bound by imperial decree" (Dey, 2000) to bring Pei-Pei back to China. The simple act of reading aloud from the imperial scrolls they carry, symbolic substitutes for the body of the emperor, brings Chon immediately to his knees in submission. Only when Pei-Pei defiantly burns the scrolls during the final fight does Chon finally relinquish the grip that the East, with all its mythical and real connotations, continues to hold over him in the West. Drawing again from Eng and Han, I read the final, celebratory moments of *Shanghai Noon* as Chon successfully transferring his libido from these reified objects and investing that energy into new objects such as his new name, "John Wayne." Into the void left by Chineseness steps the princess, the values of the American Dream and the liberatory potentials of American multiculturalism. At the same time, the freed slaves that Pei-Pei has championed disrupt the amnesia of nineteenth-century American history, making that strand of the Victorian available for a new generation of viewers at "home" and "abroad."

On seeing Chon kowtow to the imperial scroll during the final fight scene of *Shanghai Noon*, O'Bannon yells in disappointment, "I thought we were past this!" (Dey, 2000). This idea of getting "past" the contradictions and pathologies of the immigrant experience may be, however problematically, possible in the "melting pot" culture of the U.S., as Chon and Pei-Pei's success demonstrates, but obviously requires further examination when the duo begin their second neo-Victorian adventure in England, 1888. Returning to the neo-Victorian center in *Shanghai Knights* recasts O'Bannon's question to one asked by Anne Anlin Cheng, "is there any getting over" or past "race?" (Cheng, 2001, p. 103).

Called to London by Chon's sister, Lin, Chon and O'Bannon begin their investigation of the death of Chon's father, the keeper of the Chinese imperial seal, who has been murdered in the Forbidden City by English aristocrat, Lord Rathbone. Chon soon learns Rathbone's theft of the seal in its ornate dragon box has been commissioned by Wu Chow, the emperor's bastard brother in exile. Acting on a childhood trauma of the Empress Dowager striking him whenever he tried to touch the seal, which his brother played with like a toy, Wu Chow's legitimacy is dependent on his possession of the seal. In return for the seal, and thus the dragon throne, Wu has agreed to assassinate ten members of the British royal family so that Rathbone can become king of England. The clandestine plot between Rathbone and Wu recalls the stance of the Opium Wars and its contemporary counterpart, the rhetoric of Hong Kong's reunification process, but expresses this polemic relationship as a united front against the threat of diaspora that Chon and Lin represent. In a scene reminiscent of *The Opium War*, Rathbone appears in Parliament to explain the inscrutability of the Chinese. Ravaged by the opium wars and barbaric enemies like the Boxers, Rathbone intones that, "China is not well" (Dobkin, 2003). As evidence of China's unhealthiness, Rathbone reveals a tiger in a cage that was presented as an inappropriate gift to Queen Victoria. In this context, the appearance of an Asian tiger in a British institution to signal Chinese weakness must be a reference to the Asian economic "tigers," those primarily overseas Chinese powerhouses that have economically and racially threatened both China and Britain.

This imperial story, however, is subordinated to Chon's personal quest to avenge his father's death and to overcome the guilt of abandoning his sister and father in China. Read together, the two storylines stress the intimacies between national ties and kinship. The movie opens with Lin's receipt of a reconciliatory letter and a photograph of her successful brother in the West. Busy locking up the imperial seal, the father dismisses the missive, effectively disowning his son and insinuating that Chon's immigration is disloyalty to both father and country. In America, playing with the puzzle box sent by Lin after his father's murder, Chon explains the importance of the seal to Chinese power, creating a filial line from Genghis Khan through successive imperial reigns. At the same time, he tells a personal story of the seal: entrusted to his family's care for over twelve generations, Chon had been groomed as a child to inherit his father's protective detail.

The trauma of illegitimacy expressed by Wu Chow and Rathbone shifts here to the powerful ties of filialty and guilt that bind Chon, the immigrant son, in real ways to his father and in fictive ways to his homeland. Unable to resist the compulsion to repeat his father's footsteps, unbroken for twelve generations, that would also maintain the symbolic power passed down from emperor to emperor, Chon enters into the melancholic structure of diaspora again. The movie's emphasis on filiation and affiliation can clearly be seen in a fight scene that takes place inside Madame Tussaud's Wax

Museum. As any moment of physical conflict in Chan's films requires address, this scene gains significance when Chon fights Wu Chow's henchmen for the seal amid wax reproductions of Queen Victoria and Genghis Khan. Hong Kong resurfaces explicitly in this scene, symbolically represented in the seal's preciousness, its enclosure within the ornate box, and its movement through the spaces of the film. Stolen from China, it finds its way into Rathbone's secret storeroom of imperial spoils, and is found hidden under the Queen Victoria statue's skirts at the wax museum. At the end of the movie, a grateful Queen Victoria sends the newly knighted Arthur Conan Doyle to return the seal to China. Confronted with the public face of Englishness and whiteness in Queen Victoria and the great unifier of a cultural and racial proto-Chineseness in Genghis Khan, Chon encounters two representatives of the essentialist myths of blood and race. Chon's inability to inhabit whiteness is obvious; he is, as Bhabha succinctly puts it, "almost the same but not white" (Bhabha, 1994, p. 89). However, this scene also suggests that Chon might not be yellow enough either to be "the same" as Genghis Khan. One of the dilemmas facing Chon (and Hong Kong) as he struggles for the seal is similar to Ien Ang's revision of Rey Chow's question, "can one say no to China?" Can Chon, "when called for, say no to Chineseness" (Ang, 2001, p. 41)? Can he resist, or at least mediate, the powerful and intangible bonds to blood and race that turn the positive and destabilizing effects of diaspora into what Ang has criticized as a "transnational nationalism" (Ang, 2001, p. 85) in which diaspora comes to mean resinicization through myths like Genghis Khan?

While Chon battles the siren call of Chineseness, he and Lin acknowledge, but ultimately refuse, any identification with Britain despite its impact on Asian immigration. Unlike its prequel, *Shanghai Knights* ignores the representation of a Chinese community in Britain; Chon and Lin's quest remains a solitary one and aside from Wu Chow and his warriors, the siblings are lone Chinese in Victorian London. Even in Whitechapel, where Roy, Chon and Lin take shelter, no effort is made to represent the orientalist fantasies of the East End, the reality of its immigrant population, or its present status as a well-established and influential Chinatown. This powerful absence might well serve as commentary on the 1981 British Nationality Act, one in a series passed to manage decolonization, which clarified the definition of British nationality by turning former overseas "citizens" into "subjects," thus eliminating partiality or the right of abode to those in "dependent territories" like Hong Kong.[13] Like the seal's subordinate position tucked away in Queen Victoria's garter, the Act was perceived to have the deliberate goal of preventing panicked Hong Kong people from swamping Britain, a perception fuelled by minor concessions made by Thatcher in the 1990s allowing entry to a few thousand Hong Kong executives, professionals and their families. The amendment to grant British citizenship to all the residents of Gibraltar, which held a "special position in the EEC" (*British*, 1981), but not to the 3.3 million British overseas passport holders in Hong Kong only exacerbated claims of racial discrimination (Hong Kong Legislative Council, 1992). The film's historical inaccuracy illustrates the trauma of Britain's immigrant policies and exhibits an unwillingness to engage in any further recalling of that strand of immigration history.

Thus, *Shanghai Knights* unabashedly and sometimes childishly smashes its way through British and Victorian iconography. For example, Lin, uttering some choice epithets, kicks Jack the Ripper off a Whitechapel bridge when he tries to attack her, thus reversing his colonizing presence in a historically immigrant quadrant of the city. After defeating Rathbone and Wu Chow at the end of the film, Roy and Chon slide down the hands of Big Ben, ripping through a giant Union Jack draped from the tower in celebration of Queen Victoria's jubilee so as to slow their descent.[14] The pair land, conveniently enough, in the royal carriage across from a bemused Queen Victoria, played by heritage film veteran, Gemma Jones. The duo destroy the national obstacles, such as the Union Jack, that tend to construct and restrict the terrain of neo-Victorianism and prevent the frank confrontation of the Victorian with its alternate histories. When the trio finally leaves England, workmen fixing their damage to the clock tower yell out one of the film's refrains, "bloody tourists!" (Dobkin, 2003), a stereotypical response of fairly benign British xenophobia. However, the phrase functions as a poignant reminder that Chon/Chan can only ever be a "bloody tourist" in Britain. If Hong Kong reminds China of its victimhood, it should also remind Britain of its own racism from Enoch Powell's infamous "rivers of blood" speech to the anti-Asian riots in northern England in 2001 and publications such as *Over-Crowded Britain* (2003) by Ashley Mote, a small, hysterical book claiming that immigration dilutes Britishness. Finally, when not physically destroying the symbolic objects that occlude postcolonial history, *Shanghai Knights* performs radical acts of revision. Charlie Chaplin's brand of graceful slapstick, according to the film's version of history, originates from his childhood encounter with Chon Wang's martial artistry, and the literary character "Sherlock Holmes" owes his origins to several of Roy's improvised disguises. Though humorous and unlikely, such appropriations of quintessential English characters promote the potential subversiveness of neo-Victorian "screen memories."

The film's violence toward national iconography critiques the nation-based frameworks of reference in depictions of the Victorian. Thus enclosed, the film suggests, Britain remains boxed in, unable to reach any diasporic intent or point of view. The visual vocabulary of the film is governed by the image of the box: in the fight scene in a London marketplace, for example, Chan appears hemmed in by vendors' carts; Chon and Roy emerge as stowaways from a box trunk, and a sharp cut deposits the viewer with Chon who is playing with the puzzle box he has inherited from his father which arrived in Carson City wrapped in another box. Not to be opened until Chon has learned the value of patience, the puzzle box traverses the same global flows as the seal thus creating a series of enclosures that complement the film's concerns with the bonds of blood and race. The puzzle box serves as a double to the decorated box that houses the imperial seal and must accompany it back to China and, to Roy's pocket watch, a cheap imitation bequeathed to Roy by his uncle who supposedly stole it from Abraham Lincoln. These interrelated objects proffer no easy solution to the matrix of Britain/China/U.S./Hong Kong relations that underlie this version of the Victorian. However, the puzzle box offers a potential mode of recovery from the unhistorical cultural bonds that manipulate Chon. Unlike its twin, the puzzle box is destined to be destroyed. On the way to London, Roy offers repeatedly to smash it open, but Chon prefers to bide his time and remain patient. The box remains intact until the end of the film when Roy, true to his word, smashes the box for Chon. The message from father to wayward son is written in calligraphy on a rock: "family is forever ... I am proud you cast your own stone" (Dobkin, 2003). Chineseness or "the rock with some gibberish on it" (Dobkin, 2003), according to Roy, professes itself to be small and *port*able, capable of expressing multiple identities outside of the perceived norm of Chinese essentialism.

The box contains what Roy deems a "good message" (Dobkin, 2003) from an authoritative father figure who sanctions the immigrant son's (but not necessarily, by extension, the immigrant daughter's) travel to and settlement in distant lands. The message to "cast your own stone" marks the father's approval of diaspora. The box with its stone, like a traveler's baggage, redefines the concept of the Chinese diaspora that remains tied to a cultural set of attributes or a geographical center. Chon's inheritance of the stone replaces the larger ancestral or cultural heritage that fictively separates or, boxes in, Chinese from each other and from non-Chinese. The stone that can eventually be cast breaks the ties of what can be an impossible and even nonexistent memory that holds diasporic subjects across generations to an "imaginary homeland" and moves Chon close to what Aihwa Ong has called "flexible citizenship" (Ong, 1999, p. 6). The "good message" approves an act of forgetting rather than the consistent acts of memory that constitute the abstract notions of loyalty, filialty and honor and allows for a recovery from the sense of betrayal and guilt that can mark the dislocations of diasporic subjectivity.

While the stone's message is translatable and portable, instances arise in the movie that resist translation and portability. Crashing Rathbone's costume party in order to gain access to the seal, Roy arrives dressed in purloined naval regalia masquerading as a British admiral. Chon enters dressed unconvincingly as an Indian maharajah. When Chon complains that his disguise will be a failure because he is obviously Chinese, Roy snaps back that the disguises are the same thing. To ease Chon's concerns, Roy instruct him on how to nod and bob his head while saying "cheerio," as if practicing a cultural stereotype will cement his authenticity. Seeing through their disguises, Rathbone confronts Chon with his dream that the Chinese, like India, will "one day embrace British rule" (Dobkin, 2003). Chon defiantly replies that Chinese pride, familial duty and honor will provide strong resistance to such a "proper" colonial narrative. While cultural euphemisms such as "family" and "honor" can displace more radical differences like human rights or Communism, they are merely "habits," Rathbone suggests, that the British can "break" (Dobkin, 2003). This episode visually provides a knot of entangled imperial memories: the British use of Indian opium to "enslave" China, America's own often occluded status as an empire that can instruct India and China, and an intrinsic difference in the British withdrawal from India that has led to its independence and emancipation in a way that Britain's withdrawal from Hong Kong will not. Chon's costume serves as a reminder that Hong Kong's decolonization process is emphatically not "the same" as the rest of the British Empire and resists translation or certain acts of integration. Both *Shanghai Noon* and *Shanghai Knights* stress such moments of the unportable; throughout *Shanghai Noon*, for example, Chinese laborers and imperial guards, Jewish immigrants and Native Americans, pass by each other with the briefest moments of contact or mere visual recognition. These moments offer the potential for shared experiences of dispossession and alienation, but while these groups occupy the same space, the film remains silent as to whether or not, aside from pointing out sameness-in-difference, there can be any unified commitment to the politics of change.

Revised by Jackie Chan and refracted through the location of Hong Kong neo-Victorianism can provide an emancipatory solution. Freed from the triangulated and strangulated memory of the Opium Wars, neo-Victorianism emphasizes productive fractures rather than cohesive but wounded national identities that either exclude, or supposedly encapsulate, all Chinese who have exceeded China's borders and have therefore become "Westernized" regardless of history and experience. Chan's films provide new "screen memories" of the Victorian that can express different modalities of hybridity – from imperial guard to sheriff, from sojourner to migrant, and even the cultural mimicry of Chon's disguise as a maharajah – that stress the kinds of co-optation and transcendence available in the space between empires. Chan's films expand neo-Victorianism to address questions of race beyond whiteness to other essentialist constructions not conventionally under the genre's jurisdiction. The *Shanghai* series, in particular, begs the questions: can Britishness and Chineseness as constructed by conventional neo-Victorianism survive Hong Kong? And by extension, can Americanness?

Since 1997, Hong Kong has struggled for universal suffrage and other political and electoral reforms, testing the limits of the fifty years of unchanging capitalism guaranteed by the PRC under "one country, two systems." The links between Hong Kong's economic prosperity and democracy are "confusing" (Chow, 1998b, p. 102) as democracy and other forms of political advancement are continually sacrificed as Hong Kong continues, beyond colonialism, to thrive without them. For Chow, the PRC's commitment to maintaining Hong Kong's capitalist system is similar to flooding the island with opium, hoping that the addiction will numb any desire for real change: the devotion to "making a living" becomes a "kind of opium . . . that turns people into addicts, deprived of freedoms and rights and ultimately of their ability to think" (ibid., p. 105). If democracy can be regarded as the opium of the West and capitalism, paradoxically, as the opium of China, then the forgetting of the Opium Wars for Hong Kong has huge implications and possibilities for its future. Using the neo-Victorian to stage a relevant history for Hong Kong, popular cinema emphasizes its *entrepôt* success and its role in immigration and diasporic history as a base for the cross-cultural flow of people. Recalling Hong Kong as part of such alternate histories prevents it from being the last chapter of British colonial history, merely another chapter in the establishment of "greater China," or from being an improper postcolonialism that cannot be discussed.

Chapter 5

Neo-Victorianism and Science Fiction: "Steampunk"

In the previous chapter, I deliberately set aside my discussion of Jackie Chan's most recent return to the Victorian in his 2004 film, *Around the World in Eighty Days*, directed by Frank Coraci, because, despite its nineteenth-century setting and emphasis on technology, it significantly complicates neo-Victorianism's generic boundaries and appropriative strategies. Chan's film "writes back" to Jules Vernes' 1873 novel, originally published in French, in which the fastidiously English Phileas Fogg, accompanied by his French servant Passepartout, must win a bet to circumnavigate the globe in an astounding eighty days. An outsider's study, the novel presents an "obsessive interest in the English character," especially the "vexed concept of English masculinity" (Sinnema, 2003, p. 135), themes that remain available in Chan's film and the two earlier adaptations of Vernes' novel for the screen, the 1956 Hollywood blockbuster starring David Niven and Mexican actor, Cantinflas (Anderson, 1956), and a 1989 television miniseries (Gay, 1989) with Pierce Brosnan and Eric Idle in the leading roles. While the novel and Chan's film predecessors leave British might and influence on a global scale largely untroubled, the new version grants Passepartout, played by Chan, greater, if not equal, agency. The imperial story told in Fogg's bet to traverse the globe still occurs but it is initiated and facilitated by the postcolonial Other, Fogg's valet-in-disguise, Passepartout, or the Chinese fugitive Lau Xing.

The substitution of Lau is the first of many revisions made to the original novel. Having robbed the Bank of England to retrieve a jade Buddha stolen from his village by an evil Chinese female warlord, General Fang, Lau has no choice but to escape the law by becoming Fogg's valet and scientific guinea-pig. In exchange for the British military aid required to plunder the jade reserves beneath Lau's village, Fang has deposited the Buddha into British hands as payment. Pursued by British police and Fang's henchmen, Fogg's bet becomes the fastest way for Lau to return the Buddha to China in time to save his village. As the title of the film suggests, the Victorian is mobilized to chart the dispersal of Britishness *and* Chineseness "around the world." Fogg's epistemological engagement with multiple cultural Others provides him with a renewed sense of identity and collective responsibility. Thus revised, the imperial adventure becomes the origins of a new multicultural future for Britain; as Fogg tells Queen Victoria, the film's *deus ex machina*, "I saw the world, I learnt of different cultures. I flew across an ocean. I wore women's clothing. Made a friend. Fell in love" (Coraci, 2004). At the same time, Lau completes his journey "around the world" with only the most "portable" (to borrow again from Rey Chow) Chinese qualities: friendship, family and kung fu. As his alias, a pun on ethnic passing and passports, suggests, Lau/Passepartout remains diasporic, recovering a definition of globally situated Chineseness that interrogates its geopolitical reality.

In a drastic update of both his original and copies, Fogg invents such anachronistic devices as air-conditioning, roller blades, a steam-powered gurney and a flying machine. While Fogg's Englishness is defined by his ability to live with utter devotion to the efficiency of his inventiveness coupled with a healthy belief in the scientific principles of Britain's imperial progress, Lau's otherness is initially characterized by a physical "musculinity" (Tasker, 1993, p. 3) in service to Western technology. Hired upon sight, Lau is immediately strapped into a steam-powered turbine contraption complete with jetpack and goggles and launched ludicrously into flight as part of Fogg's effort to break speed records. While the film firmly inhabits the postcolonial neo-Victorianism I've discussed so far, its deployment of recent technology in a nineteenth-century setting also situates it within the genre of "steampunk," a notoriously nebulous and inconsistent subgenre of science fiction, considered an offshoot of cyberpunk. Steampunk conventionally records and explores a speculative past or creates an alternate history based upon the premise that the nineteenth century was able to harness the power of steam to mechanically create, before its time, such devices as computers and Fogg's jetpack. As a subculture with a healthy online and physical presence (see, for example, the annual *U.K. Steampunk Convivial* or the *Brass Goggles* blog and online community), the steampunk scene also celebrates and performs Victorian scientific culture as a DIY aesthetic, its practitioners often adopting the "punk" politics of tinkering and subversive invention as counter-cultural ideology, if not a lifestyle. At its heart, steampunk explores the ways in which technology and science are implicated in the cultural patterns and problems of our daily lives and those of our nineteenth century counterparts. While steampunk's untimely historicity shares similar ontological decenterings and ruptures with neo-Victorianism, its hybrid technologies offer different understandings of technological progress. In its exploration of how technology, cultural identities and racial inequality are imbricated, *Around the World in Eighty Days* emphasizes the partnership – but also the easy slippages – between steampunk and neo-Victorianism.

Eventually, it is Lau who inhabits and furiously peddles the flying machine, made from the cannibalized parts of a steamship, carrying Fogg and his French companion, Monique, back to London in time to win the bet by completing their journey ahead of schedule. Capable of moving beyond constricting definitions of nationhood and geographic boundaries, Chan develops into a new kind of transnational hero: the cyborg. One of the central images of the film, Chan's cyborg body becomes a loaded image and metaphor capable of addressing neo-Victorianism and steampunk's own muddied roots and, as I will discuss later, the sometimes uncritical entanglement of both genres. Specifically for Chan, the cyborg contains the contradictory characteristics of the immigrant: infinite adaptability, mimicry, improvisation and contingency, but not a "full" or complete identity. As Passepartout *and* Lau, Chan's body represents the viscous ties of diasporic Chinese communities caught between identification with the Chinese nation state and the hegemonic, modern West. While *Around the World* celebrates ingenuity and the dangers of inventiveness, as parsed by the trio's protective goggles, the film's steampunk gadgetry also brings to the fore how technology is both raced and gendered, especially with respect to labor: what powers Western technology, as the image of Lau encased in the flying machine demonstrates, is the body of the (usually Asian) Other. Yet, the cyborg figure also illuminates ambivalence over the exportation of technology from the West to the rest: the film suspends judgment on Lau's potential exploitation in the machine, or whether he has successfully harnessed Western technology to achieve his own Chinese ends.

These power dynamics are also affected by geography as the film visits other former imperial locations such as China, India and Turkey, all now crisis zones of economic expansion. As Barney Warf argues, the counter-factual histories captured in steampunk necessarily suggests that "received categories of structuring space are no more 'real' or proper than the arbitrary lenses that we use to make sense of that past" (Warf, 2002, p. 34). On the one hand, the film's locations suffer from a tangential relationship to modernity perceived as European or located in the West. On the other, the essentialized or comedic depictions of these sites barely mask Western anxieties over the technological and economic advances of precisely these locations in the present. For example, the film's highly Orientalized portrayal of China – mountains, pagodas and rice paddy fields, an emphasis on family and intergenerational collective living – arguably bolsters Western modernity. Overwhelmed by tradition and stuck in the past, the imagery implies, China will never reach the same developmental level as the West and remains steampunk's Other. However, the film also resists this reading by staging the longest fight scene in the village between the mythical Ten Tigers, Lau's martial arts clan, and Fang's henchmen, the Black Scorpions.[1] Transformed into a contested field by intense physical activity and violence, the village scenes complicate accusations of orientalism in the deliberate return to the purity of kung-fu unfettered by the technology so prevalent in the rest of the film. These scenes raise questions about Chan's own collusion as a global actor in the trafficking of orientalist imagery, what Arif Dirlik has called the act of "self-orientalization" (Dirlik, 1997, p. 111), an acknowledgment of how "EuroAmerican images of Asia may have been incorporated into the self-images of Asians" (ibid.) and which "invent" (ibid.) and produce traditions previously considered to be original or authentic. Chan participates in and thus legitimizes the orientalist imaginary of the West in the construction of "China," but can he be faulted in depicting an Asian character anxious to embrace the possibilities that Western technology offers?

Steampunk's rearrangement of time *and* space acknowledges competing industrial and technological centers to Britain and examines them as spaces of anxiety. Read technologically and geographically, steampunk can restore to neo-Victorianism's focus on layered temporalities an equal interest in overlapping and performative spaces. The study of steampunk enhances neo-Victorianism's ability to trouble the cartography of empire because it explicitly remakes the Victorian but rarely imagines a new version of the nineteenth century without empire in it. Thus, steampunk's radical ahistoricism, in fact, serves as a powerful reminder of history, asking us to check our memories of the Victorian against history or further interrogate the historical gaps that steampunk reveals. In this chapter, I will re-evaluate two well-established examples of neo-Victorian science fiction, *The Difference Engine* (1991) by William Gibson and Bruce Sterling and *The Diamond Age or, A Young Lady's Illustrated Primer* (1995) by Neal Stephenson, and examine the (neo-) "Victorientalist" anxieties of their imagined geographies. Finally, I will turn to Otomo Katsuhiro"s *anime* film, *Steamboy* (2004) as it complicates and revises the "Victorientalism" in these two other Western examples. Through the twin lenses of steampunk and neo-Victorianism, I also examine the ways in which race is entangled with technology and how places and people are rarely understood on their own terms "but only insofar as they slot into the global scheme of things as spaces that are at this 'stage' of development relative to an idealized European past" (Agnew, 2003, p. 36). At stake in steampunk's partnership with neo-Victorianism, I argue, is the ability to connect the imperial project from the Victorian past with the potential neo-empires of the present and future. Before turning to my discussion of these texts, I want to outline in greater depth the troubled relationship between neo-Victorianism and steampunk as it represents a serious consideration of the ethics of appropriation encoded within these two genres, each one struggling to define itself as discrete.

Steampunk: An Orientation

Adopting London as its primary setting or Victorian England as a social or cultural base, much steampunk provides fodder for neo-Victorian and Victorian Studies alike. Steampunk recalls such touchstones as the upheavals of the industrial revolution; the celebration of global display at the 1851 Great Exhibition; inventions such as the railroad, the telegraph and the typewriter, that overhauled conceptions of space, time and the human-machine interface; the cultivation of workmanship against mass production in the Arts and Crafts movement; and, of course, the imaginative creativity and vision of nineteenth-century science fiction as celebrated, for example, in Alan Moore's graphic novel series, *The League of Extraordinary Gentlemen* (1999 – present).[2] Neo-Victorian scholars like myself find that the Victorian in steampunk mirrors both aesthetic and academic desires and are often untroubled by the appropriation of a pre-existing, separate antigenre under the umbrella of neo-Victorianism. It becomes easy to ignore the numerous exceptions to steampunk: how would *Boneshaker* (2009), a novel by Cherie Priest set in an alternate Seattle in 1863; or the Hollywood adventures, *Wild Wild West* (1999) and *Cowboys and Aliens* (2011), two mainstream examples of another steampunk variant, "Weird West;" or Jean-Pierre Jeunet's 1995 film *City of Lost Children*; or the mash-up novel *Android Karenina* (2010), count in neo-Victorianism's paradigm? How far outside the realm of the Victorian can technology travel before it eclipses the bounds of steampunk and becomes invisible to neo-Victorianism? Many steampunk authors and participants express their belonging to steampunk through technology: be it steam, brass, or mechanics, these are considered nineteenth-century materials and were most prominent in London during the industrial revolution, making the Victorian simply the most relevant, but not the only, setting for steampunk to occur. To forget the "technology level" and focus only on "the Victorian," as "dman762000," a poster to *The Great Steampunk Debate* forum, argues vehemently, is to do violence to the genre: "if you're going to limit steampunk to just the Victorian era then lets [sic] just call it neo-victorian and be done with it" (*Great Steampunk*, 2010).[3] The comment foregrounds how technology should be privileged in establishing the definition of steampunk, not the recovery of the Victorian. It also speaks to how the term "neo-Victorian" has limited, if not controlled, the scope of steampunk's reach.[4]

Nonetheless, a study of steampunk adds to neo-Victorianism's history of the present. Steampunk satisfies the nostalgic desire for a version of a Victorian past through which we can remember and experience a time of "undisciplined culture" (Clayton, 2003, p. 190), prior to the segregation of the arts and sciences, mass production and the reification of the "expert." The prevalence of vampires, werewolves, zombies and etiquette in Gail Carriger's steampunk series, the *Parasol Protectorate* (2009 – present) novels, for example, demonstrate both steampunk and neo-Victorianism's hybridizing impulses and "undisciplined" disrespect of boundaries. Multiple volumes and websites like *The Steampunk Workshop* now offer "how-to" guides in crafting art, toys and fashion using the steampunk aesthetic and retro-adapting or enhancing existing technology such as laptops, mobile phones and USB flash drives with brass gears, cogs and wood. Such an interest in tinkering, as Bowser and Croxall suggest, speaks to how we have become estranged from the lived details of our everyday technology and alienated from the globalized sources and labor conditions from which this technology is derived (Rachel A. Bowser and Brian Croxall, 2010, p. 17). Thus, the Victorian in steampunk can also recall the history of the labor movement and industrial reform including antitechnological resistance such as Luddism, featured by Gibson and Sterling in the anarchic elements of *The Difference Engine*. The recent appearance of steampunk erotica and "bodice rippers" suggest a need to explore the extension of technology into our reproductive and sexual lives. At the same time, steampunk can serve as a present-day cautionary tale for past technology gone dystopically wrong: in the aftermath of SARS, for example, the Australian short film series, *The Mysterious Geographic Explorations of Jasper Morello* (2005), told in silhouette animation reminiscent of Indonesian shadow puppetry, begins with a navigator of an airship searching for a cure for his plague-ridden home, Gothia. In many ways, steampunk dramatizes Kucich and Sadoff's argument about the choice of the nineteenth century as a "rupture" for the West's time and space-compressed, gadget-obsessed and technologically saturated moment.

Steampunk's *ad hoc* technological impurities and the radical anachronism of present/future technology appearing in a Victorian quotidian can be seen to literalize the neo-Victorian agenda, especially its postmodern attributes. In general, steampunk's play with temporality fits almost seamlessly with the generic conventions and literary games of neo-Victorian fiction; both offer, as Brian McHale has observed, a "new way of 'doing' history in fiction" (McHale, 1992, p. 222). Steampunk novels serve a pedagogical function in that they help us belong to the present differently; according to McHale, they "help us historicize our present by reimagining it as an alternate future for a past that never actually happened: it makes us aware of our historical situation by imagining the historical past otherwise" (ibid., p. 223). Explicit in its constructions of alternate history, Steffan Hantke has argued that literary steampunk, like neo-Victorianism, is "preoccupied with its own fictionality" and "privileges ontological over epistemological questions" (Hantke, 1999, p. 250) and ultimately takes as its "allegorical object . . . postmodernity itself" (ibid., p. 253). Some steampunk examples may also imagine an enforced regression to the Victorian in technology or in cultural attitudes via a postapocalyptic future. Set in 2025, S. M. Stirling's *The Peshawar Lancers* (2003), for example, relocates the center of the British Empire to India; after a series of catastrophic meteorites in 1870 have devastated the earth, the "Angrezi Raj" (ibid., p. 470) has recovered the steam and mechanical technology necessary to "getting back to where we were before the Fall" (ibid., p. 49). Steampunk's alternate histories, as I have already noted, also imply alternate cartographies that reveal moments of possibility prior to the partitioning of current sites of crisis, significantly altering the memory – and geography – of empire I have been tracing so far. Radically reversing the usual conception of center and periphery, a novel like *The Peshawar Lancers* illustrates steampunk's strength in making postcolonial arguments, specifically probing the racial ethics implied in "getting back to where we were."

Several blogs have been devoted to establishing this new memory and extending the map of empire by discussing the so-called "Victorientalism" of steampunk and calling for a move "beyond Victoriana" to consider multiracial content as well as multicultural steampunk variations.[5] By "Victorientalism" posters do not usually refer to the term that Erin O'Conner has applied rather unflatteringly to what postcolonial critics do, "the mining of a distant, exotic, threatening but fascinating literature to produce and establish a singularly self-serving body of knowledge elsewhere, a body of knowledge that ultimately has more to tell us about the needs of its producers than about its ostensible subject matter" (O'Conner, 2003, p. 227).

Here, O'Conner refers to the damage done to Victorian literature particularly by Gayatri Spivak who has created a hermeneutics of reading for empire so impenetrable that the nineteenth-century novel has been divorced from any "thematic subtleties, structural indeterminacies and genuine intellectual rigor" (ibid., p. 220). Unfortunately, with a slight change in context, the accusation of "mining" and exoticism can easily be launched at neo-Victorianism itself! Steampunk discussants, however, are guided by a healthy understanding of Said's concept of "orientalism," relying on his argument that the idea of "the Orient" is produced, usually by the West, and governed by an "imaginative geography" (Said, 1979, p. 54) that is subsequently distributed throughout various discursive, political and textual practices (ibid., p. 12). The visual vocabulary of imperialism that dominates steampunk texts and culture (modified pith helmets, military uniforms and weaponry, maps, the gear and trappings of space and terrestrial exploration, Asian(– inspired) materials and costuming) and a certain position toward the Victorian that leaves in place orientalist structures and understandings of "the East" has prompted a re-examination of the steampunk archive. A paucity of non-Western steampunk examples and a proliferation of uncritical orientalisms across the genre and subculture are revealed. Thus, the authors of and contributors to blogs such as *Beyond Victoriana* and *Silver Goggles* form the frontline in compiling examples of nativist or multicultural steampunk and searching for other "punk" moments, so to speak, in the technological past of Others. These scholars and commentators actively examine the (mono-)racial politics of steampunk and critique its neo-orientalizing moves; they analyze, for example, cosplay and the often pleasurable amnesia in inhabiting a racial Other if one is white and the center if one is not. Perhaps generated by steampunk's too close generic identification with the neo-Victorian, these bloggers seem to be responding to a traumatic effect, or, a profound forgetting in steampunk that the nineteenth-century consisted of alternate experiences of empire and that other empires rivaled the British. This concentrated effort to probe "Victorientalism" in the steampunk community points to where steampunk can productively intersect with neo-Victorianism on questions of race and empire.

If steampunk represents a *carte-blanche* opportunity to recreate the Victorian practically freed from the constraints of history, the prevalence of "Victorientalism" asks us to consider the ethics behind that move. *The UK Steampunk Network* (host of *The Great Steampunk Debate*) offers a necessary warning: in addition to "rediscover[ing] the adventure, mystery and imagination in the modern world" prior to mass production and "vast meta-companies," it behooves us to remember that "the Victorian Age . . . was a time of exploitation, sexism, racism, and attempted genocide" (*Steampunk Network*, n.d.). Their manifesto urges participants to "recapture the triumphs without the tragedies" while also learning "from the mistakes of our grandparents and great-grand parents" (*Steampunk Network*, n.d.). The manifesto suggests that steampunk can enhance neo-Victorianism's mnemic apparatus and can be considered a structure of relation to the nineteenth-century past that consists of nostalgia and a return of the repressed certainly, but also provides an aesthetic that consists of an ethics of appropriation. However, what pitfalls lie in a recovery from the "mistakes" of the past that depends on the invention of a new Victorian "without the tragedies?" Steampunk's combination of technology, alternate history and geography reveal commitments and resistances to certain geopolitical visions in neo-Victorianism that indicate a will to empire in the present.

Empires: *The Difference Engine* and *The Diamond Age*

In this section, I re-evaluate two canonical examples of neo-Victorian science fiction that explicitly compare Victorian Britain to the U.S. William Gibson and Bruce Sterling's more conventional steampunk novel, *The Difference Engine*, has often been read alongside Neal Stephenson's *The Diamond Age*, but their relationship to each other has never been made clear. Considered to be within the scope of steampunk's reach, but also regarded as cyberpunk, postcyberpunk and nano-punk, what links Stephenson's massively complicated novel to *The Difference Engine*, aside from the explicit adoption of the term "neo-Victorian," I argue, is its exaggeration and radical reinvention of world geography. Written by North American authors (Gibson is Canadian), both novels address geopolitical anxieties by projecting anxieties backward onto an alternate nineteenth-century past or, in the case of *The Diamond Age*, forward onto a future that has chosen, in a move that closely resembles our own deliberate misreadings of the Victorian, to return to the moral codes of the Victorian era as an alternative to the chaos of a globalized world dominated by nano-technology. Gibson and Sterling seek to suppress the development of the U.S. as a coherent nation while *The Diamond Age* imagines a deterritorialized world entirely unconstrained by the nation state. Both novels belong within steampunk and bear upon the discussion of neo-Victorianism, I argue, because they participate in a dialogue about the topography of Empire in the present.

Gibson and Sterling's novel, *The Difference Engine*, often considered the exemplar of literary steampunk, rebuilds the nineteenth century from

Charles Babbage's "blueprints" (Gibson and Sterling, 1991, p. 22) as if his invention of the analytical engine, the proto-computer, had in fact succeeded. The result is a technologically mixed society "rife with inventors" (ibid., p. 49) in which high-speed steam gurneys and "four-wheeled velocipede[s]" (ibid.) vie for dominance against horse-drawn vehicles and the London underground and where "kinotropic" (ibid., p. 34) advertising and displays rival conventional sticking bills. The novel takes for granted the panoptic possibilities that a technology ahead of its time will create: Londoners carry engine-stippled citizen cards, each one labeled with a citizen number recorded into the databanks of the centralized Engine, housed at the Central Statistics Bureau. Every transaction is noted and filed and as files, every transaction can be tampered with for a fee and manipulated by the expertise of engine-knowledgeable "clackers" (ibid., p. 21). In this alternate nineteenth century that has supplanted the Victorian, Lord Byron is Prime Minister, kept in power by a new meritocracy of Radical Lords: Lord Babbage himself, Lord Brunel and Lord Engels, to name a few. The Romantic poets Wordsworth and Coleridge are founders of a utopian, pacifist religious group, the Pantisocrats of the Susquehanna Phalanstry, while John Keats has turned his poetic genius to the new art of "clacking." In this version of history, Wilkie Collins appears as the Luddite leader, "Captain Swing," whose goal is to carry on the legacy of Ned Ludd, overturn the meritocracy, and transform the technology of oppression into one of liberation for the English working class. Divided into "iterations," the novel follows the threads of several characters, their crossings and contact with The Modus, an engine program designed by Ada Lovelace nee Byron, rumored to be a gambling device, instrument of sabotage, and able to calculate an engine's potential for "self-referentiality" (ibid., p. 421). The iterations also rewrite Disraeli's industrial novel, *Sybil* (1845), by including the character of Sybil Gerrard, prostitute, adventuress and daughter of a Luddite martyr. At the same time, the novel introduces fictional characters such as Edward Mallory, paleontologist, discoverer of the famed "Land Leviathan," Fellow of the Royal Geographical Society and amateur gun-runner; and historical personages like Laurence Oliphant, who, in the novel, is a gentleman, journalist and professional agent of the Special Branch and Central Statistics Bureau charged with the business of securing the British empire against foreign and domestic crimes. The novel ends with multiple perspectives of an alternate London, 1991, in which, with the help of the Modus Program, England's central Engine has reached "almost-life" and becomes what Oliphant and Ada Lovelace dream of and fear, an "Eye [that] at last must see itself" (ibid., p. 429).

Critics approaching *The Difference Engine* have rightly focused on its provocative evocation of a Victorian technoculture and the potentialities of and ambivalence toward a kind of cyborgian world view that comes to a head in the two versions, one dystopic and "unhuman" (Spencer, 1999, p. 428) and the other more hopeful, of the Eye offered at the end of the novel. Tracking the novel's ambivalent technopolitics, Nicholas Spencer cautions against "resorting to a humanist antitechnologism" (ibid., p. 423) asking readers to focus instead on who owns technology and its neutrality rather than passing judgment on its value or usefulness. Similarly, Herbert Sussman warns against reproducing the "art/machine dualism" (Sussman, 1994, p. 18) that dominates our understanding of art past and present. Instead, Gibson and Sterling's alternate history offers "a new nexus of man-machine, a new machinic phylum" (ibid., p. 3) that can productively and subversively destabilize the boundaries between human and machine. Drawing attention to the plot's failed Luddite resistance and privileging instead the sabotage enacted by individual "savants" and "clackers" of the novel, Sussman continues that only "subversive use of the cyborg itself can destabilize disciplinary control by the state and bring about positive alteration within the machinic phylum" (ibid., p. 11). Faced with the choice between "panoptical use of the intelligent machine" and the "enhancement of intelligence and creativity" that the cyborg can engender, the novel's steampunk version of the Victorian functions as the "analogue of our own time" (ibid., p. 20).

If the technology and ethics of the scientific culture portrayed in *The Difference Engine* offer an "analogue of our own time," as Sussman has argued, little work has been done to extend the metaphor and situate the novel's geographical and imperial context to "our own time." *The Difference Engine's* alternate geography is as striking as its alternate history. The novel actually begins with a fictional map depicting "the world of *The Difference Engine* 1855:" while the British Empire, Europe, Asia and Africa retain their boundaries, what has changed is the generally fragmented nature of the U.S. The most pressing international concern in Gibson and Sterling's alternate Britain is the extension and control of her power in North America and how to ensure her domination as the imperial center of the world. Exercising its technological capabilities and playing socialist and nationalist factions off one another, Britain divides America into warring areas – the Republic of California, the Republic of Texas, "unorganized territory," the United States of America, the Confederate States of America, and the Manhattan Commune under the control of the Communards and their new immigrant leader, Karl Marx. As Mick Radley, the novel's political adventurer instructs, Britain leads the world in its manipulation of "the balance of power:"

> it worked for Britain in Europe for five hundred years, and it works even better in America. Union, Confederacy, Republics of Texas and California – they all take a turn in British favor, until they get too bold, a bit too independent, and then they're taken down a peg. Divide and rule, dear . . . If it weren't for British diplomacy, British power, America might be all one huge nation. (Gibson and Sterling, 1991, p. 32)

As much as the novel succeeds in disrupting American hegemony and preventing America from being "one huge nation," it can only do so by allowing its alternate Britain to reach its panoptic, arguably dystopic, conclusion.

Britain's unsurpassed power in *The Difference Engine* also means that it is not the U.S. who opens up Japan to Westernization in the nineteenth century. In the novel, the Japanese ambassador, Mori Arinori, based on the statesman educated in Britain and the U.S. who brought Western philosophy and education back to Japan in the 1840s, crows, "we have great obligation to Britain! Britain opened our ports with iron fleet. We have awaked, and learnt great lesson you have teached us" (ibid., p. 169). To which Mallory, the novel's reluctant hero, condescendingly retorts, "it's a bit of a hard slog, though, civilization, building an empire. Takes several centuries, you know . . ." (ibid.). In his dismissal of the Japanese guests, Mallory evokes a geopolitical and Orientalist argument that the globe be ordered imaginatively according to a nation's proximity to the pinnacle of Western technology. A reversal of Japan's economic boom in the 1990s, this alternate Japan requires catching up to the West and its future, the novel suggests, is to repeat Britain's past. Oliphant experiences "a certain enjoyably melancholy sense of paradox" (ibid., p. 358) at watching Mori eat toast and refrains from commenting on the Japanese man's enthusiastic endorsement that, "soon power of steam and the Engine must pervade our land. English language, following such, must suppress any use of Japanese" (ibid., p. 360). The cross-cultural anxieties implied by this relationship between Oliphant and Mori, I will argue later, haunt the return to the Victorian in *Steamboy*.[6] As in *Around the World in Eighty Days*, steampunk raises the question of whether or not to mourn the processes of self-orientalization when the Other seeks technology.

By juxtaposing this alternate "backwards" Japan of the past with the powerhouse Japan of the 1990s, the novel affirms that imagined geographies sustain empire beyond the formal end of colonialism. Mallory's amazement at the geisha doll/proto-automaton that the Japanese delegation will present as a gift to Her Britannic Majesty underscores this point. Revealing himself as the stereotype of the Victorian racist and misogynist, Mallory ignores the doll because he is fooled by the reality of her "mask-like composure" (Gibson and Sterling, 1991, p. 168). Duped by her perfection, Mallory entertains the idea that she is either "paralyzed" or a "dummy" and dismisses her as a primitive but exotic example of Japanese art and development. Rather than having the breast implants of the futuristic female cyborg, the doll performs the fantasy of the passive, Oriental woman: she pours whiskey "with either hand" for the dignitaries but only after the Japanese ambassador takes a crank, "stuck the device into the small of her back and began to twist it, his face expressionless" (ibid.). Represented by the seemingly seamless body of the doll, Mallory's anxiety about Asian creativity anticipates how Western desire has and will continue to shape the supposedly borderless region of Pacific communities like the "Pacific Rim" or its more hybrid and constructed counterpart in the present, "Asia-Pacific." However, this scene also addresses the ways in which these regions "crank" out libidinous fantasies of "Asia" for consumption by the West, and how counter-hegemonic localisms, seen in the doll's clever melding of "bamboo, and braided horse hair and whalebone springs" (ibid.) are forged.[7]

Gibson and Sterling's treatment of the Japanese can certainly be explained within the context of "techno-orientalism." Cyberpunk and steampunk found their toeholds in science fiction at the same time that Japan became an economic and technological powerhouse. Using examples such as *Blade Runner* (1982), *The Matrix* (1999), and Gibson's earlier work like *Neuromancer* (1984), David Morley and Kevin Robins demonstrate that the explicit orientalism of cyberpunk resonates with the "Japan-bashing" of the 1990s. Growing out of an implicit sense of resentment, envy and nostalgia, "techno-orientalism" tended to construct the Japanese as "unfeeling aliens . . . replicants and cyborgs" (Morley and Robins, 1995, p. 170). Morley and Robins argue that "Japan had come to exist within the Western political and cultural unconscious as a figure of danger, and it has done so because it has destabilized the neat correlation between West/East and modern/premodern" (ibid., p. 160). Such binary constructions tend to deliberately ignore the history, structures and relationships between Asians and technology, particularly products and practices deemed emergent or revolutionary. Encouraged by Donna Haraway's examination of female Asian labor in her foundational cyborg myth, one can also view techno-orientalism as Greta

Ayu Niu does, as a "practice of ascribing, erasing, and /or disavowing relationships between Asian peoples and subjects" (Niu, 2008, p. 75). By the time Gibson and Sterling's *The Difference Engine* and Neal Stephenson's *The Diamond Age* were published, Japan had become the West's future rather than its inscrutable, primitivist Other, and the four Asian "Tigers" – Hong Kong, Singapore, Seoul and Taiwan – had come to represent, at best, its present.

However, I want to argue for another way of reading the relationship between technology and nation in steampunk beyond "techno-orientalism" that can only be made available by neo-Victorianism's critical lens. Gibson and Sterling approach the U.S.'s oft-discussed amnesia or repression of its imperialist actions obliquely through the Pax Britannica.[8] Using simple acts of reversal and substitution whereby America is the weaker, pretechnological Other, *The Difference Engine* demonstrates how British/American power maintains itself through informal kinds of imperialism rather than colonization and settlement. The instructive similarities between the British Empire and the U.S., I argue, signal less a concern with techno-orientalism and more an acknowledgment of and anxiety about the U.S.'s role within what we now call "Empire" or "new imperialism." Michael Hardt and Antonio Negri's controversial tome, *Empire* (2000), clearly articulates the newness and potentialities of this globalized vision:

> The passage to Empire emerges from the twilight of modern sovereignty. In contrast to imperialism, Empire establishes no territorial center of power and does not rely on fixed boundaries or barriers. It is a decentered and deterritorializing apparatus of rule that progressively incorporates the entire global realm within its open, expanding frontiers. Empire manages hybrid identities, flexible hierarchies, and plural exchanges through modulating networks of command. (Hardt and Negri, 2000, pp. xii–xiii)

Hardt and Negri tend to remain abstract and, at times, mute on the "old forms of domination" (ibid., p. xv), violence and suppressions of "old" imperialism that undergird Empire. Loosely characterized as a new world order created by an unprecedented global flow of goods, people, ideas, information and capital, Empire is nonetheless sustained and sponsored by the military and economic hegemony of the U.S. Power, however, is distributed and administered globally and indirectly by international economic and political institutions such as the World Bank and the United Nations (Harvey, 2005, p. 10). Bolstered by the ideals of free markets,

Empire's ideologies are an unwieldy combination of democracy and capitalist imperialism. Empire may appear to operate under deterritorialized conditions, for example, the nebulous and decentralized "War on Terror," but also tends to exhibit its power in territorial actions such as the invasion and occupation of sovereign nations like Iraq or Afghanistan. Read together in a postmillennial context, the anachronisms of *The Difference Engine* and *The Diamond Age* offer a thoughtful portrait of Empire as a contradictory field: an atavistic form comprised of what can be considered nineteenth-century characteristics of imperialism – militarism, liberal ideals, absolute power, racism – combined with the technology, democratic ideals, pre-emptive action and the limitless capitalist expansion of "new" empire (Mooers, 2006, p. 2).

The Difference Engine thus emphasizes and interrogates the territorial elements of imperialism that Empire seeks to replace. Mallory's archeological expeditions to Wyoming, for example, turn out to be a plot by the "Commission on Free Trade" to supply "American savages" (Gibson and Sterling, 1991, p. 108) with guns. Officially, the Commission exists "to study international trade relations" but as a "clandestine" arm of Britain's foreign policy, it serves to arm "the enemies of nations with whom Britain is not officially at war" (ibid., p. 208). British power, as represented by Oliphant and his vast network of international and domestic spies, allows various American factions, such as "Franco-Mexican army under the command of General Houston" (ibid., p. 31) and the "Communards" in "Red Manhattan" (ibid., p. 365), to act as free agents toward some kind of heavily managed nationhood but only insofar as they are following British "civilization stage directions" (Sardar, 1996, p. 18). Described as a space "without . . . a single mile of British railroad, and lacking the telegraph, or indeed, Engine resources of any kind" (Gibson and Sterling, 1991, p. 42), the American frontier rather than a colonial *terra nullius* illustrates how Empire's deterritorialized scope is structured by equally powerful imagined geographies based on nations' failures to achieve modernity. While Mallory may dismiss Texas as "a damned wilderness, seas and continents away" (ibid., p. 186), the murder of Texian nationalists in London, who have linked their plans with the Manhattan Commune and the Luddite uprising in London, strikingly underscore that the imagined geography of "us" and "them," "civilization" and "barbarian," valued by Mallory may not be so easily sustained.

Further debates about Empire emerge in the summary of Neal Stephenson's *The Diamond Age*. Describing a world in which nanotechnology and cyberspace are *faits accomplis*, nation states are no longer able to support themselves as separate national cultures defined by racial or geographic borders. Instead, this new world order subscribes to the Common Economic Protocol, a code that "governs all kinds of economic interactions between people and organizations," respects the "indigenous justice system of CEP signatories," but "does not aspire to sovereign status" (Stephenson, 1995, p. 40). America is conspicuously absent in the novel, recalled only in the hegemonic presence of "Neo-Victorian" culture, code for the technologically and culturally dominant "New Atlantis" tribe or "phyle" (ibid., p. 33) that co-exists among others like the dominant Nipponese and Hindustanis but also the "Ashantis, Kurds, Armenians, Navajos, Tibetans, Senderos, Mormons, Jesuits, Lapps, Pathans, Tutsis, the First Distributed Republic and its innumerable offshoots, Heartlanders, Irish, and one or two local CryptNet cells" (ibid., p. 490). Without distinct nations, the novel offers multicultural memberships to "phyles" collectively gathered on artificially generated "claves" situated on "Leased Territories" (ibid., p. 66) off the coast of China but connected to Shanghai's "Coastal Republic" (ibid., p. 78) by a massive "Causeway" or "a Feed network" (ibid., p. 70). Technologically superior, the Western phyles have arranged themselves around China, and by controlling the use of energy Feeds necessary to every mode of production "spew megatons of nanostuff" into the hands of peasants inhabiting China's "Middle Kingdom" (ibid.). Rather than fostering the sale of opium, the New Atlanteans have "addicted" the Chinese to the wealth of the Feed. To break the oppression, the Chinese seek the more utopian Seed technology, more suited to Chinese culture and informed by Confucian philosophy. In Stephenson's extrapolation, China revolts from the contagion of excess global flows and divides itself into "Celestial," "Middle" and "Outer" kingdoms, essentially replaying the Boxer Rebellion in response to the overwhelming technological inequities. At the end of the novel, the Luddite "Fists of Righteous Harmony" (ibid., p. 373) emerge from the Celestial Kingdom to smash the Feed lines and drive the foreigners literally into the sea.

In a complicated plot line that rivals a Victorian triple-decker in form and content, *The Diamond Age* centers around the theft and subsequent circulation of copies of *The Young Lady's Illustrated Primer*, a gift from a leading Equity Lord of the Neo-Victorian phyle, Lord Alexander Chung-Sik Finckle-McGraw to his grand-daughter. The Primer is Finckle-McGraw's attempt to systematically inculcate "subversion" (Stephenson, 1995, p. 81) into culture, hoping in the long run to reintroduce the same kind of ingenuity and creativity that formed the phyle in the first place. Designed by nanotech engineer and hacker, the appropriately named John Percival Hackworth, the Primer functions as an interactive, reader-specific, hypertextual Bildungsroman, following or "bringing up" its reader to adulthood. Having learned to be subversive, the Primer's reader will realize that despite its hypocrisy and contradictions, the New Atlantean phyle is the "best in the long run" (ibid., p. 356). Hackworth's crime, which transforms him into the inscrutable Dr X's pawn in the fight between Feed and Seed, is his duplication of the original Primer, hoping to make available to his own daughter, Fiona, the qualities of subversion he had programmed for Finckle-McGraw.

On Hackworth's way back from Shanghai to the Coast Republic, a gang of street urchins steal the Primer and the book falls into the hands of a little orphan girl from the Leased Territories named Nell. Thanks to the Primer, Nell successfully assimilates into the Neo-Victorian phyle and her membership is guaranteed by her interpellation of the Neo-Victorian values written into the Primer's program. However, her copy of the Primer is narrated entirely by a "ractor" (ibid., p. 86), a contraction of interactive and actor, named Miranda whose subtle, human tweaks to Hackworth's codes liberate Nell from the domination of the phyle onto another path between "conformity and rebellion" (ibid., p. 356) on the wild streets of Shanghai. Blackmailed by Dr X, Hackworth is forced to duplicate the technology behind the Primer and modify it to be "more suitable for the unique cultural requirements of the Han readership" (ibid., p. 180). The copies of the Primer are used to raise and educate 250,000 Chinese girl orphans rescued from the famine-ravaged Chinese countryside. Problematically denied the subversive qualities of the Primer by Hackworth's "hack," the content of the girls' Primer is subordinated to Nell's thus forming her connection to and leadership of the 250,000-strong Mouse Army. *The Diamond Age* concludes with a return to a simpler storyline: the resolution of familial ties. As Shanghai falls to the triumphant Fists, Nell rescues Miranda, who has been trying to contact her via the "Wet Net" of the Drummers, a group-mind built around an ideal of unity artificially created by technology, with the help of Carl Hollywood, a hacker and owner of the theater where Miranda worked. In doing so, Nell disrupts further computation on the Seed technology embedded into the Primer's narrative by Hackworth and released into the Drummers' bloodstream by Miranda's presence. The regeneration of the family unit at the end of the novel fails to solve the neo-colonial context in which the Primer as a neo-Victorian text is immersed and the novel seems to draw comparisons between the power hierarchy of the family and imperialism itself. Eventually, the conclusion of the novel does not challenge what Longan and Oakes have designated the "Orientalizing duality" (Longan and Oakes, 2002, p. 54) of the book's Chinese setting.

Obviously, techno-orientalism is rampant in *The Diamond Age*. Niu, for example, finds the novel's "illustrations of Chinese characters' beliefs in essentialism, superiority, and technological determinism" to be "particularly egregious" (Niu, 2008, p. 79). As cyberpunk evolves into newer and more refined relationships to technology and posthuman subjectivities, Niu argues, the more techno-orientalism requires attention lest the relationship between labor, gender, race and technology be erased. The complicated plot of *The Diamond Age* often obfuscates how it denies technological advances and expertise to its Chinese characters: even the venerable Dr X, a "reverse engineer" and a "honer," a master manipulator of mites and nanosites "hacking them for all they were worth, getting them to do things the forgers had never envisioned" (Stephenson, 1995, p. 76), has to rely on Hackworth's ingenuity to access Seed technology. Skipping corners in order to maximize their appropriative value, the Mouse Army's Primers are simply cheap Chinese knockoffs: Dr X does not recognize the cultural value that the Neo-Victorians have placed on uniqueness and individual ownership instead, the Chinese hack and replication of the data in the girls' Primers have been for the good and common knowledge of the collective. For the Mouse Army, the Primer has taught them many lessons as a *textbook* but not in the same intimate, nurturing and highly individualized way as Nell, Fiona Hackworth and Elizabeth Finckle-McGraw, who emerge as the true cyberpunk subjects of *The Diamond Age*. The intensity of the Mouse Army's female readership of the Primer functions as a gloss on the feminization of globalization's work force: in Donna Haraway's influential revisioning of the female cyborg, it is the Asian woman who functions as the nodal point of labor, production, consumerism and eroticism in the technological sphere. Like the Japanese doll in *The Difference Engine*, the Mouse Army recalls Haraway's own neo-Victorian/steampunk image: the "nimble fingers of 'Oriental' women" paired with the "old fascination of little Anglo-Saxon Victorian girls with doll's houses" evoke a history of women's "enforced attention to the small" (Haraway, 1991, p. 154) so crucial and exploited in the workplaces of global capitalism. The Mouse Army emerges from the CK to claim Nell as their leader, support her rescue of Miranda, and witness her recognition by Victoria II as "Princess Nell," her white, Western individuality and subjectivity is enabled and reified, according to Michael Longan and Tim Oakes, by the mechanical collective behavior of the Chinese girls (Longan and Oakes, 2002, p. 55).

Explaining the importance of Seed technology to Hackworth, Dr X argues that "since the time of the Opium Wars," the Chinese have "struggled" but failed "to absorb the *yong* of technology without importing the Western *ti*"

(Stephenson, 1995, p. 547). Having the Seed would break the "centuries of chaos" caused by Feed capitalism that has caused China to remain trapped, repeating the cycles of violence and revolution that structure its past even as the rest of the world has advanced toward postnational time. Dr X offers Hackworth a Confucian utopia suspiciously similar to the one portrayed in the village of *Around the World in Eighty Days*:

> Peasants tended their fields and paddies, and even in times of drought and flood, the earth brought forth a rich harvest: food, of course, but many unfamiliar plants too, fruits that could be made into medicines, bamboo a thousand times stronger than natural varieties, trees that produced synthetic rubber and pellets of clean safe fuel. In an orderly procession the suntanned farmers brought their proceeds to great markets in clean cities free of cholera and strikes, where all of the young people were respectful and dutiful scholars and all of the elders were honored and cared for. (Stephenson, 1995, p. 458)

Longan and Oakes find this description to be the most deceptive, finding in its details a static, timeless, essentialized China that will only intensify a "Han subjectivity determined by cultural geography" (2002, p. 49) and reinforce the grip of the West. Disappointed, Longan and Oakes note that in the novel's Orientalist logic, "inwardness, cultural purity, and suspicions of outsiders are regarded as the only means by which an alternative to Western power can be envisioned" (Stephenson, 1995, p. 49). In a novel that is so triumphantly postnational, the return of the repressed of the nation state bears some thought. *The Diamond Age* rehabilitates orientalism as an important diagnosis of "Western power:" the nation state resurrects itself, in the form of nineteenth-century China, with all its cultural myths and essentializing practices necessary, to protect against and reject Feed technology or, the radical fluidities of global capital. The vision of China in the novel resists perception of the cartography of a new Empire as smooth and its dispersed structure of domination as supposedly without any links to the nation state or geography.

The Diamond Age uncannily anticipates apologist rhetoric for Empire reminiscent of neo-liberal historians and neo-Con politicians: when Finckle-McGraw questions Hackworth about his Oath to Victoria II, Hackworth answers:

> My life was not without periods of excessive, unreasoning discipline, usually imposed capriciously by those responsible for laxity in the first place.

That combined with my historical studies led me, as many others, to the conclusion that there was little in the previous century worthy of emulation, and that we must look to the nineteenth century instead for stable social models. (Stephenson, 1995, p. 24)

Praising Hackworth for his loyalty, Finckle-McGraw counters, "But you must know that the model to which you allude did not long survive the first Victoria?" To which Hackworth dryly replies, "We have outgrown much of the ignorance and resolved many of the internal contradictions that characterized that era" (Stephenson, 1995, p. 24). Having judged the twentieth century and found it lacking in moral order, New Atlanteans like Hackworth have returned to the Victorian, which, despite its hypocrisy, is at least free of moral relativism. The novel's understanding of the neo-Victorian explicitly links neo-imperialism with the kind of revisionary historical thinking practiced by Hackworth and that leads to future realities such as: "it was no longer necessary to send out dirty yokels in coonskin caps to chart the wilderness, kill the abos, and clear-cut the groves; now all you needed was a hot young geotect, a start matter compiler, and a jumbo Source" (ibid., p. 19). The cautionary tale told by steampunk seems clear: when we recall the Victorian aesthetically or as narrative are we not too in danger of retaining structures that support whiteness and imperialism? Can there be an empire without imperialism? Can we have the "triumphs" of the past without the "tragedies?"

Since the publication of both these texts, there has been a marked tendency in steampunk to match the British nineteenth-century past to an American neo-imperial present that grants the genre an acute relevance and a privileged place in neo-Victorianism. *The League of Extraordinary Gentlemen*, Alan Moore's on-going graphic novel series, for example, participates explicitly in the contemporary dialogue about Britain's new role in the American Empire. Moore bases his series on "a collection of monsters" [1999, I, p. 2] from Victorian science fiction – Edward Hyde, Allan Quartermain, Captain Nemo, Mina Harker nee Murray and Hawley Griffin, the Invisible Man – using literary characters whose status as Others or whose encounters with colonial Others make them more appropriate characters (than say, Byatt's literary critics) to explore the nineteenth century's ability to address the rhetoric and images of the current climate of neo-nationalism, fundamentalism, terrorism and cultural conflict. In the second volume of the series (2004), the neo-Victorian narrator deliberately mimics the conventional rhetoric of patriotism: Martian tripods, those "queerly-behaved foreign devils," invade London in an attempt to eradicate the cultural values and "time-honoured English *way of life*" of the (English) Other [Moore, 2004, I, p. 24, italics mine].[9] Unlike the original Wells novel, *The War of the Worlds* (1898), the tripods are not killed by an indigenous germ but by a biological weapon engineered by Dr Moreau and unwittingly delivered to London by the League. Disgusted by the government's use of biological weapons on English soil, Nemo's departure forces Mina to disband the League at the end of the second volume. By explicitly reviving the imperial anxiety that England itself is the source of its own racial and political downfall, *The League of Extraordinary Gentlemen* addresses the question of racial anxiety and ambiguities underlying the rhetoric of patriotism and terrorism. As a post-9/11 text, *League* depicts a government capable of restricting civil liberties and committing its own acts of violence in the name of national security. Similarly, Bryan Talbot's graphic novel, *Grandville* (2011), a visual mash-up of steampunk, nineteenth-century French science fiction illustrators, Rupert the Bear, and *Reservoir Dogs*, builds an anthropomorphic world from conspiracy theories surrounding the events of 9/11. Having reduced the "Socialist Republic of Britain" to a "small and unimportant country" (Talbot, 2011, p. 17) after the Napoleonic War, France has become the dominant world power of the nineteenth century. Agents of the French secret society, the Knights of the Lion, have orchestrated the Robida Tower attacks in order to correct a "society grown decadent and godless" and create a "common enemy. A terrifying spectre to fear and hate" (ibid., p. 61), steal "Britain's oil" (ibid., p. 85), and justify a never-ending war that would police the universalization of capitalism so indicative of Empire.

Steamboy: Japan's Victorian Past

In this section, I answer *Beyond Victoriana's* call and turn to Japan, a surprisingly robust producer of the steampunk aesthetic. If we enter steampunk on the side of Gibson and Sterling's Japanese doll or Stephenson's Mouse Army, the terrain begins to look very different: it becomes no longer feasible to speak of the Western present as the East Asian future and we can begin to uncover new configurations and exclusions in neo-imperial futures. Refracted through nineteenth-century Britain, the appearance of steampunk in Asia reflects a concern with another geopolitical entity, the Pacific Rim. Like Empire, the Pacific Rim, according to Christopher L. Connery, denotes a contradictory "centeredness" (Connery, 1994, p. 41) that does not encompass any central power, yet the domination of the

Pacific Rim by Japan and China has necessitated a re-imagination of global categories in which the U.S. is no longer as prominent. As Dirlik has argued, during the late nineteenth century, Japanese growth paralleled and was modeled on Euro-American colonialism and the concept of the "Pacific" was defined by a capitalist order devised using Euro-American rules (Dirlik, 1998, p. 22). Japan, Dirlik continues, "sought to carve out an Asian space within this construct" (ibid., p. 27) without necessarily offering an alternative to it. Subsequent reinventions of "EuroAmerican activity that was oriented to an Asian world economy" (ibid., p. 29) by Asians has tempered, if not ousted, Western control and thus new configurations – Pacific Basin and Asia Pacific, for example – are made available. Japanese steampunk, I suggest, depicts these shifts and negotiates them through its treatment of technology: *Steamboy's* portrayal of Victorian technology presents a distinctly Japanese anxiety with modernity and/as Western science and uncertainty about what Japan's position should be on the world stage. The mapping of Japanese concerns onto a nineteenth-century British setting imbued with nineteenth-century American capitalism makes steampunk an ideal vehicle for Japan to explore its origins as a "modern" nation and, as steampunk taps into the memory of British imperialism, perhaps even Japan's role as a colonizer within Asia.

In 2004, more than ten years after his cyberpunk masterpiece, *Akira* (1988), Japanese director Otomo Katsuhiro turned to the Victorian in his animated film, *Steamboy*. *Steamboy* is a far cry from *Akira*, which dealt explicitly with the aftermath of Hiroshima following in the footsteps of other postapocalyptic *manga* such as Nakazawa Keiji's *Barefoot Gen* (1973–85) and movies like the Godzilla franchise. Otomo recreates the Victorian in *Steamboy* – the rail yards and factories of Manchester, the domestic interior of the Steam household, and the opening of the Great Exhibition by Queen Victoria – with the obsessiveness of a British heritage film. In addition, Otomo brings the future into the nineteenth-century setting with the trappings of steampunk: steam "tractors," submarines, airships, steam-liner, -tanks, -motorcycles and jetpacks are deployed regularly. Along with the *manga* and *anime* series *Emma: A Victorian Romance* (Mori, 2002–6), a class-based drama set in 1895; *Black Butler* (Toboso, 2006 – present), a dark supernatural thriller with anachronistic elements set in the underbelly of Victorian England that explores the relationship between a demonic butler and his twelve year old employer, the head of the mysterious Phantomhive dynasty; and to a lesser extent, the pan-European nineteenth-century references in the *anime* space opera, *Last Exile* (Chigira, 2003), *Steamboy* represents a surprisingly entrenched Victorian in the Japanese imagination.

If one takes into account the highly gendered cosplay/lifestyle "Gothic Lolita" phenomenon, Japanese popular culture's engagements with the Victorian become even more pronounced.

Set in 1866 in Manchester and London during the Great Exhibition, *Steamboy* follows the adventures of a young boy, Ray Steam, who has been entrusted with the "steam ball," a source of immense energy invented by his grandfather, Dr Lloyd Steam, and Ray's father, Dr Edward Steam. With an enormity of detail that only *anime* can capture, *Steamboy* depicts a version of the Industrial Revolution powered by massive, yet unpredictable, steam engines. The steam ball device will harness the energy of pure liquid in a concentrated space and revolutionize the industrial landscape. Ray and the steam ball are caught between the fictionalized engineer Robert Stephenson, an inventor and politician, and the O'Hara Foundation, the American corporation and international arms dealer. Standing in brazenly for an immoral capitalism and America's technological advancement, the Foundation has employed the Steam men to construct and power the "Steam Castle," a giant flying tower armed with steam-powered weapons and "steam troopers," which spectacularly destroys the Crystal Palace and most of London at the end of the film. The Steam Castle bides its time within the O'Hara Foundation's pavilion at the Crystal Palace until the Foundation decides to unleash a demonstration of its powers for the international delegates gathered for the opening of the Exhibition. Along with Miss Scarlett, the O'Hara Foundation's spoiled and bratty representative, Ray must rescue London from destruction. In *Steamboy*, the Western past – Victorian and technological – is also Japan's past.

In order to depict this appropriation, *Steamboy* generates a series of visual and cultural displacements through which viewers can indulge in the fluidity between various geographies and national memories. By juxtaposing the Crystal Palace, a privileged site in steampunk and both Victorian and neo-Victorian studies, with the Steam Castle, its monstrous, *anime* equivalent, Otomo combines the universalization of Western culture in the nineteenth century with Japan's own militant past funded by and encased within an American structure. Although both are constructed out of steel and glass, the O'Hara Foundation's pavilion-cum-Steam Castle dwarfs the Crystal Palace; separated by a multitude of windows, spectators often peer at each opposing structure in awe and surprise. Each structure and every gaze becomes framed within the other, suggesting interlocking histories and technologies. However, while the film invites such visual encounters, they remain mediated and governed by glass; the multiple pasts remain, as Judith Roof has argued about the Victorian "technology of display" (Roof, 2000,

p. 104), out of view, "frustrated by glass and arrangement, the very technologies designed to bring them into safe and informative view in the first place" (ibid.). The film tropes on such issues of transparency by making use of mirrors and reflections. In one of the film's more touching scenes, Ray and Scarlett sneak into the Crystal Palace and indulge in a rare moment of childish freedom. Scarlett becomes seduced by her own reflection, sometimes distorted, in the Exhibition hall's mirrors. Similarly, mirrors surround the Steam Castle's main control hub as part of its navigation system thus framing and magnifying Edward Steam's face as he pilots. As viewers we see an American girl comprehend her adulthood and a British scientist confronting his cyborg body, but we are constantly reminded that this takes place within the context of a Japanese version of the Victorian. These magnifications and reflections provide opportunities for the recognition of the multiple sites and identities that have historically, at some point or another, contributed to making "Japan."

Read simplistically, *Steamboy* functions as a conventional anti-Western narrative: the steam ball quite accurately represents a nuclear fission reactor and thus can be interpreted as an indictment of Western technology following the trauma of Hiroshima and Nagasaki.[10] However, the partnership between the O'Hara Foundation and the Steam men, who are simultaneously coded British and Japanese, and between Miss Scarlett and Ray Steam, emphasizes that the relationships of the Pacific, as Dirlik has argued, are dominated by Anglo-American and Asian confrontations (Dirlik, 1998, p. 22). As John Whittier Treat writes, "Hiroshima does not lie at the center of American life, though some have suggested that it should. America, on the other hand, has been a constant presence – force – in Japanese life since 1945 and has been constantly 'represented,' if you will, by the often heavy-handed demonstration of its national power" (Treat, 1994, p. 238). The traumatic date, 1945, can be contested, however, in favor of Commodore Perry's arrival in Japan in the service of American expansionism in 1853. It is possible that *Steamboy* loosely recalls this more "Victorian" date in its explicit reference to Scarlett O'Hara and Margaret Mitchell's 1937 novel, *Gone With the Wind*. This unusual intertext suggests that the global narrative of neo-Victorianism could tentatively encompass American texts written prior to *The French Lieutenant's Woman* and *Wide Sargasso Sea* that bear no reference to contemporary neo-Victorianism. Indeed, given the popularity of Mitchell's novel and the MGM film that spawned multiple remakes and theatrical revision in Japan, a Japanese audience might not make the same strict distinctions.[11] By offering a shared text such as *Gone With the Wind*, *Steamboy* invites its global viewers to experience an Anglo-American Japanese version of history, one that began with Laurence Oliphant's influence over the young scholar, Mori Arinori, in the mid 1860s, but that unfortunately culminates in the tragedy of Hiroshima and Nagasaki. In most postwar cultural production, the image of the mushroom cloud stands in for "an abstraction of US technological prowess and Cold War ascendancy . . . [and] also as a screen memory of the human cost of the bombings" (Hong, 2009, p. 136). In *Steamboy*, however, the iconic mushroom cloud is replaced by a frozen cloud of steam released by the Castle as the Steam men rush to recalculate pressure gauges and measures in order to protect what remains of London. The final scenes of the film show the massive columns of ice piercing the city disintegrating harmlessly into snowflakes when touched by curious London children. This rehabilitation of the mushroom cloud to harmless snowscape suggests the process of recovery, simultaneously "hosting" (ibid., p. 146) the memory of the American occupation of postwar Japan alongside the trauma of the Hiroshima/Nagasaki bombings thus expressing a commonality across cultural and national imaginaries.

This mode of recovery, unfortunately, leaves little room for thinking critically about Japan's own imperial complicity and I would like to argue that steampunk in a Japanese setting might offer an alternative to a victimized Japanese position and address more fully its own imperial status. Anxieties about science and technology are played out in the generational structure of the film. Dressed in rags and imprisoned in his invention for most of the film, the elderly Dr Lloyd is essentially a pacifist who wants science to "reveal universal principles . . . not assist humanity in its folly" (Otomo, 2004). His contribution to the Steam Castle's design is a children's amusement park, the addition of carousels and fireworks to what is essentially a weapon. Once the Steam Castle's deadliness becomes a reality, Dr Lloyd seeks its destruction and urges Ray to "save science from the wicked and preserve the future!" (ibid.). For Lloyd, the "soul of man is not ready for science such as this" and the consequences of his invention are that "war and confusion will rule the world" (ibid.). In contrast, Lloyd's son, Edward Steam, functions as one of the film's cyborg figures. Hideously disfigured by a steam-blast and thus fitted with mechanical prosthetics, Dr Lloyd accuses Edward of selling his "soul," and thus his humanity, to the capitalists in the belief that science, even in the form of weapons, serves as progress. For Eddy, the goal of science is to "make all humanity equal" so that "man will be freed from long, hard labor and will prevail over even nature's greatest disasters;" his inventions will "deliver this enormous power to the entire world" (ibid.). That this vision is to be "delivered" via the

O'Hara Foundation's funds and global reach as military weapons for profit does not affect his zeal or his ethics. In words that echo the ethics behind the invention of the atom bomb, Dr Eddy aids his father and son, Ray, in destroying the Steam Castle only because he is assured that once "mankind has seen … a marvel like this … even if it were then to be destroyed … would soon be made again … science will not halt in its march" (ibid.). Dr Eddy's prophecy is realized in the final montage of *Steamboy* which looks forward to an apocalyptic WWI. However, it is important to note that science, in this context, is specifically *Western* science and in addition to referencing the traumas of WWII, the film's version of the Victorian is also Meiji-era Japan (1868–1945), a period of great flux and instability when science and technology were harnessed explicitly to the project of nation so that Japan could compete with the West. If one of the more embedded memories of industrialized Britain in the contemporary imagination is the image of a steam train cutting a path through the English countryside, it can easily be transcribed, as *Steamboy* demonstrates, to nineteenth-century Japan.

According to Hiromi Mizuno's parsing of Japan's "scientific nationalism" (Mizuno, 2009, p. 11), nineteenth-century Japan's relationship to modern science was inextricably and problematically linked with its imperial mythology and distinctiveness as a nation. The goal of the Meiji government was "to be recognized by the West as a modern, civilized nation, as the Western powers were, and to celebrate the nation's particularity to build a national identity" (ibid., p. 2). In order to end Japan's isolation and to compete with other colonial and capitalist powers, the Meiji leadership sought a modern economy and industry by embracing Western technology often through partnerships with Victorian Britain.[12] One of the most far-reaching features of the Meiji era was the official abolishment of feudalism and the "rehabilitation" (Checkland, 1989, p. 215) of the ruling samurai class to the nation's modernizing efforts. If Japan's "unequal treaties" with the U.S. and other Western powers were to be broken, "Japan needed to catch up with Western science and technology" (Mizuno, 2009, p. 3). "Science" was valued for its supposedly universal properties, its ability to be applicable everywhere, but its supposedly Western origins were in competition with Japan's ideology of distinctiveness which was heavily woven into the constitution, municipal and civic structures and everyday life. *Steamboy's* technologically advanced nineteenth-century Britain/Japan thus addresses the argument raised by *The Difference Engine* and *The Diamond Age* and recast as a postcolonial concern in *Around the World in Eighty Days*: for countries deeply immersed in local networks and systems of belief like Japan, can there be a non-Western science?

Increasingly dominated by "technocrats," Mizuno's term for elite engineers with both the aspiration and access to political power, Japan embarked on a trajectory of "scientific nationalism," where technology and science became "the most urgent and important assets for the integrity, survival and progress of the nation" (Mizuno, 2009, p. 11). Successful in wars against China and Russia and the colonization of Korea and Taiwan, Japan soon emerged as the East's modern power. Western science had become Japanese science. An anticolonial relationship toward the West soon developed in response to the growing oppressiveness of imperial ideology and the strength of the technocrats' control over the government (ibid., p. 3). According to Mizuno, the Japanese plan to colonize Asia in the early twentieth century emerged out of the need for Japan to be independent of Western domination: "Japan needed to have unrestrained access to the resources of Asia; in return, Japan would provide Asia with the science and technology necessary to protect Asia from Western imperialism" (ibid., p. 44). *Steamboy's* borrowing of British imperial space to cast its Japanese story reflects the historical interrelation of science and nationalism as told by Mizuno. In the film, for example, Stephenson's character best fits the definition of a "technocrat:" as a politician and a scientist, he believes "while science exists to make people happy – the basis of that happiness – the nation – must be preserved!" (Otomo, 2004). Deposited into characters such as Stephenson and his traitorous assistant David, the memory of British imperialism and superiority enabled by science is recalled to host a critique of Japanese colonialism. Thus, although the debates over the role of science between Dr Lloyd and Dr Eddy revolve around the innocence of technology – that its dangers lie in the hands of those who wield it – they nonetheless take place within the context of national and imperial power. Just as the two men are encircled by the Great Exhibition and imprisoned by the Steam Castle and the O'Hara Pavillion throughout the film, technology is always harnessed to national agendas and global markets. The Steam men's argument that science can "deliver power to the entire world" becomes agonizingly similar to Japan's mission to colonize Asia for resources and labor under the banner "the New Order of Science-Technology" (Mizuno, 2009, p. 43)

As Edward Steam's goal, it seems, is to bring about a Victorian "New Order of Science-Technology," *Steamboy* shies away from claiming him as a positive cyborg figure capable of overcoming dualistic reductions or breaching the boundaries between human and machine. Like Frankenstein's monster in appearance, Eddy must insert his mechanized arm into the cannibalized parts of a steam organ that function as the Steam Castle's control panel in order to activate the weapon. Transformed into a cyborg by his interactions with Western science, the incoherence of Eddy's body offers a strong parallel to the anxieties and concerns over the multiracial, often monstrous, subject as object. As Elizabeth McMahon has suggested, the cyborg and the colonial subject partake in the process of "abject becoming" in which both are exiled from society but also embody "creative" potentials in their position "outside the law as well as the somatic and psychic revolution it effects for those brought into intimate contact, though the limits of this enabling agency remains contingent and uncertain" (McMahon, 2007, p. 212). Born out of the major nineteenth-century discourses of scientific naturalism and the "spectacle" of "man-made identities" (ibid., p. 211), what McMahon calls the "colonial cyborg" contributes to a more nuanced understanding of the relationship between colonizer and colonized. The *post*colonial cyborg body with is greater emphasis on technology and, I argue, geography, draws on Bhabha's concept of hybridity and depends upon Haraway's description of the cyborg's potential to embody the politics of "transgressed boundaries, potent fusions, and dangerous possibilities' (Haraway, 1991, p. 154). Haraway's cyborg and postcolonial theory share a commitment to "permanently partial identities and contradictory standpoints" (ibid.) and both eschew "*all* claims for an organic or natural standpoint" (ibid., p. 157) in favor of a "maze of dualism" or an "infidel heteroglossia" (ibid., p. 181). "Cyborg writing" and postcolonial fiction both seize "the tools to mark the world that marked them as other" (ibid., p. 175). For my purposes, the postcolonial cyborg bodies represented in *Steamboy* interrogate the seaming together of a monolithic "Asia" and the vulnerability of those seams to tearing.

While Lau Xing/Passepartout embodies the positive aspects of Haraway's posthuman and postcolonial vision of the cyborg, *Steamboy* works to posit Eddy as inhuman, forsaking the "soul" (Otomo, 2004) for profit. Unable to embrace Eddy's destabilizing border condition, the film takes the side of Ray Steam, the other cyborg in the film, seeing in the child rather than the father a *more* human, rather than posthuman, interaction with a threatening technological field. Ultimately, Ray's qualities of bravery, innocence and the ability to understand and improve technology at a single glance make him the ideal candidate for deciding the steam ball's fate. In contrast to his father, Ray's cyborg identity is improvisational: his various jet pack inventions are an alternative to his father's more mechanical and monstrous parts. For Ray, technology is subordinated to human creativity and as WWI sweeps across Europe, in part due to the inventions of Dr Lloyd and Dr Edward the film implies, Ray becomes the globally conscious "Steamboy." Performing heroic acts of rescue throughout the film, Ray embodies a younger generation that is not politically apathetic and withdrawn from society (like the so-called *otaku*), but capable of being a critical and historically informed participant in international affairs. Focusing on Ray's qualities and intuitive understanding of technology, however, offers another more contemporary reading. So far, I have argued that *Steamboy* locates Meiji-era Japan as the prehistory to Hiroshima and Nagasaki, the technological rupture that has defined visions of a demilitarized future in the region. Yet, *Steamboy* was conceived in the 1990s when Japan reinterpreted its postwar pacifist constitution to allow its Self Defense Forces to be deployed as part of the United Nations' noncombat forces to conflict areas around the world. The film's 2004 release coincided with the Japanese government's decision to send the SDF to Iraq for humanitarian relief, a move that provoked public concerns over constitutional violations as well as a resurgence of nationalist sentiments.[13] Thus, the generational structure of the film can also be read as a simplistic but thoughtful representation of a posttraumatic, potentially remilitarized Japan.

Around the World Again

The ability to dramatize technology and its relationship to geography makes steampunk a natural partner to neo-Victorianism and enhances its potential to offer a critique of neo-imperialism. Steampunk aims to recover the stories of those who remain technologically underdeveloped and therefore judged as "less" because they are shut out of the teleological thrust of history. Addressing steampunk reveals a new imperative for postcolonial neo-Victorianism: it cautions against being too enamored of technological novelty and the future it may shape and draws attention to the politics of the past – the so-called "old imperialism" – that globalization seems suspiciously anxious to sweep away. Interrogating the relationship between steampunk and neo-Victorianism elaborates on the temptation to emphasize triumphs without the tragedies in our appropriation of the past. Read critically, however, steampunk's ability to liberate its readers, viewers and participants from chronology and cartography locates new vectors within neo-Victorianism's expanse that reinforces the ability to resist empire in the here and now.

Chapter 6

The Neo-Victorian-at-Sea: Toward a Global Memory of the Victorian

In this book, I have discussed how the Victorian has become a potent textual and cultural shorthand for empire – and Empire – in the contemporary global imagination. By cementing a memory of the nineteenth century as the height of the British imperial project, neo-Victorianism allows for the creative and critical juxtaposition of imperialism in the past with neo-imperialist formations in play in a supposedly postcolonial present. Neo-Victorianism becomes an opportunity to stage the Victorian in the present as a means of recovery of and recovery *from* the memory of the British Empire that impedes the imagination of a post-imperial future. Often tied to the nation state and processes of decolonization around the former British Empire, especially in former settler colonies, I have demonstrated throughout this book that the further neo-Victorianism moves from Britain, the more capable it becomes in addressing new sites of production with differently charged and equally fraught positions toward the West. Locations such as Japan and China, for example, expand neo-Victorianism's purview to incorporate new experiences such as diaspora and techno-orientalism. While playing a crucial role in narratives of recovery, the deployment and appeal of the Victorian in such locations often obscure their imperial imperatives and valorize their perceived position as the victims of Western aggressors. In this conclusion, I would like to pursue the implications of a global vision for neo-Victorianism by exploring some novels that explicitly engage with a metaphorical and real space of globalization: the sea. A global memory of the Victorian emerges attuned to the conditions and experience of transnationality but the vastness of the sea – the attention to space as well as time – also puts pressure on neo-Victorianism's effectiveness in resisting or critiquing power now, especially more informal or invisible forms of coercion and control divorced from sovereignty or direct political or territorial domination.

Neo-Victorianism Now: A Frozen Archive

One particular discovery in 2010 helpfully recaps the politics of memory underlying the postcolonial neo-Victorian project and provides an example of the new shift in direction for neo-Victorianism that I am tracing. As part of the Canadian government's plan to establish a "long-standing presence in the Arctic that can enhance issues of sovereignty" (Canwest, 2008), Canadian archeologists set out on yet another mission to locate the remains of the Franklin Expedition, the fatal search for new routes through the Northwest Passage led by Sir John Franklin in 1845. Two ships, the *Erebus* and *HMS Terror*, and a total of 150 men left England under Franklin's command and were never seen again. All that remains is a fractured history of starvation, disease, death and cannibalism as Franklin's men abandoned their vessels after his death and attempted to cross the ice on foot. All international attempts to recover Franklin and his ships from the moment news of their disappearance was received in nineteenth-century London to the present have been unsuccessful. In the summer of 2010, in probably the most dramatic neo-Victorian moment ever, the Canadian team located the almost entirely preserved wreck of *HMS Investigator*, an English ship sailing under the leadership of Captain Robert McClure that set out on one of many failed searches for Franklin in 1848. Trapped in packed ice, McClure and his men were luckily rescued from the Franklin Expedition's fate by the Royal Navy. This amazing historical find barely masks the controversial impetus behind the current Canadian mission: to establish Canada's unbroken sovereignty over any new arctic territory and shipping lanes that will become available by the effects of global warming. In what is literally a case of uncharted waters, Russia, Denmark, Norway and the U.S. join Canada in the neo-imperial jockeying over who will have jurisdiction over newly exposed seas and whatever resources may lie in or under them.[1]

Driven by a desire to recover a lost past it literally inherits from Britain (the British ceded any of Franklin's remains to Canada in 1997) (Canwest, 2008), the Canadian mission reconstructs both a fatal journey of adventure and scientific exploration undertaken in the name of empire and fragmented records of cross-cultural contact between Europeans and Inuit tribes. The mission simultaneously raises neo-imperial problems: already threatened by climate change, will the fragility of Inuit culture and heritage be protected and their rights championed as part of the "true North, strong and free?" Will the Inuit be dispossessed of their land in the push for resources and riches? What kind of north/south colonialisms occur as the result of Canada's Arctic policy? Thus, the romance of solving one of the greatest mysteries of the nineteenth century will also mean the establishment of a new Canadian maritime empire that may repeat, if not rival, that of its former imperial master. These important concerns are anchored to the image of the shipwreck or, more specifically, the ubiquitous image of the ship terrifyingly trapped in ice associated with nineteenth-century Arctic exploration. This image, I argue, might also reflect the current "frozen" state of the archive neo-Victorian studies has, for better or for worse, canonized: can neo-Victorian studies and production put Britain (and Franklin) to rest and embrace some new paradigm that will not just repeat the imperial games of the past?

Andrea Barrett's 1998 novel, *The Voyage of The Narwhal* – a novel that barely counts within the paradigm of neo-Victorian fiction because it unfolds in nineteenth-century Philadelphia and an unspecified icy North – implicitly stages this neo-Victorian dilemma. Consumed by the search for Franklin and marooned in the Frozen Sea, the battered crew of the *Narwhal* does not discover "even the smallest scrap of new coastline" (Barret, 1998, p. 92) and are scooped by Elisha Kane's surprise rescue and triumphant return to Philadelphia. Increasingly disillusioned, the suspicious men "experience the search for Franklin's remains as just . . . distraction" (ibid., p. 98) from expedition commander Zeke Voorhees's voracious quest for fame. Anchored to an increasingly ghostly British presence, the sailors are "distracted" from national agendas such as Zeke's ambition to lead the U.S. in the "allied sciences" (Driver, 2001, p. 3) of geography, surveying and navigation that make up imperial knowledge. At the same time, other versions of the Victorian such as the Irish Famine, which sparked a different kind of sea voyage, have been forgotten while in the Arctic, "where no one might ever have seen them, three young Englishmen had each been given a careful and singular grave" (Barrett, 1998, p. 90). Tied to the search for coastline and the boundaries of an open polar sea, the expedition's mission – neo-Victorianism's mission – becomes increasingly unclear: "Commander Voorhees made it sound as if we were going to rescue *survivors*," one character complains, "yet it seems we're only going after corpses" (ibid., p. 50).

As if to answer this call for "survivors" rather than "corpses," there has been, I argue, a sea change in postmillennial fiction's treatment of the Victorian. Recently, a concentration of neo-Victorian novels have been fixated on and structured by the sea voyage rather than the more "settled" locales of some of the neo-Victorian texts that I have discussed thus far. Texts such as Matthew Kneale's *English Passengers* (2000), Harry Thompson's *To The Edge of the World* (2003), Andrea Barrett's short stories from *Ship Fever*

(1996) and *Servants of the Map* (2003) and Amitav Ghosh's *Sea of Poppies* (2008) are concerned with *journeys* rather than the founding acts of settler colonialism themselves: a privileging of what Gilroy has termed "*routes* over roots" (Gilroy, 1993, p. 133). I refer to this new trend of oceanic travel and ship narratives as the "neo-Victorian-at-sea." The neo-Victorian-at-sea establishes the ocean, rather than Britain, as the liquid site of empire reframing British imperialism as a "vast and evolving political space" (Klein, 2002, p. 2). The neo-Victorian-at-sea serves as a reminder that the British Empire was above all an "empire of the seas" (ibid.), forcing us to rethink even further the usual structures of center and periphery that mark most postcolonial fiction. In this chapter, I read the neo-Victorian-at-sea as a search for new critical directions as authors practicing postcolonial politics move beyond conventional neo-Victorianism's bounded territorial spaces and status as national literatures. However, despite this enervation of the field, a palpable sense of crisis about the increasingly strict constraints of genre surfaces from a study of the neo-Victorian-at-sea.

The Neo-Victorian-at-Sea

At first glance, the turn to the sea (and I include its setting of the sea, ships and ports) and its *dramatis personae* (pirates, sailors, human cargo) seems, perhaps, over-determined for neo-Victorian fiction. For a postcolonial project invested in forms of cultural memory, the sea, *pace* Derek Walcott, *is* history, tossing up the detritus of monuments and the submerged histories of colonial atrocities. The sea functions as the "grey vault" (Walcott, 1979, p. 25): at once watery archive, graveyard and theater of memory. In keeping with postcolonial imperatives, the neo-Victorian-at-sea can make that "grey vault" available for recall and restitution in the present. In keeping with the many critics engaged in historicizing the sea and revising its status as mere metaphor, empty, timeless and thus ahistorical, the neo-Victorian-at-sea associates itself with other ventures that regard the sea as a new paradigm capable of "accommodating various revisionary accounts . . . of the modern historical experience of transnational contact zones" (Klein, 2002, p. 2). Tracing the spatial significations of the Pacific Rim and the unequal circulation of capital, labor and people upon which they are predicated, Christopher L. Connery pushes back against the mythologies and sublimations of "the oceanic feeling" (Connery, 1996, p. 289) that reduces the sea to poesis. More recently, Heather Blum's work locates a history of labor in the sea: sailors-cum-authors were "both producers and consumers of intellectual as well as manual labor" (Blum, 2008, p. 12) and thus offer an epistemological challenge to the study of literary culture during the antebellum period. Similarly, the revisionary studies of the regionalism of the Indian Ocean explore its pre-European globality as facilitator of cultural exchange and trade between India, Africa and Asia.[2] All of these rehistoricizations of the sea, including the neo-Victorian-at-sea, owe a debt to Paul Gilroy's reclamation of the Black Atlantic and slavery's disruption to the narratives and conventional periodicizations of modernity. In Gilroy's analysis, the "contact zone" of the Atlantic meant that the intellectual and cultural traditions reified as discrete or authentic are, in fact, transcultural, polyphonic and hybrid. Gilroy highlights ships as the avatar of modernity, in particular, as "a living, micro-culture, micro-political system in motion" (Gilroy, 1993, p. 7); a repository of the economics and half-remembered experiences of the slave-trade; a space for the orchestration of temporal and even geographical resistances; and a powerful chronotope and counter-culture to Western orthodoxies and constructions of modernity. While Gilroy's canvas of the Black Atlantic has been revised and expanded to include other African experiences and to be more translocal and trans-national in scope, his ideas still underpin interventions in the standard stories of globalization as modernity, available and accessible to all.

Despite *The Black Atlantic's* impact on literary and cultural studies and the prominence of the sea in Jean Rhys's *Wide Sargasso Sea*, a foundational text of postcolonial neo-Victorian fiction, neo-Victorianism approaches the sea in the millennium with a surprising sense of belatedness. Constrained by the self-imposed parameters of the Victorian, neo-Victorian studies and fiction embraces Foucault's hugely influential re-readings of sexuality in the nineteenth century and yet is sometimes reluctant or feels unable to turn to Gilroy's *The Black Atlantic*. Novels set in a preabolition nineteenth century and prior to the reign of Queen Victoria – Caryl Phillip's *Cambridge* (1992) or Andrea Levy's *The Long Song* (2010) – do not often fall under neo-Victorianism's scrutiny, thus the incorporation of slavery appears uneven. The slave narrative's specificities as a form also act as a significant deterrent to neo-Victorianism's usual colonizing tendencies, thus the "neo-slave narrative" exists as its own separate subgenre.[3] Hemmed in by chronology, neo-Victorianism finds it too late to celebrate or critique the spectacle of Britain's naval might and tragedies in the early nineteenth century, thus excluding the sea novels of Patrick O'Brian (the most well-known of the Aubrey/Maturin series being the 1970 novel, *Master and Commander*) or Julian Stockwin's *Kydd* (2001 – present) series. The turn to the sea, however, can rejuvenate the field's archive and generic capabilities as the Victorian can now also be read as maritime empire and a memory of empire that is also shared between Britain, Africa, Asia and the Americas.

What enables the neo-Victorian-at-sea, I believe, are current geopolitical imperatives that refocus our attention from the Atlantic to the South and other China Seas and the Indian Ocean. This shift offers vastly different stories, epistemologies, patterns of migration and trade as "old diasporas" interact with "modern empires" (Hofmeyer, 2010, p. 722) touched by the Victorian but not necessarily *of* the Victorian. In response to this new global vision, a key feature of the neo-Victorian-at-sea has obviously become the ship, derived from another Foucauldian concept, the ship as heterotopia. In his unfinished essay, "Of Other Spaces," Foucault traces the links between the nineteenth-century "great obsession" with the accretions of time and history to our designation as an "epoch of space" (Foucault, 1967, p. 22). Drawing on the language of displacement, Foucault writes, "we are at a moment . . . when our experience of the world is less that of a long life developing through time than that of a network that connects points and intersects with its own skein" (ibid.). To explain the contradictory ways in which we are newly emplaced, Foucault appeals to the concept of heterotopias. Governed by certain principles, Foucault deems sacred and profane spaces as varied as cemeteries, the Oriental garden and motel rooms, as examples of heterotopia. A history of such "counter-sites" that are "without geographical markers" (ibid., p. 25) and a study of their contradictory and disruptive uses would allow for the identification of "heterotopic sites" (ibid., p. 26) where otherness is constructed and flourishes. Most attractive to the neo-Victorian-at-sea is Foucault's final assertion that "the ship is the heterotopia *par excellence*" (ibid., p. 27). Ending on a note of imaginative escapism, he elaborates, "in civilizations without boats, dreams dry up, espionage takes the place of adventure, and the police take the place of pirates" (ibid.). Building on the ship as the "great instrument of economic development" (ibid.), the argument that Foucault did not want to explore, Cesare Casarino argues that the concentrated return to sea narratives in the late-nineteenth century was a method of registering, via an existing representational form, a "world system that was increasingly arduous to visualize, the more multiple, interconnected and global it became" (Casarino, 2002, p. 10). As the political economy of the late-nineteenth century transitioned from mercantile to industrial capitalism, literary production turned toward the familiar sea narrative in order to "get across the radically new" (ibid., p. 6). The neo-Victorian-at-sea arguably reflects a similar crisis: the return to the sea narrative responds to a need to make sense of global consumption, trade and labor, and the mass movement of people via a previous moment of globalization made possible by imperialism. By focusing on the sea, the novels that I will be examining in this final chapter resist the urge in much neo-Victorian fiction to return to the prominence of the nation state and posit instead an unbounded globality that might unravel neo-Victorian studies by expanding it to its limits.

From "Black Line" to "Black Water": *English Passengers* and *Sea of Poppies*

In what follows, I offer a reading of two novels, Kneale's *English Passengers* and Ghosh's *Sea of Poppies*: both novels invite us to disassociate the Victorian with its landed qualities and transform it instead into a memory of the voyage, a series of encounters with other cultures and peoples without the tyranny of origin. Written in 2000, *English Passengers* offers yet more "island stories" to complicate the British colonization of Australia by dramatizing the extinction of full-blooded aboriginals in Tasmania. Led by the rebellious Mother, the remaining aborigines are forced to relocate their dwindling numbers to Flinders Island in the mid-nineteenth century. Mother's half-white son, Peevay, a product of her rape by a white convict, narrates these sections of the novel. As Peevay slowly learns English, his hybridity becomes a powerful weapon against colonial oppression as he organizes "PEEVAY'S MOB" (Kneale, 2000, p. 433) by educating them about "writing and LAWS, white men's tricks and BIBLE CHEATING and more" (ibid., p. 434). Against this land-based politics of memory, *English Passengers* also focuses on the ill-fated voyage of the smuggling ship, *Sincerity*, and its crew from the Isle of Man, a semi-colonized space in the history and geography of the British Isles. The *Sincerity* carries a mutinous group of over-zealous English explorers determined to discover the Garden of Eden in Tasmania. Told as a series of missives, journals, letters and other documents of a "traveling culture" (Clifford, 1997, p. 17), *English Passengers* can be regarded as an example of what Paul Carter has called "spatial history" that is "neither static nor mindlessly mobile ... where traveling is a process of continually beginning, continually ending, where discovery and settlement belong to the same exploratory process" (Carter, 1987, p. xxiv). However, unlike Carter's celebration of the dialectic of land and sea, *English Passengers* seems unable to commit to the shift in representational strategies offered by the neo-Victorian-at-sea. I read the interweaving of the *Sincerity's* voyage with the portrayal of aboriginal dispossession as an expression of anxiety and suspicion over what can be lost by the turn to the sea; as the *Sincerity* is shipwrecked off the coast of England, we are offered only a momentary glimpse of a community beyond a hegemonic landed understanding of the Victorian.

English Passengers presents the ship as an alternative archive and poses the question: what would the Victorian look like told from the position of the voyage? Neo-Victorianism relies on an archive constituted of texts and artifacts: novels and film from Byatt's *Possession* onward have fetishized the archive and thus, a certain neo-Victorian thingy-ness lends a particular thickness or authenticity to the reconstruction while also correcting what currently counts as the historical record. The ship in the neo-Victorian-at-sea offers an opposing archival act to conventional neo-Victorian texts; it is quite happy to jettison the same texts and things – the signifiers of Englishness and Victorianness – that might interfere with its own, often illegal, trading agendas. Captain Quillian Illian Kewley and his Manx crew, for example, scoff at the "shame" of having to take on passengers and even "worse, Englishmen all of them" (Kneale, 2001, p. 79). The crew extend their scorn to the loading of the English expedition's stores of the "best potted ham, hermetically sealed salmon, hotch-potch from Aberdeen, and whole cases of sherry, whiskey and champagne . . . folding tables and chairs, table linen, crockery and some finest Sheffield silver cutlery . . ." (ibid., p. 43) into the *Sincerity's* hold. While the English passengers – the Reverend Wilson, an ardent supporter of theories such as "Divine Refrigeration" (ibid., p. 21) and other proofs against the "atheisms of Geology" (ibid., p. 24); surgeon and racial scientist Dr Potter, based on Dr Robert Knox; and the young botanist, Timothy Renshaw – struggle to maintain their various English practices aboard ship, they are also overwhelmed by the "sea technicalities" (ibid., p. 108) of sailing life. A combination of bad food, bad weather, lack of privacy and sleep deprivation causes Wilson to lament:

> I do believe that, with the exception of a field of battle, there is hardly a place on earth more poorly suited to the gaining of rest than a sailing ship . . . Timbers creak, ropes and blocks would squeal, officers would bellow, boots would thump and the crew themselves would begin singing at the top of their voices, seeming unable to tug at any rope without wailing some unspeakable shanty song. (ibid., p. 109)

Removed from the regularities of English life, the ship becomes a "field of battle" between those on deck and those who should remain below, between languages and between nations. Englishmen and Manxmen compete over space and morality: Wilson's construction of a "sea lectern" and a "sea pulpit" out of champagne and cutlery boxes for his sermons on deck, for example, directly contradicts Captain Kewley's command that "this is a ship, not a preaching house" (ibid., p. 114). Only the appearance of an ambiguous pirate or customs ship on the horizon and an ensuing cannon fight restores Kewley's authority and prevents Wilson from delivering his sermon on "the sea! The sea! That great wilderness…" (ibid., p. 120). The "sea technicalities" seem to be, at the onset of the novel, an antidote to the English passengers' religious zeal and theories of racialism. One of the greatest strengths of the ship is its ability to undo Englishness – a vehicle that breaks it down and disinters it from its national roots.

The *Sincerity* and its Manx crew deliberately undermine Englishness and, by extension, the territorial nature of the neo-Victorian project. Under Captain Kewley's command and careful scrutiny, the crew has secretly stocked a separate cargo of contraband goods. Kewley's design of the *Sincerity* mocks the sincerity of neo-Victorian reconstruction itself. Loose blocks behind "the two busts, of Albert and Victoria" which, significantly, "seemed somehow a touch less anchored," trigger the "hinged trap door" (Kneale, 2000, p. 35) to the secret hold. Kewley continues:

> Now I'll tell you why all those serious-faced customs men never found a thing. It was because the *Sincerity* wasn't just some piece of cheap faked-up carpentry, no. From the dining-cabin floor down, the *Sincerity* was two entire vessels, one inside the other. The inner hull was those timbers I'd bought from the boat that was being broken up, and though I'd had it thinned out little, still it didn't sound hollow if you gave it a thump. It even looked weathered and damp, just like it should. As for the gap between the these two hulls, this was no more than eighteen inches – more and the hold would have looked too curious – but eighteen inches right round the body of a ship holds a might store of bales of tobacco and flasks of brandy. (ibid.)

The *Sincerity* functions differently than neo-Victorianism's oft-criticized theme-park approach to the nineteenth century. Dismissing the goal of some neo-Victorian texts to recreate or adapt the nineteenth century, the *Sincerity* is neither "some piece of cheap faked-up carpentry" nor does it "sound hollow" or inauthentic. The *Sincerity* rejects a postcolonial neo-Victorianism too as we are asked not to focus on the recovered "inner hull" or hidden ship but the "eighteen inches" of space between the two ships nestled one inside another. The *Sincerity's* energy is entirely devoted to the "dark" space that girds the ship, with its "rich smell of wood and leaf and spirit to sweeten your nostrils" (ibid.). As the avatar of the neo-Victorian-at-sea, the *Sincerity's* eighteen-inch gap describes an intimate illegitimacy or, again, the traffic and spaces *between* empires. The *Sincerity's* gap also replaces the Isle of Man itself: now a semi-colonized territory, Kewley remembers Man Island as once "free and independent" from "interfering English politicians" (ibid., p. 4). Peel City rivaled Liverpool, Manchester and London as a vibrant port with ships sailing into it "direct from every corner of the world, from Europe and Africa, from Indies West and East" (ibid., p. 5). The neo-Victorian-at-sea moves the neo-Victorian agenda away from careful reconstruction of the Isle of Man to the ship itself thus recasting the island as a global space and describing a culture forced by colonialism into a diasporic identity with the sea.

Structured by the concept of the "contact zone," the neo-Victorian-at-sea explores the loss of traditional dialects and native language through coerced and voluntary participation in an empire of English. These novels stress the polylinguistic aspects of travel and how they relate to the questions of recovering – and recovering from – colonialism. Multilingualism, as Tina Steiner has argued, becomes a way of introducing conflict and a system of power and coercion subsumed under the smooth multicultural canvas of a "trading lingua franca" or by the perceived "peaceful traditions of the oceanic trade" (Steiner, 2008, p. 49). *English Passengers*, for example, dramatizes the extermination of aboriginal dialects but also the extinction of other ways of being British. Kneale reveals in the appendix to the novel that the Manx dialect "gradually declined during the nineteenth century, and the last native Manx speaker died in the 1970s" (Kneale, 2000, p. 443). Manx was a language made up of Irish and Scottish Gaelic peppered with the words and phrases that register the Manx obsessions: "disapproval, the sea, herring and superstition" (ibid.). In the early pages of the novel, Captain Kewley can still gloat about Manx's uniqueness, that "hardly a soul on earth besides other Manxman will understand a word" and that "to your Englishman it's as clear as purest Chinese" (ibid., p. 203). *English Passengers* reflects the linguistic varieties lost under the violence of colonialism – indigenous Tasmanian culture and life certainly – but also how the effort to bring an anarchic language under control is brought about by eliminating competing forms of the vernacular in favor of an authoritative but still undetermined standard English. The "British" center is consolidated by the governing of any forms of what Evelyn Chi'en has called "weird" (Chi'en, 2004, p. 4) or "broken" (ibid., p. 64) English that could offer a counter-discourse and the seed of otherness within the supposedly "United"

Kingdom. As long as the *Sincerity* remains afloat, characters are offered linguistic opportunities and experiences related to the fluidity of the sea.

Once the novel reaches land, so to speak, and drops anchor in Tasmania, however, it asks us to confront the ethics of such a watery world view. We are forced to reconsider the transnational and liberatory potentials of the ship against the violent extermination of Tasmanian aborigines. While the routes and rhythm of ships' travel dominate the structure of the novel, the narrative on land presents us with trauma narratives indicative of postcolonial neo-Victorianism: the novel includes a description of the Black Line, for example, a British-sanctioned raid of the island by settlers, ex-convicts and soldiers to round up aborigines for deportation ostensibly for their own protection. Told from the point of view of several fictional and historical British characters such as George Alder, the Governor of Van Dieman's Land, the Black Line creates a powerful narrative disruption from the *Sincerity*'s liquidity. As accusations of "deliberate murder" (Kneale, 2000, p. 144) are launched against Alder, we come to realize the tensions between the two narrative threads, one aqueous, the other territorial:

> While I had been arguing with the fellow we must have ridden over a ridge, as now a fine view stretched out ahead. It was an exhilarating spot, with gulls hanging high in the wind and the crash of waves all around. To the left lay the sea, to the right also, with the thick line of men glinting and stamping away in each direction, as far as the shores. In front of us lay a wide expanse of open grassland, rolling gently down to the water, and looking a little like some wild part of the Devonshire coast. We had reached the very end of the peninsular, and our great march. (ibid., p. 145)

Here, the reader is faced with two scenarios: despite being surrounded by the sea, the vista is monopolized by the "great march" of whiteness and violence that transforms the Tasmanian environment into a semblance of "the Devonshire coast." In the end, the Black Line forestalls any celebratory notion of diaspora that the *Sincerity* may represent, looking across the "fine view" of the Tasmanian landscape, Governor Alder muses that "the most noticeable thing about the scene . . . was that it was wholly and utterly empty of aborigines" (ibid.).

It should be noted that *English Passengers* loosely fictionalizes the experiences of indigenous historical personages: Kneale mentions in his epilogue that Peevay's Mother, for example, is based on aboriginal resistance fighter, Walyer, "who fought the whites and was greatly feared by them"

(Kneale, 2000, p. 439). The desecration of Mother's corpse is also based on the events surrounding the death of "Truganini" or "Tru-ger-nan-ner" mythologized by colonial authorities and historians as "the last of the Tasmanians" (quoted in Barlow, 1998, p. 59) and enshrined as a powerful and poignant symbol of authenticity and extinction. After her death, her skeleton was placed on display at the Royal Society of Tasmania Museum well into the twentieth century. Like Walyer, Truganini is an iconic figure who literally embodies the political narratives of indigeneity, nation and feminism (Perera, 1996, p. 396). At the same time, her remains establish "evidence" of a fictive authenticity that mobilizes historical and legal challenges to Native Title and other land claims. In the novel, the ever-rebellious Mother, who is renamed "Mary" by her English captors, dies at the moment her photograph is about to be taken, deliberately toppling the record-making device as she crashes to the ground. Mary's disruption of modernity via imperialist surveillance merely troubles but does not change the politics of extinction surrounding her death. Her attempts to evade the gaze of scientific imperialism only spurs Dr Potter to body-theft because "the aborigines of the colony being so greatly reduced, their bones are known to attract the interest of museums and scientific institutions within Europe" (Kneale, 2000, p. 328). As "Mother Mary," her remains become relics offering conduits to imperial rather than religious power.[4] Looting such relics imbues Potter with the worldly, material power to claim legitimacy for *his* version of the Victorian, that is, "wholly and utterly empty of aborigines" (ibid., p. 145). Thus, the voyage of the *Sincerity* – the neo-Victorian-at-sea – sits uneasily beside the potent land-based politics of memory that Mary's/Truganini's remains represent.

Ambivalence toward the neo-Victorian-at-sea's project can be seen in the complicated plot surrounding Mary's remains and the fate of the *Sincerity* and her Manx crew. Some summary here is necessary to illustrate the novel's uneasiness with its global implications. Happily abandoning their English passengers to the Tasmanian outback on their disastrous mission to search for the Garden of Eden and having finally found a buyer for their cargo, the crew of the *Sincerity* eagerly prepare for their return to the Isle of Man. As they are about to set sail however, Captain Kewley spots the bedraggled group of English explorers on the shore and, overcome by guilt, brings them aboard ship. With their numbers depleted by a vengeful, murdering Peevay, who has finally had his "killing war against num, thirty summers late" (Kneale, 2000, p. 380), the English passengers and Potter's contraband collection of aboriginal specimens are reunited with the *Sincerity*. Driven mad by religious zeal and by Peevay's systematic hunting of his men,

Reverend Wilson breaks free of his prison in the hold to smash and reveal evidence of "Potter's evil" (ibid., p. 382), the papers, aboriginal artifacts and specimens, including Mary's remains, that Potter has gathered on the expedition. Having snuck aboard ship, Peevay manages to steal his mother's bones in the melee and bring them ashore for burial with the "saddest goodbyes" (ibid., p. 387), thus re-interring the Victorian and its capability for telling a Tasmanian story with the "correct dignity" (ibid.). When the passengers discover that the *Sincerity* is, essentially, a smuggling ship, the English decide to mutiny, imprison Captain Kewley and the crew, and sail, almost single-handedly back to England. In sight of England, the ship becomes wedged between two massive rocks and sinks after months of neglect in a massive storm. During the escape, Dr Potter is murdered and his body entombed within the shipwreck. Exiled from the Isle of Man by his criminal record, Kewley travels to London and stumbles across the book launch and exhibit for *The Destiny of Nations*, Potter's racist diatribe, paid for by his supporters who have also excavated the wreck of the *Sincerity* for Potter's scientific artifacts. In the glass case, under the heading "Unknown Male Presumed Tasmanian Aborigine Possible Victim of Human Sacrifice" (ibid., p. 438), Kewley identifies Potter's skeleton from the fatal blow to his skull and by his beard, a tell-tale "fine shade of red" (ibid.). As the novel cannot entertain the possibility of aboriginal survivors in Tasmania, it takes its revenge on Potter's corpse.

In an online interview with *Boldtype*, Kneale has expressed his interest in capturing the "craziness of the Victorian British mind" and the "dangerously misguided notions of the nineteenth century" (McDonald, 2000) in *English Passengers*. Peevay's burial of Mother and Potter's future as an exhibit of the "barbarism" of the "Black Type" (Kneale, 2000, p. 392) he so abhorred offer a fitting anticolonial ending to Kneale's anticolonial novel. Its events culminate in the recovery of and the recovery from the imperial past and appear to fulfill the expectations of postcolonial neo-Victorian narratives. However, this does not account for the sinking of the *Sincerity*. Caught between massive rocks off the shore of England, the eighteen-inch gap of the ship, Kewley makes sure to mention, is crushed along with the neo-Victorian-at-sea's potential. Poised between neo-Victorianism and the neo-Victorian-at sea, or stuck between two rocks and a hard place, the novel remains uncertain about the loose, vagueness of heterotopic space and the real geography of imperial power represented by Tasmania and poor Kewley's final journey to London via the regulatory controls of public transportation.

In contrast to *English Passengers*, Amitav Ghosh's novel, *Sea of Poppies*, with its focus on the Indian ocean, is nothing but celebratory in its use of the voyage to achieve its recovery work, specifically, revising Gilroy's argument in *The Black Atlantic* for the Indian diaspora. Perhaps surprisingly, India has not been a robust producer of neo-Victorian narratives, overshadowed, it seems, by 1947 rather than 1857.[5] But, the neo-Victorian-at-sea allows for this redress: *Sea of Poppies*, the first part of a trilogy, dramatizes the export of Indian, and to a lesser extent, Chinese labor around the British Empire, reframed by Ghosh as "Greater India." Using opium as a vector, Ghosh restores to centrality the figure of the "coolie" and thus a history of slavery to the Victorian, problematically imagined as over before neo-Victorianism begins its memory-work. The novel traces the journey of the *Ibis*, its crew of "Chinese and East Africans, Arabs, and Malays, Bengalis and Goans, Tamils and Arakanese" that had "nothing in common, except the Indian Ocean" (Ghosh, 2008, p. 13) and its cargo of indentured workers. Written in 2008, the novel finds for a diasporic, transnational present a version of the Victorian past accountable to international contracted labor originating in India, China and Africa, and migration to destinations beyond the "properly" colonial spaces prized by neo-Victorian studies. *Sea of Poppies* features an interwoven array of cultures and composite identities sponsored by the routes and spaces *between* empires.

Unlike *English Passengers*, however, once the *Ibis* is boarded, *Sea of Poppies* never lands. Emphasizing the enclosed spaces of the ship, Ghosh weaves together the lives and fortunes of various characters to make up the diasporic tapestry of the novel and to express the trauma of migration. The novel introduces characters like Deeti, an Indian woman, rescued from suttee, who escapes her life and her caste with her lover to join the *Ibis* for a new life "where the holy Ganga disappeared into the Kala-Pani, 'the Black Water'" (Ghosh, 2008, p. 3); Neel Rattan Halder, a Bengali aristocrat and landowner who is tricked into forgery and bankrupted by the unscrupulous Benjamin Burnham, owner of the *Ibis* and opium trader; transported as a convict, Neel shares his cell with Ah Fatt, a Parsi-Chinese laborer and former opium addict; and Paulette, orphaned by the death of her French botanist father, who stows away disguised as a coolie rather than marry the buffoonish Mr. Kendalbushe. Together, their stories on the *Ibis* recover the history of the indentureship of over two million coolies who defied the traditional Hindu ban against leaving the sacred waters of the Ganges in order to labor on plantations in the Mauritius, British Guyana and beyond. The *Ibis's* de facto leader, second mate Zachary Reid or "Malum Zikri" (ibid., p. 15), forms the link between decks. Throughout the novel, he conceals his racial identity as the "son of a Maryland freedwoman" (ibid., p. 10) in order to pass as white. Zachary's "metif" (ibid., p. 464) identity and the *Ibis's* own refurbishment into "a hold that was designed to carry slaves will serve just as well to carry coolies and convicts" (ibid., p. 74) underscores the links between the slave trade of Gilroy's Black Atlantic and the plurality of Indian labor and migration. In Zachary, Ghosh confronts *négritude* with "coolitude," Khal Torabully's influential reclamation of the pejorative term "coolie" to symbolize instead, "the possibility of a composite identity to ease the pain and enrich culturally the lands in which he/she settled" (Carter and Torabully, 2002, p. 144). Using the dominance of the *Ibis* as heterotopia, Ghosh highlights "coolitude's" function as a memorial strategy, addressing the coolie's need to restore to memory the "cultural implications of the Voyage" (ibid., p. 141) which were not, as the *Ibis's* travelers realize, "experienced in full consciousness" (ibid., p. 342) at the time of its undertaking.

The novel infuses the Victorian with what Torabully calls a "marine essence" (Carter and Torabully, 2002, p. 158) and reconstitutes the ship as a means to enable the "metaphorical construction of a new identity" (ibid.). *Sea of Poppies* champions the sea voyage because the majority of the neo-Victorian-at-sea's memory-work occurs during passage, rather than in the aftermath of arrival. Thus, Ghosh describes the interactions between the Anglo-Chinese criminal, Ah Fatt, and the Indian convict, Neel, as the most intimate of friendships that can only develop in the darkest of shared cells. With a sparse English as the only mode of communication between the unlikely pair, "the genius of Ah Fatt's descriptions lay in their elisions, so that to listen to him was a venture of collaboration, in which the things that were spoken of came gradually to be transformed into artifacts of a shared imagining" (Ghosh, 2008, p. 345). Through such moments of "collaboration," Neel begins to register cosmopolitan values, "that Canton was to his own city as Calcutta was to the villages around it" (ibid.). The pidgin language of the sea, accompanied by silences, provides a "shared imagining" whereby the ship, rather than the place of arrival, becomes the initial space and experience of multiculturalism outside of India. *Sea of Poppies* thus revisits neo-Victorianism as elision rather than postmodern rupture or break so that the ship and duration rather than destination and origin are privileged. Thus, the reader comes to realize with Deeti that the *Ibis* was "the Mother-Father of her new family, a great wooden *mái-báp*, an adoptive ancestor and parent of dynasties yet to come" (ibid., p. 328).

Both Kneale and Ghosh are interested in recapturing and partly reconstructing a panoply of Englishes. Sometimes reverent and sometimes mocking, *Sea of Poppies* delivers a world without English enriched only by locality and dialects. On the *Ibis*, characters learn to communicate in a variety of Englishes and:

> in Laskari – that motley tongue, spoken nowhere but on the water, whose words are as varied as the port's traffic, an anarchic medley of Portuguese calaluzes and Kerala pattimars, Arab booms and Bengal punchways, Malay proas and Tamil catamarans, Hindusthani pulwars and English snows – yet beneath the surface of this farrago of sounds, meaning flowed as freely as the currents beneath the crowded press of boats. (Ghosh, 2008, p. 96)

The *Ibis* represents the multitudinous linguistic attempts at transgression, constructions of new subjectivities and the breaking with origin: not one India, not one Africa, not one China, not one Britain. To elaborate on language's ability to achieve liberatory ends, Ghosh appends to the American edition of *Sea of Poppies* the text of "The *Ibis* Chrestomathy," begun by Neel, which rivals the chronotope of the ship in the representation of linguistic and intellectual transnationalism. Neel's Chrestomathy functions "not so much a key to language as an astrological chart, crafted by a man who was obsessed with the destiny of words" (Ghosh, 2008, p. 473). Checked against the "complete and authoritative lexicon of the English language" – the Oxford English Dictionary – the Chrestomathy exists as a genealogy and an almanac of how words in "Bengali, Arabic, Chinese, Hind, Laskari or anything else" (ibid., p. 474) become naturalized, thus disappearing, into official English. The chrestomathy also forms a poignant collection of lost words like "zubben" (ibid., p. 515), a word which Neel can find "no evidence [of] in any of my dictionaries. But I know I have heard it often used, and if it does not exist, it should, for no other expression could so accurately describe the subject of the Chrestomathy" (ibid.). Neel's life work mirrors the journey of the "many migrants who have sailed from eastern waters towards the chilly shores of the English language" (ibid., p. 473). Carried on by Neel's descendents, "wordy-wallahs" (ibid., p. 474) drafted to continue his legacy, the Chrestomathy offers a recovery of a history of the English language as a "sea-language" (ibid., p. 483) richly rooted in nautical terms and carrying with it a submerged history of colonialism and migration. The Chrestomathy also restores a linguistic coherency to the present as "so long as the knowledge of his words was kept alive within the family, it would tie them to their past and thus to each other" (ibid., p. 474). Like the ship, language becomes another contact zone that resists the monolingualism of nation and empire.

In addition to the linguistic attack on English, the novel challenges conventional narratives of migrations from East to West, as Inderpal Grewal has noted, by preferring journeys from the East to the East (Grewal, 2008, p. 183). Telling the story of his childhood, Ah Fatt describes being inspired by the "famous and beloved title, *Journey to the West*," a gift from his Parsi tutor in China. Ah Fatt's dream of wanting to "go West" – to "Mr Moddie's very own homeland – Hindusthan, or Jambudyipa as it was called in the old books" (Ghosh, 2008, p. 387) – dismays his father who thinks it is the "real West – to France or America or England" (ibid., pp. 387–8) that should drive his son's desire to travel. Ah Fatt's journey, like that of the *Ibis* and many of her passengers, disrupts the dyad of West and non-West and argues for continuities between communities that share histories of anticolonial struggle and trade. Such vignettes have led critics like Grewal, among others, to critique Ghosh for romanticizing, especially precolonial, "narratives of cosmopolitan tolerance and peaceful coexistence engendered by trade" (Grewal, 2008, p. 180). Some of Ghosh's fiction exhibits an uncomfortable tendency to forget that profound intolerance and difference existed prior to nation and colonialism's redrawing of national and diasporic lines. However, Ghosh's foray into neo-Victorianism in *Sea of Poppies* can counter such criticisms: if the Victorian recalls primarily a memory of empire, as I have argued, then any depiction of trade, migration, mobility and even language itself, must be saturated by colonial power relations. Certainly, the cosmopolitan values of the novel do not extend to Zachary, for example, who remains blind to the similarities between his own heritage of slavery and the future of his human cargo in the hold.

The recurrent theme of cartographic failure in the neo-Victorian-at-sea suggests a sustained concern with the direction of neo-Victorianism and its reach. Almost all of the novels I have discussed so far contain, as part of their introductory materials, maps of their journeys. As a privileged system of postcolonial texts, maps are intimately linked to imperial expansion, epistemology and legitimacy. Graham Huggan, among others, has argued for the necessity of "decolonizing the map" (Huggan, 1987, p. 147) to resist hegemonic, Western constructions. It is imperative, according to Huggan, for postcolonial texts to "reconceptualize the map itself as the expression of a shifting ground between alternative metaphors rather than as the approximate representation of a literal 'truth'" (Huggan, 1987, p. 153). Yet, the neo-Victorian-at-sea rejects this conventional postcolonial argument of deconstructing the map and insists instead on the absolute failure to map at all. In *English Passengers*, the crew of the *Sincerity* relies on outdated charts, one which marks the Cape Colony "as Dutch . . . which took us back to

Napoleon himself" (Kneale, 2000, p. 107), and, after an almost blind sailing to the antipodes, decide to set their course according to "a little sketch map drawn by some doctor friend of Potter's" (ibid., p. 272). Barrett's *Voyage of the Narwhal* offers an even more striking example of cartographic catastrophe; unable to imagine a conventional voyage or narrative, the ship remains stalled in ice for much of the novel. Frozen in place and unable to navigate, the crew eventually has to abandon the *Narwhal* to conclude the journey on foot across the ice. Even *Sea of Poppies* concludes with a cliffhanger, leaving the reader unclear if any destination is to be reached. The neo-Victorian-at-sea's depiction of cartographic failure appears at odds with its insistence on the map itself and this uncertainty is worth exploring further.

The failure to map emphasizes the very themes and shifting memories of the Victorian as empire I have been tracing in this book. Do we remember – and experience – imperialism in the present as more territorially bounded, akin to the "old imperialism" offered by conventional neo-Victorian texts that takes place through the acquisition and control of sovereign nations – as the wars in Iraq and Afghanistan underscore? If we choose the sea, do we eschew the prominence and enhancement of state power in favor of Hardt and Negri's concept of a decentered, globalized, deterritorialized Empire? Moreover, these novels map, in their paradoxical failure to map, the qualities of a defined and thus potentially exhausted genre. The sea, I argue, can also be read as a metaphor for the metaphor of genre. The maps of the neo-Victorian-at-sea express the crisis that neo-Victorian studies might have run out of space and texts to colonize and yet is simultaneously opening and constructing new markets for consumption. Thus, we can chart the trajectory in the ever-proliferating academic writing about the neo-Victorian toward other nineteenth centuries and an inching later and later into the Edwardian and beyond, seeing in the awkwardly named "neo-forties" fiction the traces of neo-Victorianism. The neo-Victorian-at-sea can mark both the apotheosis and the unraveling of neo-Victorianism, with the sea indicating an anxiety over what Derrida has called the "floodgate of genre" (Derrida, 1980, p. 66) that opens up a madness of classification and distinctions. The contradictory mapping practices of the neo-Victorian-at-sea therefore outlines the "law of genre" which also implies a counter-law, "a law of impurity or a principle of contamination" (ibid., p. 57), that is, a genre's internal history of its own production that causes it to dissolve. The implications of this kind of genre-death for postcolonialism's partnership with the neo-Victorian are striking. On the one hand, the natural tendency of neo-Victorian studies to canonize postcolonial neo-Victorian texts and authors seems counter-productive given postcolonialism's investments in resisting totalizing narratives. On the other, a postcolonial approach continues to reveal the powerplay behind neo-Victorianism's insistence on or expansion of the genre and calls our attention, as neo-Victorian scholars, to the ways we are being asked to police the borders of difference.

Somewhere Beyond the Sea: Neo-Victorianism's Future

I have demonstrated that in their negotiation of globalizing forces, *English Passengers* and *Sea of Poppies* redraw the boundaries of a generically and geographically viable neo-Victorianism. As content drives the changes in form, I want to conclude with a brief discussion of two texts – China Miéville's *The Scar* (2002) and David Mitchell's *Cloud Atlas* (2004) – that illustrate a commitment to a global, deterritorialized Victorian and might serve as a forecast for the future of neo-Victorianism. *Cloud Atlas* is framed by the nineteenth century while *The Scar* merely "feels" Victorian because of its retro-futuristic technological backdrop. Both novels focus on sea journeys; both feature alternative worlds built around cycles of colonialism, corporative exploitations and other forms of asymmetrical power; and both trouble the distinction between temporal elision and rupture as their structure of relation to the past. Both might be classified as novels that "play" under the sign of the Victorian, however, to claim these novels as neo-Victorian arguably violates meaning in the texts. So, what new mnemic strategies can be gained from such radical explorations of the nineteenth century's imbrication in the present and what might the Victorian continue to facilitate in these two novels?

To encompass his Marxist politics and his novels' *outré* literary status, China Miéville has coined the unwieldy terms "New Weird" (Cooper, 2009, p. 213) and now, "radical fantasy" (Jameson, 2002, p. 273) to describe his "Bas-Lag" trilogy. Bas-Lag, the "most boldly and meticulously realized alternative world in fiction," according to Carl Freedman, "serves the ultimate purpose of providing a locus where ideas of socialist revolution can be experimentally concretized" (Freedman, 2005, p. 238). The poetics of the collective and dialectical political agenda of Miéville's trilogy reminded reviewers of steampunk, specifically "Marxist steampunk" (quoted in Kendrick, 2009, p. 259), and critics of what "steampunk ought to be" (ibid.). Based on what Miéville deems a "chaos-fucked Victorian London" (Gordon, 2003), the description of the sprawling cityscape of New Crobuzon in all three novels remains in keeping with steampunk's alternate histories of imperial centers. Vaguely reminiscent of functioning city-states in our own time and space, characters experience New Crobuzon as a "profane steam-powered god" (Miéville, 2000, p. 623): a network of neighborhoods, often differentiated by species, with uneven access to the city's wealth and power. Populated by hybrid creatures such as garudas, khepri, cactacae, amphibian vodynoi; multidimensional monstrosities; sentient techno-entities; and perhaps, most importantly, cruelly and mechanically-modified human criminals called the Remade, the Bas-Lag world maintains a self-conscious interest in postcolonial politics, race and labor processes. The novels' combination of the occult and scientific technology, what Miéville calls "thaumaturgy," resonates strongly with neo-Victorianism's depiction of the Victorian as an improvised and "undisciplined" (Clayton, 2003, p. 7) scientific culture. The steampunk qualities and the metropolitan and frontier landscapes anchored by New Crobuzon often code Miéville's trilogy as "neo-Victorian," even as they appear as a node of contention in the online discussions of *The Great Steampunk Debate* and *Steampunk Scholar*.[6] While Miéville's work may be far removed from the neo-Victorian fiction I have discussed so far, I argue that his deployment of the neo-Victorian, even as mere effect, nonetheless affirms that the nineteenth century is still required as a touchstone for the discussion of empire.

For my purposes, Miéville's second Bas-Lag novel, *The Scar*, correlates most closely with the neo-Victorian-at-sea. Following the conspiratorial events and political purges of *Perdido Street Station* (2000), linguist Bellis Coldwine flees New Crobuzon on board the *Terpischoria* with its "hold full of prisoners; peons; indentured laborers and Remade" (Miéville, 2002, p. 2) for a new life on Nova Esperium, one of the Crobuzon Empire's isolated colonies. Hired as a translator between Crobuzoner officials and the Salkrikaltor cray, Bellis becomes party to the knowledge of the theft of a rig, the Sorghum, capable of drilling precious rock-milk from the sea floor. During negotiations, the cray insist that the *Terpischoria* change course to return a mysterious passenger, Crobuzoner informant, Silas Fennec, to the capital. The next day, pirates, led by the ruthless and inscrutable Uther Doul, attack the ship and her passengers, both free and Remade, are press-ganged to join the massive flotilla city of Armada. Patrolled from the sky by dirigibles and aerostats, towed through the ocean by a fleet of tugs and vessels, Armada has inched slowly through Bas-Lag's oceans, gradually increasing in size, might and wealth through centuries of piracy.

Bellis describes Armada as a city constructed out of "old boat bones" (Miéville, 2002, p. 75): thousands of purloined ships are refitted and reshaped, lashed together to form Armada's bulk, each ship "built up, topped with structure; style and materials shoved together from a hundred histories and esthetics into a compound architecture" (ibid.). Despite its carnivalesque appearance and population of "women and men in lush, ragged dress . . . street children, the cactacae and khepri, hotchi, llorgirs, massive gessin, and vumurt and others," Armada's hybridity is "stark and uncharming" (ibid., p. 78). Newly-kidnapped "citizens" of Armada are swiftly processed by the city's massive bureaucracy, provided with housing, given employment and incorporated into Armada's economic system. While the hundreds of Remade criminals rejoice in their new freedom, Bellis and her human passengers soon realize that citizenship on Armada means unacceptable exile from New Crobuzon. In keeping with the tropes I have identified in the neo-Victorian-at-sea, *The Scar* engages with the multilinguistic aspects of global space: communication on Armada is conducted in the hybrid discourse of Salt, "the sailors" argot, a found language riveted together from the thousand vernaculars of the Basilisk Channel, Ragamoll, and Perrickish, the tongues of the Pirate and Jheshull Islands' (ibid., p. 21). Like the many sailors of the neo-Victorian-at-sea, *The Scar* also presents mapping as a failure: Bellis and Silas "tried to trace a route home" (ibid., p. 199) and fail, thus jumpstarting the series of disastrous events that lead the Crobuzoner navy to Armada. Finally, Armada, like many neo-Victorian ships, will never reach its destination.

Administered from various ridings, Armada's leadership lies centralized in the Lovers, an enigmatic and powerful couple, scarred by freggios in the mirror image of each other. Their plans for Armada are simple: use thaumaturgy and sorcery to conjure a mythical sea-creature, the avanc, from a hole in the sea "that stretched down below the reach of any geo-empath" (Miéville, 2002, p. 362); harness its immense body to the massive chains attached to Armada's main ships; control its progress through the water with a constant injection of mined rock-milk; and coerce their adopted city to sail to a geographical impossibility and "ontological condition" (Palmer, 2009, p. 231) simply called the Scar, a rift in the world made by extraterrestrial beings, a place where reality is "pounded" by "great waves of puissance" (Miéville, 2002, p. 476) and "thick with seams of what might be, all the possible ways" (ibid., p. 542). The novel's vast plot is too detailed to cover here, however, both Bellis and her reluctant Remade accomplice, Tanner Sack, soon realize that they have been ensnared in an elaborate plot of intrigue and power master-minded at first by Silas Fennec, and then by Uther Doul: one, a Crobuzoner spy in the land of the fearsome Gengriss, in search of a "free market to power" with "trade, colonies and all that they entailed" (ibid., p. 521) and the other, a scholar and warrior in the ways of "possibility mining" (ibid., p. 543), the ability to tap the Scar's simultaneities of "the way things weren't and aren't but could be" (ibid.) in the name of absolute power.

The Scar offers a complicated allegory of globalization's uneven geopolitical realities that still partially draws on the Victorian to explore neo-imperial cosmopolitics. As Christopher Kendrick argues in his article on the novel's fictive geography and exploration of capitalism's stages of development, New Crobuzon functions as the major competitor for world power, its "appetite for trade, raw materials and colonies figures a familiar or traditional sort of capitalist imperialism" (Kendrick, 2009, p. 267). With its cultural and political dominance secured by trade and military, especially naval, prowess, New Crobuzon operates as a typical, nineteenth-century sovereign state. However, if this novel is to effectively allegorize the vast scope of the "global ethnoscapes" (Appadurai, 1996, p. 33) that Appadurai claims are a characteristic of modernity and if it is to challenge the forces of global capitalism, then other strategies, other landscapes beyond the Victorian as empire, must be employed or, at least, entertained. Against New Crobuzon's more familiar Victorianness, Armada becomes an alternative, it exercises its authority as a "pirate city, ruled by cruel mercantilism, existing in the pores of the world, snatching new citizens from their ships, a floating Freetown for buying and selling stolen goods, where might made right" (Miéville, 2002, p. 77). As its name suggests, Armada alludes to a history of maritime militarism, including piracy, from the sixteenth century onward that has gone hand in hand with the rise of capitalism and that can best be described as "preimperialist" (Kendrick, 2009, p. 267) in scope. Armada's quest to harness the potentialities of the Scar, however, described by its sole survivor as a massive irregular fissure opening up into empty space, leaking possible realities into its environs, "seems to aim at a kind of virtual presence to all points of the map, which puts one in the mind of fantasies of globalization" (ibid.). To other critics, the chaos and rupture caused by the Scar conjures up moments of contact between the colonial and the postcolonial and recalls encounters between Europeans and the New World (Dillon, 2007, p.14). To these already entangled systems of power, the novel adds a tiered understanding of global economies and cultures: the Gengris occupy an alien frontier space in the novel where feared apparatus of terror, "salp vats" and "weapons farms," (Miéville, 2002, p. 519) are a reality. Racinated and orientalized by the dominant Crobuzoner imagination, they are commonly described as the "grindylow, aquatic demons or monsters or degenerate crossbred men and women" (ibid., p. 125). The Gengris stalk Armada throughout its journey for unknowingly harboring Silas Fennec and his theft of strategic plans and maps to complete a "feasibility study" (ibid., p. 521) of Grindylow territories and holdings in order to build a Crobuzoner canal and open up the empire to new markets and trade routes. Seeking knowledge of the avanc, Armada also visits the dreaded Anophlean Islands, once a powerful but mindless empire ruled by monstrous and insatiable mosquito-like females, now reduced to a largely impotent colony cut off from the rest of the world. Even in this Remade context, colonialism and the process of Othering prevail as the dominant modes of making sense of the world; even Remade, the novel suggests, describing empire still requires the Victorian to anchor power hierarchies that are deeply embedded, systemic processes.

Deceived by Fennec that New Crubuzon, "her city which she treasured with a ferocious, unromantic love" (Miéville, 2002, p. 105), is under threat from an imminent Gengris attack, Bellis convinces Tanner Sack to aid her in delivering a message to New Crubuzon enclosed with a secret tracking device for Armada. After confessing their treason to Uther Doul, both Bellis and Tanner receive brutal floggings as punishment for their betrayal of Armada, their scars a permanent reminder of Armada's wrath. For Bellis, our neo-Victorian representative, if you will, scars and wounds are traumatic, violent acts of forced memorialization committed in the name of authority and power. Her scars illustrate that Armada's apparatus of suppression severely dampens its ability to function as what Appadurai calls a "grassroots" (Appadurai, 1996, p. 168) postnational formation that might be "more diverse, more fluid, more ad hoc, more provisional, less coherent, less organized, and simply less implicated in the comparative advantages of the nation-state" (ibid.), capable of offering resistance and critique from below. When the Crobuzoner navy attacks Armada and is crushed by Armada's suicide tactics, Bellis and Tanner realize too late the brutality of both their homeland and their adopted state. The events of the novel redefine and negativize the acts of recovery I have been tracing, reinforcing the idea that violence lies at the root of the power of appropriation, that the present's appropriation of the past is merely the proliferation of scar material, and that what seams memories together in any imperial context is accretions of pain.

The Scar recalls the Victorian in order to resist the Victorian, in the sense that the novel rejects any kind of ideological imperialism in its quest for a utopian vision of plurality. If New Crubuzon and Armada remain undefeated and unchampioned, it is because the novel refuses to favor utopia, singular notions of community, individual action or hubris, or definitive versions of past and future. Violence occurs, the novel suggests, when characters act with singular vision in mind: the Lovers' quest for the absolute power of the

Scar is challenged by the return of Armada's scout, a possible Hedrigall and his experience of an alternate Armada's annihilation, or Bellis and Tanner's patriotism which earns them both a flogging, the violent and permanent marks of Armada justice. Instead, it attempts to achieve balance in all its social alternatives, hoping to finesse the "possibility mining" advanced by Uther Doul, even if Doul remains cold, calculating, asexual and ultimately without allegiance. Insofar as *The Scar* is and is not neo-Victorian, it suggests that perhaps no account of neo-imperialism can occur without a consideration of the British Empire in the nineteenth century. However, the Victorian in *The Scar* has been Remade; Miéville has "wound[ed] it and heal[ed] it in a new reconfiguration" (Miéville, 2002, p. 575) so that it exists as merely a trace of the previously enabling relationship between neo-Victorianism and postcolonial politics. The weakness of the Victorian in *The Scar* necessitates that it is only one of many weapons in Miéville's arsenal of revolutionary strategies in addressing how individual choice and collective action can resist and facilitate globalization's forces.

The Scar concludes on the eve of Bellis' anticlimactic release to New Crobuzon and her reflections on her journal, an open "Possible Letter" (Miéville, 2002, p. 577) that will never be delivered to an unknown recipient and thus, forestalls the future. While Armada never reaches the Scar, it has been abandoned by one of the Lovers and will never be the same again and while Bellis' return as a prodigal remains ambiguous, she too has changed:

> I cannot be used anymore. Those days are over. I know too much. What I do now, I do for me. And I feel, for all that has happened, as if it is now, only now in these days, that my journey is beginning. I feel as if this – even all this – has been a prologue. (ibid., p. 578)

Bellis' Remade relationship to New Crobuzon suggests a decentered and alienated but newly committed individual capable of a cosmopolitan awareness. By cosmopolitan, I mean that Bellis can position herself, at the very least, outside of the structures of nation and is open, however vulnerably and ambivalently, to different ways of being in the world. Thus, *The Scar* accompanies David Mitchell's *Cloud Atlas*, to which I will now turn, which also utilizes the trope of the sea to explore cosmopolitan ideals in the context of the realities of globalization. If, as many have argued, globalization is a *fait accompli*, we have become incapacitated by the restructured forces of capitalism and technology and helpless in any kind of individual or collective political action. In such a reading, cosmopolitanism emerges as an antidote. The various divisions of cosmopolitan studies are too many to enumerate here, but several constants persist: whether it is the rhetoric of global community, "world citizenship" (Nussbaum), "planetary humanism" (Appiah) or "planetary conviviality" (Gilroy), all require a radical leave-taking of nation as the only model for "imagined community." In its global scope, however, cosmopolitanism must not lose sight of the local, the disenfranchised and the diversity of dissent. In addition to valuing human life and rights and nurturing global community, cosmopolitanism, in whatever guise it takes, targets totalitarianism and fundamentalism of all kinds.

The appearance of the Victorian in the cosmopolitan novel like *Cloud Atlas* can enable what Rebecca Walkowitz has called a "critical cosmopolitanism" that entails "an aversion to heroic tones of appropriation and progress, and a suspicion of epistemological privilege, views from above or from the center that assume a consistent distinction between who is seeing and what is seen" (Walkowitz, 2006, p. 2). According to Walkowitz, critical cosmopolitanism requires a constantly mobile, doubled, if not entangled, consciousness capable of ethical acts and self-reflection in the global sphere. If, as I have argued, the Victorian deftly encodes the discourse and experiences of imperialism into its visual and textual presence, then, its deployment in a novel such as *Cloud Atlas* cautions us that cosmopolitanism, in its evocations of global designs and as a politics of inclusion, can be evoked to "support or tolerate imperialism" (ibid., p. 4) in the present. At the very least, the return to the Victorian in a cosmopolitan context can represent the stubborn attachments to locality and the past. Conversely, the demands of cosmopolitanism can unveil a critique of neo-Victorianism's deficiencies in imagining more future-driven, nuanced ways of being with the world.

Elegantly simply, *Cloud Atlas's* unique experimental structure supports its complex arguments about time, history and cosmopolitan commonality. Essentially six fragmented but complete and connected novellas, the novel advances more or less chronologically from the 1850s, beginning with an excerpt from "The Pacific Journal of Adam Ewing," toward the novel's center with a narrative entitled "Sloosha's Crossin' An' Ev'rything After" set in an indeterminate, postapocalyptic future on the Hawaiian islands. It then reverses through the narratives allowing the divided sections to conclude. The nineteenth-century story that functions both as the novel's past and, chronologically, as its beginning thus ends the novel as its future in the order of our reading experience. Except for "Sloosha's Crossin," Mitchell embeds each tale textually within the one proceeding it, like "matryoshka dolls" (Mitchell, 2004, p. 393): in the 1930s, Ewing's diary is discovered by Robert Frobisher, the composer of the *Cloud Atlas Sextet,* in "Letters From Zedelghem," which are then received by Rufus Sixsmith, the physicist who, in 1970s California, will write the report that will uncover the unsafe standards at the Swannekke nuclear power plant, which is delivered to the media by Luisa Rey, the heroine of "Half-Lives: The First Luisa Rey Mystery," edited by the hapless and aging publisher in post-imperial Britain, Thomas Cavendish, whose narrative turns out to be the plot of the "disney" (ibid., p. 213), "The Ghastly Ordeal of Thomas Cavendish," watched by the "ascended" fabricant Sonmi-451, who, after penning her revolutionary Declarations, becomes a god to the remaining "civ'lized" (ibid., p. 244) tribe on the island of Ha-Why. Clever connections also emerge in each section and proliferate as each story unfolds: *The Prophetess,* the ship that carries Ewing to Honolulu, for example, has been preserved as a historical relic in the Buenas Yerbe marina where Luisa Rey meets her would-be assassin. Suggestions of reincarnation, uncanny memories, déjà vu and the physical detail of a comet-shaped birthmark that the protagonists all share also add to the novel's interest in pursuing a global commonality across time where individual actions have real and "virtual" effects.

Each section of the novel playfully engages with specific genres, literary forms and intertexts best suited to the novel's critique of tyranny and exploitation and its interests in the limits of individual and collective conscience and resistance. The title of "The Orison of Sonmi-451," for example, should remind readers of contemporary science fiction such as *Fahrenheit 451* and "Orison's" denouement derives from 1970s movies like *Logan's Run* and *Soylent Green.* Not surprisingly, therefore, a summary of "The Pacific Journal of Adam Ewing" will reveal its reliance on sea-faring fiction from Defoe to Conrad to Melville as well as on the tropes of postcolonial neo-Victorianism and the neo-Victorian-at-sea. The novel opens in the Chatham Isles with Adam Ewing, a notary from San Francisco, following a "trail of recent footprints" on a beach to a "White man" (Mitchell, 2004, p. 3), the notorious Dr Henry Goose, who is busy searching for the teeth of cannibals for a pair of dentures that will humiliate a "She-Donkey" (ibid., p. 4) marchioness who had him "black-balled from Society" (ibid.). Dispelling the notion of an isolated experience in favor of a rapidly shrinking globe, Ewing notes, "if there by an eyrie so desolate, or isle so remote, that one may there resort unchallenged by an Englishman, 'tis not down on any map I ever saw" (ibid., p. 3). The meeting of these two men, far from home, "beyond the Indian hamlet, upon a forlorn strand" (ibid.), makes an argument for transnational experience (along with whiteness and masculinity) as the precondition for a cosmopolitan outlook. The bizarre meeting between Ewing and Goose is juxtaposed against another encounter, "below the Indian hamlet" (ibid., p. 6) this time, where Ewing witnesses the public flogging of a slave. Ewing embarrassingly "swoons" after "the beaten savage raised his slumped head, found out *my* eye & shone me a look of uncanny, amicable knowing!" (ibid.). Unknowingly, Ewing has just met Autua, the Moriori slave and stowaway, who will eventually save Ewing from being poisoned by Goose, revealed at the end of "Journal" as a vicious swindler and a quack. Autua's punishment stems from his refusal to accept his slave-status because he has "seen too much o' the world" (ibid., p. 29) as a deckhand and sailor. Here, the rerouted gaze of a slave marks a more complicated moment of the transnational where cosmopolitanism can flourish, where individuals like Autua, alienated by race, economics or migration, are, even "before national borders have been crossed . . . already the subject of a transnation" (Ashcroft, 2010, p. 72). Set in the nineteenth century, however, the germs of global citizenship that Autua represents and that Ewing will soon learn to cultivate are nonetheless shown to be brutal and locatable in colonialism and slavery.

In Autua, we find a trans-Pacific hybridized character whose travels index the transculturation of Gilroy's Black Atlantic beyond its previous boundaries. His presence on board the ship exposes Ewing to the history and demise of the idealized, indigenous Moriori on the Chatham Isles who were conquered and exterminated by Maori warriors and English settlers. Like *English Passengers*, "Journal" concerns itself with the extinction of the Moriori but remains sensitive to how colonial trauma can be politicized: Ewing briefly entertains the accusation that D'Arnoq, a preacher and a "mixed-blood mongrel of a man" (Mitchell, 2004, p. 16) embellished Moriori history "only to legitimize his own swindling land claims against the Maori, the true owners of the Chathams" (ibid.). But, like *Sea of Poppies*, the long ship journey in Autua's presence works to erode and eventually disrupt Ewing's scientific racism and ethnocentrism. Like Frederick Douglass, Autua's travels put him in contact with the ideologies of liberation and democracy that Ewing, as an American, expounds but does not yet practice. Dramatically rescued by Autua, Ewing commits himself to the "Abolitionist cause" and to a new system of beliefs: "if we believe that humanity may transcend tooth & claw, if we believe divers races & creeds can share this world as peaceably as orphans share their candlenut tree . . . such a world will come to pass" (ibid., p. 508). Despite his father-in-law's intonation that Ewing's new-found cosmopolitanism is naïve and "Whiggish" (ibid.) because his life "amounted to nothing more than one drop in a limitless ocean,"

Ewing ends his journal with a revised message of hope, "yet what is any ocean but a multitude of drops?" (ibid., p. 509).

All the major elements of neo-Victorian fiction and the neo-Victorian-at-sea are represented in "Journal" – trauma, politicized postcolonial memory, settler colonialism, imperialism, a resourceful Other who, in this case, forces Ewing to revise his prejudices, and connections to a geopolitical present refracted through a sea voyage – and harnessed to a cosmopolitan project. The results of reading "The Pacific Journal of Adam Ewing" as a neo-Victorian frame narrative are lucrative. It becomes possible, for example, to treat the nineteenth century as traumatic rupture, a moment of origin for the dystopias of the future: the greediness for "treasure, gold, spices & dominion" (Mitchell, 2004, p. 489) that underlie the civilizing missions of the Victorian as empire repeats in the conquest of the Moriori by the Maori, in the Valleymen being hunted by the Kona tribe in "Slosha's Crossin'," between "fabricants" (ibid., p. 185) and "pure-bloods" (ibid., p. 218) in "Orison of Sonmi-451" and, to a certain extent, in society's persecution of the elderly characters in "The Ghastly Ordeal of Thomas Cavendish."[7] As an explicit memory of empire, the depiction of the Victorian in *Cloud Atlas* cautions readers against the acceptance of an over-simplified, humanistic cosmopolitanism that merely masks, as Gilroy has argued in *After Empire*, "intervention in other people's sovereign territory on the grounds that their ailing or incompetent national state has failed to measure up to the levels of good practice that merit recognition as civilized" (ibid., p. 60). This explains the discourse of civilization and imperialism that runs through Mitchell's novel: recording his conversation with D'Arnoq, Ewing writes, "I questioned if such an ill as too *much* civilization" existed or no? Mr D'Arnoq told me, "If there is no God west of the Horn, why there's non of your constitution's All men are created equal, neither, Mr. Ewing" (ibid., p. 10). Such appeals to morality carry through to all the other stories, from Ayers's desire to make "civilization ever more resplendent" (ibid., p. 81) with the genius of his musical compositions to the Prescient ethics of contact, embodied in Zach'ry's relationship with Meronym, "we Prescients din't b'lief our weak flame o' Civ'lize was now the brightest in the Hole World, an' further an' further we sailed year by year, but we din't find no flame brighter. So lonesome we felt" (ibid., p. 271). The conflation of raw imperial power with moral and racial arguments in "Journal's" nineteenth-century setting correlates strongly with the "new armored cosmopolitanism" (ibid., p. 63) that Gilroy finds so problematically characteristic of twenty-first century politics. Essentially a barely disguised "ethical imperialism," contemporary cosmopolitanism, according to Gilroy, consists of a coalition of "willing national states oriented by the goal of enforcing a desiderata of peace, privatization, and market mechanisms on a global scale" (ibid., p. 62) and who legitimize and justify this business by appealing to moralistic arguments. This particular challenge of being in the same present has much in common with the embedded presents of Mitchell's novel.

Despite the strength of such readings, they privilege the nineteenth-century as the cause of the deficiencies and drawbacks of globalization and classify the novel, partly, as neo-Victorian in much the same way that by focusing on "Orison of Sonmi-451" or "Sloosha's Crossin'" might designate it as futuristic or postapocalyptic. The novel's arguments about time, however, insist that we forego such classifications. In "Half-Lives" Isaac Sachs ruminates on his attraction to Luisa Rey and on the relationship between actual and virtual pasts and futures. Using another ship, the Titanic, as an example, he describes a neo-historical project, one that any neo-Victorian scholar would recognize: "a virtual sinking of the Titanic, created from reworked memories, paper, hearsay, fiction – in short, belief, grows ever 'truer'." Such a "virtual past," according to Sachs, is "malleable, ever-brightening + ever more difficult to circumvent/expose as fraudulent" (ibid., p. 392). Like any strong neo-Victorian project, "the present presses the virtual past into its own service, to lend credence to its mythologies + legitimacy to the imposition of will. Power seeks + is the right to 'landscape' the virtual past" (ibid., p. 393). As I have argued, neo-Victorianism can itself be considered such an "imposition of will," recovering and crafting a "virtual past" for the political and psychic recovery of the present. However, *Cloud Atlas* is not a neo-Victorian novel and through Sachs, demands "symmetry" (ibid., p. 393) in its form. In addition to "virtual pasts," we are asked to consider "virtual futures" constructed out of "wishes, prophecies + daydreams" (ibid., p. 393). In the novel's temporal logic, the Victorian past transforms into its "virtual future" rendering the "actual future" not the stark, tribal landscape of "Sloosha's Crossin'," not yet. Unwritten and unmapped, the future remains open to the possible: Ewing's beliefs that "leaders must be just, violence muzzled, power accountable & the riches of the Earth & its Oceans shared equitably" (ibid., p. 508).

Reconceived as the future rather than as hegemonic past, the Victorian is decentered; it becomes no less crucial than the novel's other cautionary tales of choice between globalization's homogenization of the masses, what Gilroy calls "seriality," represented in the novel's themes of clones and repetition, and "radically individualistic view[s] of humanity" (Gilroy, 2004, p. 64) that render solidarity and collective action problematic in 1970s California, 1930s Europe, contemporary Britain, futuristic Korea, or the end of history in Hawaii. Like *The Scar*, *Cloud Atlas* plies the neo-Victorian to challenge our tendency toward progressivist models of historical thought. Instead of the temporal disjunction of the neo-Victorian, *Cloud Atlas* offers what Jo Alyson Parker calls, in her analysis of the novel's manipulation of narrative time, the continuities of the "Long Now" (Parker, 2010, p. 210), which, for me, offers a way of conceiving of neo-Victorianism as "*this* was once now." The novel creates a new structure of relation to the "now" – rather than the past – that provides a "vision of the future linked to the past and present, which is intended to make clear the importance, the necessity, of acting responsibly" (ibid.). Implied in *Cloud Atlas* is a critique of neo-Victorianism's obsessive recreations of a "virtual past;" the novel questions whether or not recreation or adaptation is compatible with the ethical imagination of "virtual futures." Instead, *Cloud Atlas* constructs a new temporal landscape, a carefully crafted "nests of presents" (Mitchell, 2004, p. 393), that allows us to conceive of the "neo" differently and ethically as the "now-Victorian" rather than the Victorian for now. Ethical action, in other words, comes from treating the past and the future as the present, as the always now.

"Lady Franklin's Lament"

There is little to suggest that neo-Victorianism will become obsolete: healthy numbers of neo-Victorian texts across media and culture are being produced and consumed by academic and popular audiences alike around the world. Even as this book was being prepared for publication, Ghosh's second installment of the *Ibis* trilogy, *River of Smoke* (2011) was released; Carol Birch's whaling adventure, *Jamrach's Menagerie* (2011) was shortlisted for the Booker Prize; new postcolonial adaptations of Brontë favorites are currently being screened at international film festivals. However, there are signs that the dominance of neo-Victorianism's mnemic and political functions for the present are being challenged by the recall of other periods (as the recent line of inquiry into "neo-historical fiction" suggests), by other genres such as "New Weird" fiction and cosmopolitanism, and by other praxis of the contemporary.

On the one hand, *The Scar* and *Cloud Atlas* indicate limited directions for, at least, postcolonial neo-Victorianism's ability to unveil neo-imperial practices and structures. If, as I have argued, the story of neo-Victorianism has also been, in part, the story of postcolonialism and postcolonial theory's ability to reveal and register the atrocities and ongoing inequities of colonialism, then perhaps the decentering of the neo-Victorian by Miéville and Mitchell provide evidence that, due to the exigencies of globalization, neoliberal capitalism, mass migration and postnational identity politics, the contours of empire in the present have shifted significantly. So significantly, in fact, that what was once a prominent mode of postcolonial recall in the nationalist discourses of the late-twentieth century, as reflected in the work of Carey, Atwood, Moore and others, may no longer be the dominant strategy for negotiating the boundaries and experiences of the "post" after the millennium. The similarities that once made us, at least in the West, those "Other" Victorians may have become increasingly unrecognizable. On the other hand, Miéville and Mitchell's work make a convincing argument that different, more innovative explorations of temporality and historicity will be required to resist the supposed linearity of globalization's narrative. Their novels challenge us to boldly experiment with our critical approaches to and expectations for the Victorian in the present to produce narratives beyond those which privilege imperialism, conquest and settlement as the origin of current global systems, especially at the margins. Until then, non-Anglocentric examples of neo-Victorianism may remain rare or neo-Victorianism may be relegated to a reading demographic located solely in the West. As new cartographies, real and imaginary, proliferate, it remains to be seen if the "N-word" and the "V-word" can be expanded beyond a contact zone with British imperialism and trade and function as a viable floating signifier for other nineteenth centuries and histories of colonialism and empires.

Notes

Introduction

[1] For a reading of the cultural value of Queen Victoria's body and statues to the formation of the empire, see Adrienne Munich's essay "Queen Victoria, Empire and Excess" (1987).

[2] Take, for example, Christian Gutleben's book, *Nostalgic Postmodernism: The Victorian Trend and the Contemporary British Novel* (2001), Simon Joyce's *The Victorians in the Rearview Mirror* (2007), Louisa Hadley's *Neo-Victorian Fiction and Historical Narratives* (2010) and Kate Mitchell's *History and Cultural Memory in Neo-Victorian Fiction* (2010): all take primarily British novels as their archives.

[3] Similarly, Jay Clayton's project in *Charles Dickens in Cyberspace: The Afterlife of the Nineteenth Century in Postmodern Culture* (2003) reveals postmodernism's indebtedness to the nineteenth century, specifically the Romantics, and simultaneously argues that the Victorian definition of "culture" haunts contemporary cultural studies.

[4] Kucich and Sadoff prefer the term "post-Victorian" as it resonates with their interests in postmodernism; concerned with the genre's implicit conservative politics, Gutleben refers to the return to the Victorian as "retro-Victorian;" while Cora Kaplan, hoping to expand the field, opts for "Victoriana."

[5] Suzanne Keen, for example, makes few distinctions between neo-Victorianism and a much larger "vogue for new historical fiction" (Keen, 2006, p. 172) in contemporary culture and the publishing industry.

[6] Across the board, there is an acknowledgment of the role that the market plays in constructing and responding to our desire for particular versions of the Victorian (the "bodice ripper" romance, for example, or Andrew Davies's sexy adaptations of Victorian novels for television) and the "more complex paradigms" (Heilmann and Llewellyn, 2010, p. 7) of neo-Victorian texts.

[7] For a history of the development of Victorian Studies, see Taylor and Wolff's *The Victorians Since 1901: Histories, Representations and Revisions* (2004).

[8] Heilmann has discussed the neo-Victorian in Sarah Waters's "neo-forties" novel, *The Little Stranger* (2009) and Alejandro Amenábar's 2001 film, *The Others* in her conference paper, "The Ancestral Home Revisited, or Neo-Victorian Spectral Returns in the Neo-Forties," most recently at the "Fashioning the Neo-Victorian" conference at the University of Erlangen – Nuremberg, 2007.

[9] See the "Aims and Scope" section of *Neo-Victorian Studies*, <http://www.neovictorianstudies.com/>.

[10] Niall Ferguson's book *Colossus: The Rise and Fall of the American Empire* (2005) is probably the most well-known and controversial comparison between American

power and the British empire. For more thoughtful approaches, see the essays in *New Imperialists: Ideologies of Empire* (2006), edited by Colin Mooers; and Porter's *Empire and Superempire: Britain, America and the World* (2006).

11. For an excellent overview of postcolonial theory's continued necessity to globalization studies, especially in the wake of Hardt and Negri's *Empire*, see Ania Loomba et al.'s introduction to *Postcolonial Studies and Beyond* (2005). An alternative view might be Amitav Kumar's provocative question, "can 'World Bank Literature' be a new name for postcolonial studies?" (Kumar, 2003, p. xx). Implied in Kumar's question is a lack of faith in postcolonialism's ability to register the complexities and new dominances of the world capitalist system.

12. Kate Mitchell's chapter, "Memory texts: history, fiction and the historical imaginary" (2010), helpfully offers a dense overview of the critical shift from historical discourse and knowledge to cultural memory in a neo-Victorian context. While we share similar critical positions, Mitchell's work pivots on neo-Victorian fiction's self-reflexive interactions with technologies of memory that produce memory while I focus on neo-Victorianism as a site-specific politics of memory.

13. Prime Minister Kevin Rudd's official apology to indigenous Australians, for example, mirrors exactly this unproblematic national model of recovery: "the time has now come for the nation to turn a new page in Australia's history by righting the wrongs of the past and so moving forward with confidence to the future" (Rudd, 2008).

14. Marie-Luis Kohlke treads similar ground in her discussion of trauma and neo-Victorianism in the introduction to the inaugural issue of the *Neo-Victorian Studies* (2008) and in the introduction (co-authored with Christian Gutleben) to a recent collection of essays, *Neo-Victorian Tropes of Trauma* (2010). Central to Kohlke's argument about trauma and neo-Victorianism is the genre's ability to bear witness to the past.

15. See Judith Herman's *Trauma and Recovery* (1992), pp. 214–36.

16. "Modern American literature" is the glaring omission in Byatt's novel and arguably in neo-Victorianism in general. I choose to read "modern American literature" as Byatt's perhaps unconscious codeword for problems arising from racial and cultural diversity, neo-imperialism, economic might – for everything, in other words, that the English might have to apologize for. Understanding U.S. power via the British Empire is both explicit and implicit in many of the neo-Victorian texts I have chosen, however, the ways in which neo-Victorianism dovetails with the recovery of a history of slavery in nineteenth-century America in neo-slave narratives like Toni Morrison's *Beloved* (1987), Charles R. Johnson's novel, *Middle Passage* (1990) or, Suzan-Lori Parks" *Venus* (1997), remains unexplored. This omission might stem from the ethical issues surrounding the term "Victorian" that I discuss in this chapter.

17. For example, Peter Carey's *Oscar and Lucinda* and *True History of the Kelly Gang*; Kate Grenville's *The Secret River* (Australia); Margaret Atwood's *Alias Grace*; Michael Redhill's *Consolation* (Canada) are all either Booker winners (Carey has won twice) or were on the Booker long or shortlist. I explore aspects of the relationship of literary prizes to the creation of a neo-Victorian canon and how it affects the dynamics of center and periphery in Chapter 3.

[18] See Graham Huggan's argument in his chapter "Prizing otherness: a short history of the Booker" in *The Postcolonial Exotic* (2001).
[19] This influential reading of Hong Kong's postcolonial identity can be found in Ackbar Abbas's *Hong Kong: Culture and the Politics of Disappearance* (1997a).

Chapter 1

[1] Friday 31st, August, 1888: Whitechapel. Two men find the body of a 45-year old woman, her throat cut, her body disemboweled. Identified as Mary Ann Nichols, she is commonly thought to be the first victim of Jack the Ripper. From August to November, the unknown killer claimed the lives of four more women: Annie Chapman, Catherine Eddowes, Elizabeth Stride and Mary Jane Kelly. The "facts" of the case are few: five women, all prostitutes, all killed and brutally mutilated within the confines of London's East End. The one crucial fact that is missing is the identity of the killer who disappeared out of history after murdering Kelly on 9 November. The most influential sources of Ripperology are: Stephen Knight's *Jack the Ripper: the Final Solution* (1983) heavily relied on by Moore and Sinclair; Philip Sugden's *The Complete History of Jack the Ripper* (1994) and Paul Begg's 1988 book *Jack the Ripper: The Uncensored Facts*. The most recent controversial Ripper theory has been Patricia Cornwall's *Portrait of a Killer: Jack the Ripper Case Closed* (2003) in which she argued (after spending millions of her own money investigating the case) that painter Walter Sickert was the killer. For access to the wealth of information on the Whitechapel murders, the *Ripper Casebook* website (www.casebook.org) is a remarkable archive of historical documents, bibliographic information, Ripperology and hosts several Ripper message boards and wikis.
[2] All citations from *From Hell* will designate the chapter number first followed by page numbers. Roman numerals refer to the appendices.
[3] For further discussion of the political and cultural ramifications of Margaret Thatcher's own brand of neo-Victorianism, see Raphael Samuel's essay "Mrs. Thatcher's Return to Victorian Values" (1992) and section two, in particular, of Kate Mitchell's chapter, "Contemporary Victorian(ism)s" in *History and Cultural Memory in Neo-Victorian Fiction* (2010). Much of the discussion of Thatcherism and neo-Victorianism coincides with commentary and analysis of the British "heritage industry" in the 1980s; Suzanne Keen, however, offers a different context for post-imperial historical novels with research on the changes made to the British national curriculum regarding the teaching of history in the 1970s and 1980s. The changes adopted as part of the Education Reform Act in 1988 "set a national curriculum emphasizing the basics of British history" (Keen, 2001, p. 106) in place of its previous "multicultural, anti-racist thrust" (ibid.).
[4] See the poll, "What are the most popular fictional Ripper books?" (n.d.) at the *Ripper Casebook* website. *Dan Leno* or *The Trial of Elizabeth Cree*, its American title, is voted number 11 for "best Ripper fiction."
[5] Movies about the Whitechapel murders have been made since silent film, underscoring Jack the Ripper's appeal and also his relationship to modernity, but the late 1970s and 1980s saw a glut of television documentaries and Ripper films: *Murder By Decree* (1979); *Time After Time* (1979); *The Ripper* (1985); *Jack the Ripper*

(1988). *Time after Time* is one of the more interesting films for neo-Victorianism as the story follows H. G. Wells chasing the Ripper foward in time to San Francisco in the 1960s.

[6] Munich writes, for example, in her introduction to *Queen Victoria's Secrets*, "Queen Victoria was considered as the quintessential domestic figure but also a ruler of exotic lands; she was loved as a mother, though she claimed not to enjoy her own children's company; she was viewed as a prudish moral arbiter yet was ridiculed or feared as a woman hungry for sex; in her veins flowed the bluest blood, but in her heart she felt akin to the common people. What secrets permitted the culture to accommodate Queen Victoria's contradictory meanings?" (Munich, 1998, p. 3).

[7] See Heather Nunn's argument about the problems of anti-Thatcherite critique in her article, "Running Wild: Fictions of Gender and Childhood in Thatcher's Britain" (2001).

[8] See Claire Monk's chapter, "Underbelly UK: The 1990s underclass film, masculinity, and the ideologies of New Britain" in *British Cinema, Past and Present* (2000).

[9] Sean Nixon's contribution *British Cultural Studies* (2001) outlines the origins and subsequent scripting of the "new lad" and "new man" phenomenon in the context of Blair's "Cool Britannia." Significantly, Nixon points out that these "codings of masculinity" (Nixon, 2001, p. 384) are also ethnically coded, both expanding and limiting identities and consumer roles for British men.

[10] The ending of *White Chappell, Scarlet Tracings* reinforces this argument; escaping London, "Sinclair" visits Thorpe-le-Soken, Gull's ancestral home, and finds a ruined barge that Gull's father had been unconventionally buried in. "Sinclair" believes that the discovery will "release" his wife from "dreams of minatory buildings, a wind-invaded house, long corridors of strangers" and that he will return to this place with his children, "and the connection will be made, the circuit complete" (Sinclair, 1987, p. 210). Although a connection to a "living past" has been made, it is still commodified and limited to a heterosexual economy.

[11] For Thatcher's cross-dressing gender politics, see my co-authored introduction to the collected edition, *Thatcher & After: Margaret Thatcher and Her Afterlife in Contemporary Culture* (2010).

[12] In *Atlas of the European Novel* (1998), Franco Moretti describes a similar misremembering of the Victorian city as English in the answers to a poll he conducted amongst friends about Sherlock Holmes's London: "the answers were all very firm," he records, "fog, the East End, blind alleys, the Docks, the Thames, the Tower . . ." (Moretti, 1998, p. 134), despite the fact that Holmes entered the East End only once in his illustrious career.

[13] As Raphael Samuel notes, tongue-in-cheek, "there was no such thing as a market for old photographs before the 1970s" (Samuel, 1994, p. 337) as the heritage industry provoked and produced a desire for the patina of age.

[14] See Graham McPhee and Prem Poddar's *Empire and After: Englishness in Postcolonial Perspective* (2010). Arguably, psychogeography can contribute to what McPhee and Poddar define as a "new Englishness." These besieged locations allow Britain to assume the "pose of victimhood no longer representative of mastery and power," the "perennial loser" (McPhee and Poddar, 2010, p. 16) threatened by its devolved neighbors, a united Europe and immigrants.

[15] For an in-depth discussion of the centrality of the East End to British heritage and the work of Sinclair and Ackroyd, see Alex Murray's *Recalling London: Literature and History in the work of Peter Ackroyd and Iain Sinclair* (2007).

[16] The supplemental material released with the *From Hell* DVD contains 12 minutes of footage of the Whitechapel set being built in Prague. Incidentally, the Jackie Chan movie, *Shanghai Knights*, discussed in Chapter 4, was shot on the same Czech set (http://www.jigsawlounge.co.uk/film/shanghaiknights.html).

Chapter 2

[1] In the tradition of "writing back to empire," *Oscar and Lucinda* rewrites Edmund Gosse's autobiographical novel, *Father and Son* (1907).

[2] *Oscar and Lucinda*, for example, was published to coincide with Australia's Bicentennial celebrations: at its heart, the novel is an unconventional love story between an English clergyman and an Australian heiress, both eager to literally gamble their cultural and monetary inheritances away. While the novel deplores the destruction of an indigenous history and culture (in a way that *Jack Maggs* palpably doesn't) by the establishment of Christianity, it nonetheless mourns the passing of the sentiment of Christianity with Oscar's delivery of a fragile glass church to an isolated outback parish. *The True History of the Kelly Gang* (2001) celebrated the life and writing of Ned Kelly, the underdog Irish bushranger famous for evading capture by British troops for two years. *True History* reimagines the depth and emotional life of one of the founding figures of Anglo-Australian myth and history. Carey's return to bushranger myth and his reclamation of an Irish hero as a positive image of the past offered a ready patch for the seemingly divided Australia, debating its future as a republic on the cusp of the millennium.

[3] The edited collection, *Legacies of White Australia: Race, Culture and Nation* (2003), offers multiple perspectives on the history, aftermath and persistence of the White Australia policy. In his foreword to the edition, for example, Wang Gungwu states, "the idea of White Australia may have been enshrined in the Immigration Restriction Act in 1901, but the Act simply marked the climax of at least forty years of agitation during which the idea was fully shaped and justified" (Wang, 2003, p. vii). Exploring Australia's "foreign relations" in the region, Sean Brawley observes that "one hundred years after the passage of the Immigration Restriction Act, earlier reports of the demise of the White Australia policy were premature" (Brawley, 2003, p. 93).

[4] Ien Ang, who has been engaged in mapping multiculturalism's effects on Asian-Australians, reads the official, almost overnight, deletion of "race" in immigration law by the Labor Government in 1972, as traumatic, an "absent presence" and a "radical epistemological break" (Ang, 2001, p. 103) that disavows rather than confronts the "racist past of the nation, and . . . the central importance of racial differentiation in the very historical constitution of Australia as a nation state" (Ang, 2001, p. 104). Thus, white Australians, in particular, she suggests, have lost a language and a vocabulary to describe, discuss and integrate the very real and colorful landscape of racial difference around them.

[5] In 2010, Pauline Hanson had "had enough" (BBC News, 2010) of her psychological and political exile and expressed interest in immigrating "home" to Britain.

[6] Carey's project is similar to historians like Miriam Dixson who shy away from the "black armband" approach to Australia's settler past. Dixson discusses the necessity but the unpopularity or skittishness of critics to examine the cohesive properties of popular conceptions of and attachment to nation at the expense of the disintegration of the most basic communal bonds – a problem that neo-Victorianism also explores. Because Australia has not actually reached multiculturalism yet, during such a "vulnerable time of transition," she argues, "the core culture will have to continue acting as the baseline carrier of an imaginary for the emerging Australia" (Dixson, 1999, p. 164), especially because all Australians are "indebted" to the Anglo-Celtic core culture for the foundation of Australia's civic culture. Neither Dixson nor Carey is writing in defense of whiteness but both suggest that it is a renewed civic identity that white Australia needs to strive for.

[7] Rufus Dawes was the hero of Australian author Marcus Clarke's serialized novel, *His Natural Life*, which ran from 1870 to 1872.

[8] Pierce's book includes biographical excerpts from Carey. These are both a revelation of a pattern in Carey's work of lost children, orphans and sickly babies as well as the "true story" of Carey's first marriage and the couple's decision to terminate a pregnancy. In keeping with the themes of *Jack Maggs*, this is an example of a personal trauma informing and being informed by a national one.

[9] In 2006, Kate Grenville's novel *The Secret River* was short-listed for the Man Booker Prize. Also a neo-Victorian novel, Grenville's story of an uneasy relationship between settlers and convicts and the violence of settlement in nineteenth-century Australia was, if one follows Lamb's logic, a more "appropriately" anticolonial history. The fact that *The Secret River* did not win, however, lends support to Huggan's argument that the Booker industry, consciously or not, prizes revisionist histories that still propagate, even as they "write back" to, imperial myths and cruelties.

[10] *The True History of The Kelly Gang* is based on the Jerilderie Letter, a 56-page letter that Ned Kelly attempted to have printed in 1879. In an interview with Robert McCrum, Carey explains how the letter, unnoticed in a library somewhere in America, was bought by the State Library of Victoria in Australia a month after the novel's publication (McCrum, 2001). The archiving of Jack's letters as an act of healing anticipates this effort of renewing and retrieving Anglo-Australian heritage.

Chapter 3

[1] Coral Ann Howells has been one of few critics to read Atwood's work in a specifically Canadian context and her latest project has been to treat Atwood's latest novels – *Alias Grace* and *The Blind Assassin* (2000), which is set in mid-twentieth-century Canada – as part of an attempt to "refigure Canadian identities, not only in the present for the future, but retrospectively as well" (Howells, 2003, p. 26). While Howells and I share an interest in official multiculturalism's rescripting

of Canadian identity and literature, Howells does not address whiteness as part of Atwood's project of "opening up English Canada's colonial history and its heritage myths" (ibid., p. 25).

[2] Both the Meech Lake and Charlottetown Accords were attempts at amending the constitution to recognize Quebec as a distinct entity within Canada. Both were defeated primarily because they did not extend the same recognition and status to claims of First Nation peoples (Stein, 1997, pp. 332–7). The 1990 "Oka crisis" was a fatal standoff between the Mohawks of Kanehsatake and the town of Oka, Quebec over Native title to land zoned for a golf course. After a lengthy siege lasting 78 days, one member of the provincial police who attacked the Mohawks was killed (Mackey, 2002, p. 112). Such legislations and violent confrontations disrupt the myths of Canada as a "peaceable kingdom."

[3] See McClintock's *Imperial Leather* (1995), especially her chapter on author Olive Schreiner, and Adele Perry's essay, "Fair Ones of a Purer Cast": White women and colonialism in Nineteenth-Century British Columbia" (1997), which explores white femininity's role in shaping the colonial mission.

[4] To avoid confusion, I will refer to Susanna Moodie as "Moodie" and Atwood's version of Susanna Moodie as "Mrs Moodie."

[5] For an examination of the controversy and criticism surrounding *Survival* see Paul Goetsch's chapter "Margaret Atwood: A Canadian Nationalist" (2000). Atwood herself defended *Survival* against Robin Mathew's criticism of it in an essay "Mathews and Misrepresentation" (1973), reprinted in *Second Words* (1982), a collection of her essays and nonfiction. In her introduction to her writing from 1972–6, Atwood writes, "*Survival* was fun to attack. In fact, it still is; most self-respecting professors of Can Lit begin their courses, I'm told, with a short ritual sneer at it" (Atwood, 1982, p. 105).

[6] Both *The Servant Girl* and the play, *Grace*, rehearse many of the themes later developed in *Alias Grace*, but are rich neo-Victorian texts in their own right. *The Servant Girl* is adapted from James McDermott's confession; in this version, Grace is clearly guilty in seducing and thus emasculating McDermott who responds by maiming Hannah (in *Alias Grace*, Nancy Montgomery) with an axe and stashing her body in the cellar to be strangled to death by Grace later. Realizing that he has been duped, McDermott kills Kinnaird/Kinnear, the object of Grace's obsession, and thus re-establishes his dominance over her. The majority of the screenplay is concerned with the chronology of the events but Mrs Moodie appears at the end of the script to serve a policing function, condemning Grace in the name of various Victorian scientific and criminal discourses. Atwood's crafting of the 1979 play is much more exciting than her rather flat portrayal of the same events in the 1970 screenplay. The stage is a large cross-section of the Kinnear house and the play begins to hint at the tropes of immigration, domesticity and settlement that will figure strongly in *Alias Grace*. While Grace is still largely described by Mrs Moodie in this version, Atwood begins to take greater liberties with her character. She is a young woman distinctly concerned about the boundaries of place and her motivations for murder are tinged with both the desire for and disavowal of transgression. Throughout the play, Mrs Moodie appears both in the nineteenth century and the twentieth century – in one very neo-Victorian moment, she visits a historically accurate replica of a settler village just outside of Toronto – to offer

commentary on the development, or civilization, of Canada. Both the screenplay and the play are available, with permission, from the Thomas Fischer Rare Book Library at the University of Toronto.

[7] The birth of *Alias Grace* is described by Atwood in her 1996 Bronfman Lecture, reprinted as the essay, "In Search of *Alias Grace*: On Writing Canadian Historical Fiction" (1998).

[8] The Royal Commission was put together to "inquire into and report upon the existing state of bilinguilism and biculturalism in Canada and to recommend what steps should be taken to develop the Canadian Confederation on the basis of equal partnership between the two founding races, taking into account the contribution made by the other ethnic groups to the cultural enrichment of Canada" (quoted in Fleras and Elliot, 2002, p. 72). After more than 80 ethnic or cultural groups were identified by the Commission, it recommended a policy of multiculturalism united by the official languages of English and French.

[9] The Canada First movement was a proto-nationalist group formed during the struggle between French and English-speaking Canada over the constitution of a coherent Canadian identity after Confederation in 1867. Gillian Poulter claims that the movement's objective was to "foster the growth of national spirit and promote British immigration through literature, art, and the writing of Canadian history" (Poulter, 2009, p. 3). Poulter is quick to point out the racial elements of the Canada First movement, the "unifying factor that would allow all the European inhabitants of Canada to share a common national identity" was their descent from "northern races, whether they were Celtic, Saxon, Teutonic or Norman" (ibid.).

[10] In 1985, prior to the establishment of the Multiculturalism Act in 1988, Canadian ministers promised that "this country is never going to be a melting pot... I don't think Canadians want Canada to be a melting pot" (quoted in Tenszen, 1985). By 1994, *The Globe and Mail* reported that government studies "have taken one of the great distinguishing statements Canadians use to differentiate themselves from Americans – Canadian society is a cultural mosaic; U.S. society is a melting point. They tested it for truth and found it wanting" (Valpy, 1994). Neil Bissoondath published *Selling Illusions: The Cult of Multiculturalism in Canada* (1994), his critique of multiculturalism's failure to aid in the integration of immigrants in the same year. In 2004, *The Gazette* was still reporting that "only a slim majority of Canadians believes multiculturalism policies intended to keep Canada a cultural mosaic instead of a U.S.-style melting pot help newcomers blend into Canadian society" (Naumetz, 2004).

[11] Critics like Jennifer Murray's examination of the quilt metaphor in *Alias Grace* come the closest to articulating its importance for a Canadian identity: "as a work in progress," she argues, "[the quilt] acknowledges diversity, yet as a finished product, it becomes a cover, a blanket; something which, to function effectively, must emphasize its unity" (Murray, 2001, p. 78).

[12] Atwood is familiar with Hacking's work, listing his book, *Rewriting the Soul: Multiple Personality and the Sciences of Memory* (1995), as a source in the acknowledgments of *Alias Grace* and citing him in her essay "In Search of *Alias Grace*" (1998).

[13] See Earle Birney's oft-quoted poem, "Can Lit."

Chapter 4

[1] According to Ackbar Abbas, Hong Kong's most influential cultural critic, the expiration date of 1 July, 1997 had the effect of renewing Hong Kong people's relationship to place, "an instance . . . of love at last sight" (Abbas, 1997a, p. 23). Those wanting to capture the territory's "sense of elusiveness, the slipperiness, the ambivalences of Hong Kong's cultural space deployed a 'politics of disappearance'" (ibid., p. 24). Thus, Abbas and other critics privilege Hong Kong's "new wave" cinema, dominated by auteurs such as Wong Kar Wai and Ann Hui, and its techniques of representing disappearance paradoxically as a "pathology of presence" (ibid., p. 25). Capable of juggling the contradictory and compensatory impulses of dealing with Hong Kong's imminent disappearance, "new wave" cinema adopted strategies of "timelessness (achronicity) and "placelessness (the international, the parasitic), a tendency to live its own version of the "floating world" without the need to establish stable identities" and the very urgent need to "have some kind of cultural identity in place before Hong Kong re-enters the Chinese fold" (ibid., p. 76). Increasing attention is being paid to popular cinema's negotiation of the same discourse of disappearance.

[2] See W. Travis Hanes and Frank Sanello's historical account, *The Opium Wars: The Addiction of One Empire and the Corruption of Another* (2002). For a recent interpretation of the Opium Wars" resonance in the present, see Rey Chow's excellent essay "King Kong in Hong Kong: Watching the "handover" from the U.S.A." (1998b).

[3] Ng Kang-Chung, "Role of opium remembered," *South China Morning Post*, (1997).

[4] Such comments were compiled in a *South China Morning Post* article, "Hong Kong will bury ageing Beijing elite" (Wallen, 1997). For example, *The Daily Telegraph* claimed that China is "despite its rapid economic growth" still a "fundamentally crude and backward country;" *The Independent* argued, "it is the domestic values of the departing ex-colonial power . . . which are in global ascendent, and the authoritarian, pitiless post-Marxism of the aging Beijing elite which is in retreat. Whatever happens in the next few months and years, Hong Kong will bury them, not the other way around" (Wallen, 1997, p. 10).

[5] See, Yingchi Chu's *Hong Kong Cinema: Colonizer, Motherland and Self* (2003) pp. 44–7.

[6] In Jan Morris's elegiac history of Hong Kong as the end of empire, she notes that Captain Charles Elliot, who annexed Hong Kong in 1841 as a British free port and base for trade with China, is "uncommemorated still in the colony that he founded, and his entry in the Dictionary of National Biography makes no mention of Hong Kong" (Morris, 1997, p. 25).

[7] See Ho (2000, p. 85) and John McLeod's article, "On the Chase for Gideon Nye: History and Representation in Timothy Mo's *An Insular Possession*" (1999).

[8] For an excellent overview of the Chinese reaction to the film and its national, commercial and state-funded context, see Zhiwei Xiao's article, "The Opium War in the Movies: History, Politics and Propaganda" (2000).

[9] See Jackie Chan's autobiography, *I Am Jackie Chan: My Life in Action* (1999, with Jeff Yang).

[10] See Chu's *Hong Kong Cinema: Coloniser, Motherland and Self* (2002) and Kwai-Cheung Lo's article "Double Negations: Hong Kong Cultural Identity in Hollywood's Transnational Representations" (2001) and his book, *Chinese Face/Off: The Transnational Popular Culture of Hong Kong* (2005); and Steve Fore's chapters on Jackie Chan in the collections, *At Full Speed: Hong Kong Cinema in a Borderless World* (2001) and *Transnational Chinese Cinema* (1997).

[11] See Lisa Lowe's *Immigrant Acts: On Asian American Cultural Politics* (1999), p. 20.

[12] See Ang (2001), pp. 81–4 and Allen Chun's emphatic article, "Fuck Chineseness: On the Ambiguities of Ethnicity as Culture as Identity" (1996). Both Ang and Chun question the monolithic, often inherited, understandings of cultural "Chineseness."

[13] The Commonwealth Immigration Act was passed in 1962 to stem the flow of immigrants from the Carribbean and Indian subcontinent; previous to 1962, all subjects of the British Empire had the right of abode in Britain. In 1971, another Immigration Act created a definition of British nationality for overseas territories based on patriality; this created the unique situation of Britain denying British nationals the right of entry to Britain (Hansen, 2000, pp. 126–7). The British Nationality Act of 1981, many felt, privileged the ethnic Britishness of some over the Britishness of others; it was possible for someone who had one British grandparent in South Africa to become a British citizen and claim a "close[r] connection" to Britain than someone born in Hong Kong, British territory (ibid., p. 179). The British National Overseas passport was created in the early 1990s specifically for Hong Kong; it did not give residents the right of abode in the UK, but it did give them the right to seek embassy protection and legal recourse. In 2002, the Labor administration passed the essentially "empty" (ibid., p. 214) British Overseas Territories Act that gave the dwindling number of previously "dependent" territories the right to apply for British citizenship (ibid., p. 214).

[14] The Big Ben scene anchors multiple histories: it pays tribute to British comedy, *My Learned Friend* (1941) and *The Thirty-Nine Steps* (1978) while also recalling the clock tower scene in *Project A* and the "Hong Kong clock" erected in Tiananmen Square in Beijing several years prior to reunification to "count down" the end of Hong Kong's lease to Britain. For an analysis of the manipulation of temporality over the "handover" in service of a Chinese national narrative, see Wu Hung's essay, "The Hong Kong clock: public time-telling and political time/space" (1997).

Chapter 5

[1] Sammo Hung makes a cameo appearance as legendary martial artist Wong Fei Hung, leader of the Ten Tigers, but also a Chinese patriot, healer and philosopher who fought for the rights of the oppressed against corruption and the invasion of foreign powers. Hung's appearance gestures toward other ostensibly neo-Victorian cultural texts produced outside the West such as *Once Upon A Time in China*. *Once Upon A Time In China* (1991–7) was a series of six Hong Kong martial arts films directed by Tsui Hark and starring Jet Li in the lead role. Set in nineteenth-century Canton, the first film depicts Wong Fei Hung battling

English, French and American forces plundering China and questioning the Western ideals adopted by his "13th Aunt." The series of films follows the fall of the Qing dynasty, the establishment of the Republic of China, and the immigration of Chinese to Hong Kong and the American West.
2 Because steampunk's range spreads across media to material culture, I will restrict my discussion to literary and visual culture. For a comprehensive survey of steampunk literature, culture and neo-Victorianism, see Rachel A. Bowser and Brian Croxall's Introduction (2010) the special edition on steampunk in *Neo-Victorian Studies*.
3 *The Great Steampunk Debate* is a series of forums that discuss "beliefs, politics, ethics, and how all of these things interact with steampunk (if they, in fact, intersect at all)." The organizers claim that "in recent years steampunk has become increasingly divided and fragmentary, and this could threaten the integrity of our community, if we let it" (*Great Steampunk*, 2010). Again, the same claims can be made for neo-Victorianism.
4 This concern has been voiced by "The Steampunk Scholar" in a post on the "future of steampunk." Taking stock of steampunk examples set "before the turn-of-the-century" and Lea Hernandez's "Texas steampunk manga," the "Scholar" laments that "sadly, these books are not commonly mentioned on steampunk reading lists. I'm guessing the limiting view of steampunk as neo-Victorian excluded these books from the early 'canon'" ("Leaving London," 2010).
5 The three blogs that discuss Victorientalism or are entirely devoted to multicultural steampunk that I cover here are: Dru Pagliassotti's entry "Against VictOrientalism" (2010), "Jha's" blog, *Silver Goggles*, specifically her entry, "Countering Victorientalism" (2010), and "Ay-leen the Peacemaker's" outstanding blog, *Beyond Victoriana: A Multicultural Perspective on Steampunk*, whose mission is to explore "steampunk outside of a Western-dominant, Eurocentric framework" ("Ay-leen the Peacemaker", 2010).
6 The close relationship between Mori Arinori (1847–89) and Laurence Oliphant (1882–8), his mentor in the West, is documented in Checkland's book, *Britain's Encounter with Meiji Japan, 1868–1912* (1989). Mori was sent to London as a young man as part of a national mission to "make a judgement of the advantages and disadvantages of Western industrial, economic and political development" (Checkland, 1989, p. 119) and its appropriateness for the "enlightenment" of Japan. Checkland describes Mori's difficult career as a scholar and a statesman because of his adoption of Western ideas and philosophies about which he remained conflicted for the rest of his life. This conflict, I believe, can still be traced in Otomo's neo-Victorian project.
7 The Japanese doll's counterpart in the novel is Ada Lovelace Byron, named the "Queen of Engines" in the novel and known as the "Princess of Parallelograms" in history, who worked extensively with Babbage to promote the potential of his engines. Gibson and Sterling recover Ada as an "untimely figure" whose history is intimately intertwined with Babbage. In *The Difference Engine*, Ada is a huge intellectual and symbolic presence, linking Babbage's technological vision to the political power of her father. The real Ada's close work with Babbage on the formulation and calculations of the analytical engines has allowed cyberfeminists to claim her as the first female software programmer. Indeed, Ada's translation of

Babbage's Italian collaborator Menebrea's contribution to the analytical engine and her notes on the article were generally thought to be superior to Babbage's own work (Green, 2001, p. 142). In the footnotes to his chapter, "Hacking the Nineteenth Century," Jay Clayton briefly chronicles the "controversy" over Lovelace's role either as an "unjustly neglected pioneer of the computer" or "the most overrated figure in the history of computing" (Clayton, 2003, p. 226,); this debate suggests that there is a struggle over the "invention" of a tradition in computing that can contain a larger female presence. As Sadie Plant asserts, the language used to describe our technology is remarkably close to Ada's and Babbage's vision of the new Jacquard loom as the foundation for computing: the Web, Internet and Matrix share the same images as weaving, traditionally women's work. "If weaving has played such a crucial role in the history of computing," Plant argues, "it is also the key to one of the most extraordinary sites of woman-machine interface which short-circuits their prescribed relationship and persists regardless of what man effects and defines as the history of technology" (Plant, 2000, p. 332). *The Difference Engine* recovers an alternate version of the story of technology, one which re-associates white female work with the essentially rhizomatic nature of scientific culture.

[8] See, for example, issues two and three of *Common Knowledge* (2005) devoted to the symposium, "Imperial Trauma: The Powerlessness of the Powerful." Linda Colley's introduction, as well as many of the essays, covers the various repressions and willful forgettings of U.S. imperialism. Along the same lines, Bernard Porter argues that linking the U.S. with empire "creates an amnesiac phrase not easily applied to or remembered in the present, despite how it is readily applied to everything from Hollywood to McDonald's" (Porter, 2006, pp. 4–5). This amnesia emerges, Porter continues, from "the American insistence that the word 'imperialism' only applies to the *formal* acquisition of territory overseas" (ibid., p. 64).

[9] A few years later, both Blair and Bush would draw on similar phrasing: in a speech delivered on 6 September, 2006, Bush argued that "we're fighting for our way of life and our ability to live in freedom" (2006); a few weeks later, Tony Blair would use a similar phrase, "it's an attack on our way of life" (2006), to describe the global war on terror in his final speech to the Labour Party conference.

[10] *Steamboy's* nuclear discourse will, no doubt, have to be re-evaluated in the wake of the Fukushima nuclear reactor disaster after the 2011 tsunami and earthquake.

[11] One of the earliest translations and revisions of *Gone with the Wind* in Japan was Kikuta Kazuo's musical drama, *Scaretto* (1966). *Gone With the Wind* spoke to Japan's postwar reconstruction, provided an emphasis on local/home-town nostalgia, addressed gender and sexual politics, and more importantly for this chapter, played up to an "older" version of Japanese culture being swept away by Westernization and technology (Wetmore, 2006, p. 245).

[12] See Checkland (1989), who details the co-operation between the British engineers of railways, shipyards and communication systems who lived and worked alongside their Japanese students and partners in both Japan and Britain.

[13] I am indebted here to Michael Fisch's article "Nation, War, and Japan's Future in the Science Fiction Anime Film *Patlabor II*" (2000) in which he reads Oshii

Mamoru's anime, *Patlabor II* (1993), within the context of Japan's reinterpretation of Article 9 of its postwar constitution which strictly prohibits, in perpetuity, the use of military force. Fisch argues that the film participates in a "fraught political debate" (2000) over Japan's postwar relationship with the U.S., anti-American sentiment and international and public pressure to participate in humanitarian efforts during the Gulf War. Given the re-emergence of these debates about the SDF during the Iraq war and the release of *Steamboy* in 2003–4, it seemed fitting to revisit Fisch's argument. For an overview of the controversy and Japan's changes to its political and constitutional policy during the Iraq war, please see Tomohito Shinoda's article, "Japan's Top Down Policy Process to Dispatch the SDF to Iraq" in the *Japanese Journal of Political Science* (2006).

Chapter 6

[1] In a 2010 report on "Canada's Arctic Sovereignty," for example, debate over Arctic sovereignty was presented. It was suggested that the Arctic is "becoming increasingly accessible to a number of different actors who are descending upon it with both different and not mutually beneficial agendas" (Canada's Arctic Sovereignty, 2010, p. 4). Furthermore, "non-Arctic" states in the region "could well lead to future challenges" (many of them potentially military) "to Canadian sovereignty" (ibid.).

[2] There is a growing body of work on the Indian Ocean within "Oceanic Studies," see, for example, the May 2010 issue of *PMLA* and the rich collection of essays in *Indian Ocean Studies* (Moorthy and Jamal, 2009) part of Routledge's Indian Ocean series.

[3] See Ashraf Rushdy's *Neo-Slave Narratives: Studies in the Social Logic of a Literary Form* (1999).

[4] I want to thank Susanna Throop for pointing this reading out to me.

[5] For British-Indian neo-Victorian examples of the Indian Mutiny of 1857, see Marie-Luise Kohlke's essay, "Tipoo's Tiger on the Loose: Neo-Victorian Witness-Bearing and the Trauma of the Indian Mutiny," in *Neo-Victorian Tropes of Trauma* (2010). I have found neo-Victorian texts in general originating from India rare, exceptions being the Bollywood extravaganzas, *Lagaan: Once Upon a Time in India* (Gowariker, 2001) and *The Rising: Ballad of Mangal Pandey* (Mehta, 2005), both anti-imperial narratives set in the nineteenth century, the latter depicting the events leading up to the 1857 Sepoy mutiny.

[6] As one might imagine, online discussion of Miéville's novel pushes the boundaries of what is acceptable as steampunk and neo-Victorianism. Some bloggers suggest that *Perdido Street Station* offers an alternate world rather than the alternate history so necessary to steampunk; others suggest that steampunk is expansive enough to include the novel's lapses into fantasy. Most reviewers and bloggers across the board use the term "neo-Victorian" loosely to describe the Bas-Lag setting.

[7] For a reading of *Cloud Atlas's* neo-Victorian framework and its relationship to trauma and witnessing, see Celia Wallhead and Marie-Luise Kohlke's chapter,

"The Neo-Victorian Frame of Mitchell's *Cloud Atlas*: Temporal and Traumatic Reverberations" (2010). While they read the function of the Victorian in *Cloud Atlas* as "the return of the repressed or an involuntary flashback to an originary traumatic scene" (Wallhead and Kohlke, 2010, p. 217), I argue that the novel's temporal politics are unwilling to privilege any historical moment, even as traumatic past or future.

Bibliography

Abbas, A. (1997a), *Hong Kong: Culture and the Politics of Disappearance*. Minneapolis, MN: University of Minnesota press.
—(1997b), "Hong Kong: other histories, other politics," *Public Culture*, 9, 293–313.
Ackroyd, P. (1994), *Dan Leno and the Limehouse Golem*. London: Vintage.
Agnew, J. (2003), *Geopolitics: Re-visioning World Politics*. London and New York: Routledge.
Amenábar, A. (2001), *The Others*. USA: Dimension Films.
Anderson, B. (1991), *Imagined Communities*. London and New York: Verso.
Anderson, M. (1956), *Around the World in Eighty Days*. USA: Twentieth Century Fox Studios.
Ang, I. (2001), *On Not Speaking Chinese: Living Between Asia and the West*. London and New York: Routledge.
Antze, P. and Lambek, M. (1996), *Tense Past: Cultural Essays in Trauma and Memory*. London and New York: Routledge.
Appadurai, A. (1996), *Modernity at Large: Cultural Dimensions of Globalization*. Minneapolis, MN: University of Minnesota Press.
Ashcroft, B. (2010), "Transnation," in J. Wilson, C. Sandru and S. L. Welsh (eds), *Rerouting the Postcolonial: New Directions for the New Millennium*. London and New York: Routledge, pp. 72–85.
Ashcroft, B., Griffiths, G., and Tiffin, H. (1989), *The Empire Writes Back*. London and New York: Routledge.
Atwood, M. (1970), *The Journals of Susanna Moodie*. Oxford: Oxford University Press.
—(1972), *Survival: A Thematic Guide to Canadian Literature*. Toronto: McClelland & Stewart Inc.
—(1974), *The Servant Girl*. Canada: CBC Television.
—(1979), *Grace: A Play in Two Acts*. Canada: O. W. Toad.
—(1982), *Second Words: Selected Critical Prose 1960–82*. Toronto, ON: House of Anansi Press.
—(1996), *Alias Grace*. NY: Vintage Press.
—(1998), "In search of *Alias Grace*: on writing Canadian historical fictions," *The American Historical Review*, 103, 5, 1503–16, December.
—(2000), *The Blind Assassin*. Toronto, ON: McClelland & Stewart Ltd.
"Ay-leen the Peacemaker," (2010), "About *Beyond Victoriana*: mission statement," *Beyond Victoriana: A Multicultural Perspective on Steampunk*, blog post, March 2010, viewed 2 December 2010, <http://beyondvictoriana.com/about/>.
Bal, M. (1999), "Introduction," in M. Bal, J. Crewe, and L. Spitzer (eds), *Acts of Memory: Cultural Recall in the Present*. Hanover, NH: University Press of New England, pp. vii–xvii.

Bannerji, H. (2000), *The Dark Side of the Nation: Essays on Multiculturalism, Nationalism and Gender.* Toronto, Ontario: Canadian Scholars' Press Inc.

Barlow, D. (1998), "Authenticity/hybridity and Pallawah identities in Castro's *Drift*," *Southerly*, 58, 2, 58–9.

Barnes, J. (2005), *Arthur and George.* London: Jonathan Cape.

Barrett, A. (1996), *Ship Fever: Stories.* London and New York: W. W. Norton & Co. Ltd.

—(1998), *Voyage of the Narwhal.* London and New York: W.W. Norton & Co. Ltd.

—(2003), *Servants of the Map: Stories.* London and New York: W. W. Norton & Co. Ltd.

Barthes, R. (1980), *Camera Lucida.* New York: Hill and Wang.

Baucom, I. (1999), *Out of Place: Englishness, Empire and the Locations of Identity.* Princeton, NJ: Princeton University Press.

BBC News (2010), "Australia Race Politician Pauline Hanson moving to UK," *BBC News*, 15 February, viewed 29 July, 2011. <http://news.bbc.co.uk/2/hi/8515977.stm>.

Begg, P. (1988), *Jack the Ripper: The Uncensored Facts.* London: Robson Books.

Bhabha, H. (1994), *The Location of Culture.* London: Routledge.

Bissoondath, N. (1994), *Selling Illusions: The Cult of Multiculturalism in Canada.* New York: Penguin Books.

Blackford, H. (2006), "The psychology of the handmaid: Margaret Atwood's novel parables of the possessed Canadian character", *Ameriquests*, 3, 1, viewed 12 September 2011, <http://ejournals.library.vanderbilt.edu/ojs/index.php/ameriquests/article/view/51/46>.

Blair, T. (2006), "Tony Blair's speech: text of the Labour leader's valedictory speech to the party conference," *The Guardian*, 25 September, viewed 17 October, 2009,<http://www.guardian.co.uk/politics/2006/sep/26/labourconference.labour3>.

Blake, A. (1998), "Retrolution: Culture and Heritage in a Young Country" in A. Coddington and M. Perryman (eds), *The Moderniser's Dilemma: Radical Politics in the Age of Blair.* London: Lawrence & Wishart Ltd., pp. 143–56.

Blum, H. (2008), *The View from the Masthead: Maritime Imagination and Antebellum American Sea Narratives.* Chapel Hill, NC: University of North Carolina Press.

Boldtype (1998), "Interview with Peter Carey," *Boldtype: An Online Literary Magazine*, vol. 2, no. 12, viewed 3 March 2000, <http://www.randomhouse.com/boldtype/0399/carey/interview.html\>.

Bowser, R. and Croxall, B. (2010), "Introduction: industrial revolution," *Neo-Victorian Studies*, 3, 1, 1–45.

Boyle, D. (1996), *Trainspotting.* London: Channel Four Films.

Brass Goggles (n.d.), <http://brassgoggles.co.uk/blog/>.

Brawley, S. (2003), "Legacies: the White Australia policy and foreign relations since 1973," in L. Jayasuriya, D. Walker, D., and J. Gothard (eds), *Legacies of White Australia: Race, Culture and Nation.* Crawley, Western Australia: University of Western Australia Press, pp. 93–109.

Brison, S. (1999), "Trauma Narratives and the Remaking of the Self," in M. Bal, J. Crew, and L.Spitzer (eds), *Acts of Memory: Cultural Recall in the Present.* Hanover, NH: University Press of New England, pp. 39–54.

British Nationality Act 1981. Website, viewed 12 January 2004, <http://www.uniset.ca>.
Brooker, P. (2000), "A Novelist in the Era of Higher Capitalism: Iain Sinclair and the Postmodern East End," paper delivered at *Urban Space and Representation Conference*, viewed 23 July 2003. <http://www.nottingham.ac.uk/3cities/brooker.htm>.
Brydon, D. (2004), "Reading postcoloniality, reading Canada," in C. Sugars (ed.), *Unhomely States: Theorizing English-Canadian Postcolonialism*, Ontario & New York: Broadview Press, pp. 165–79.
Burton, A. (2003), "Introduction: On the Inadequacy and the Indispensability of the Nation" in A. Burton (ed.), *After the Imperial Turn: Thinking with and through the Nation*. Durham, NC: Duke University Press, pp. 1–23.
Burton, T. (2007), *Sweeney Todd: The Demon Barber of Fleet Street*. USA: Dreamworks.
Bush, G. W. (2006), "We're fighting for our way of life," *CNN Access*, 6 September, viewed 17 October, 2009, <http://www.cnn.com/2006/POLITICS/09/06/bush.transcript/index.html>.
Byatt, A. S. (1990), *Possession*. London: Vintage.
Cameron, E. (2004), *Multiculturalism and Immigration in Canada: an Introductory Reader*. Toronto, ON: Canadian Scholars' Press.
"Canada's Arctic Sovereignty" (2010), Report of the Standing Committee on National Defence, 40th Parliament, 3rd Session, June, pp. 1–36, viewed 30 August, 2010. <Googledocs: 01_NDDN_ArcticSovereignty_7782679_Covers_ENG>.
Canwest News Service (2008), "Parks Canada to lead new search for Franklin ships", Canada.com, 15 August, viewed October 20, 2009, <http://www.canada.com/story_print.html?id=147541d1-0d04-445c-963a-f9c498b32883&sponsor =>.
Caputi, J. (1987), *The Age of Sex Crime*. Bowling Green, OH: Bowling Green State University Popular Press.
Carey, P. (1988), *Oscar and Lucinda*. New York: Vintage Books.
—(1997), *Jack Maggs*. New York: Knopf.
—(2000), *True History of the Kelly Gang*. New York: Knopf.
Carriger, G. (2009 – present), *Parasol Protectorate* series. New York: Orbit Books.
Carter, M. and Torabully, K. (2002), *Coolitude: an Anthology of the Indian Labor Diaspora*. London: Anthem.
Carter, P. (1987), *The Road to Botany Bay: An Exploration of Landscape and History*. Minneapolis, MN: University of Minnesota Press.
Caruth, C. (1996), *Unclaimed Experience: Trauma, Narrative, and History*. Baltimore, MD: Johns Hopkins University Press.
—(ed.) (1995), *Trauma: Explorations in Memory*. Baltimore, MD: Johns Hopkins University Press.
Casarino, C. (2002), *Modernity at Sea: Marx, Conrad in Crisis*. Minneapolis MN: University of Minnesota Press.
Cattaneo, P. (1997), *The Full Monty*. USA: Fox Searchlight.
Chadwick, F. (1988), *Space: 1889* [role-playing game]. Game Designer's Workshop, reprinted by Heliograph Inc.
Chan, J. (1983), *Project A*. Hong Kong: Golden Harvest.
—(1999), *I Am Jackie Chan: My Life in Action* (with Jeff Yang). New York: Ballantine Books.

Checkland, O. (1989), *Britain's Encounter with Meiji Japan, 1868–1912*. Basingstoke, UK: Macmillan Press.
Cheng, A. (2001), *The Melancholy of Race: Psychoanalysis, Assimilation and Hidden Grief*. Oxford: Oxford University Press.
Chi'en, E. (2004), *Weird English*. Cambridge, MA: Harvard University Press.
Chigira, K. (2003), *Last Exile*. Japan: Gonzo.
Chouvy, P. (2010), *Opium: Uncovering the Politics of the Poppy*. Cambridge, MA: Harvard University Press.
Chow, R. (1993), *Writing Diaspora*. Bloomington, IN: Indiana University Press.
—(1998a), *Ethics After Idealism: Theory, Culture, Ethnicity, Reading*. Bloomington, IN: Indiana University Press, 1998.
—(1998b), "King Kong In Hong Kong: Watching the 'Handover' from the U.S.A.", *Social Text* 16, 2, Summer, 93–108.
Chu, Y. (2003), *Hong Kong Cinema: Coloniser, Motherland and Self*. London and New York: Routledge.
Chun, A. (1996), "Fuck Chineseness: on the ambiguities of ethnicity as culture as identity," *boundary 2*, 23, 2, 111–38.
Clark, B. (1979), *Murder By Decree*. Canada: Canadian Film Development Corporation.
Clarke, M. (1870–2), *His Natural Life*. Oxford: Oxford University Press.
Clavell, J. (1966), *Tai-Pan*. New York: Dell Publishing.
Clayton, J. (2003), *Charles Dickens in Cyberspace: The Afterlife of the Nineteenth Century in Postmodern Culture*. Oxford: Oxford University Press.
Clifford, J. (1997), *Routes: Travel and Translation in the Late Twentieth Century*. Cambridge, MA: Harvard University Press.
Clooney, R. M. (1996), *The Politics of Home: Postcolonial relocations and Twentieth-century Fiction*. Cambridge: Cambridge University Press.
Coleman, D. (2006), *White Civility: The Literary Project of English Canada*. Toronto, ON: University of Toronto Press.
Colley, L. (2005), "Introduction: some difficulties of empire – past, present, and future," *Common Knowledge*, 11, 2, Spring, 198–214.
Connery, C. L. (1994), "Pacific rim discourse: the U.S. global imaginary in the late cold war years," in R. Wilson and A. Dirlik, (eds), *Asia/Pacific as Space of Cultural Production*. Durham, NC: Duke University Press, pp. 30–56.
—(1996), "The oceanic feeling and the regional imaginary," in R. Wilson and W. Dissanayake (eds), *Global/Local: Cultural Production and the Transnational Imaginary*. Durham, NC: Duke University Press, pp. 284–311.
Cooper, R. (2009), "Building worlds: dialectical materialism as method in China Miéville's Bas-Lag," *Extrapolation*, 50, 2, 212–23.
Coraci, F. (2004), *Around the World in Eighty Days*. USA: Walt Disney Pictures.
Corner, J. and Harvey, S. (1991), "Introduction: Great Britain Limited," in J. Corner and S. Harvey (eds), *Enterprise and Heritage: Crosscurrents of National Culture*. London and New York: Routledge, pp. 1–20.
Cornwall, P. (2009), *Portrait of a Serial Killer: Jack the Ripper Case Closed*. New York: Berkley Books.
Darroch, H. (2004), "Hysteria and traumatic testimony: Margaret Atwood's *Alias Grace*," *Essays on Canadian Writing*, 81, pp. 103–21.

Davison, G. (2000), *The Use and Abuse of Australian History*. Sydney, Australia: Allen & Unwin.
Derrida, J. (1980), "The law of genre," *Critical Inquiry*, 1, 1, Autumn, 55–81.
Devereux, C. (1994), "A process of being re-Anglicized: 'colonial' houses and 'post-colonial' fiction," *Australian and New Zealand Studies in Canada*, 11/12, 11–30.
Dey, T. (2000), *Shanghai Noon*. USA: Touchstone Pictures.
Digital China/Harvard, (n.d.), *The Opium War*, viewed 13 September 2011, <http://cyber.law.harvard.edu/ChinaDragon/opiumwar.html>.
Dillon, G. (2007), "Scarification and Survivance in China Miéville's *The Scar*," *Foundation*, 31, 101, 13–25.
Dirlik, A. (1997), *The Postcolonial Aura: Third World Criticism in the Age of Global Capitalism*. Boulder, CO: Westview Press.
—(1998), "The Asia-Pacific idea: reality and representation in the invention of a regional structure," in A. Dirlik (ed.), *What Is In a Rim?: Critical Perspectives on the Pacific Region Idea*. Lanham, MD: Rowman & Littlefield Publishers, pp. 15–36.
Dixson, M. (1999), *The Imaginary Australian: Anglo-Celts and Identity, 1788 to the present*. Sydney, Australia: University of New South Wales Press.
"dman762000," (2010), Post to Steampunk beyond 19th century Europe, Wednesday, May 12. *The Great Steampunk Debate*. Accessed March 6, 2011. <http://www.greatsteampunkdebate.com/forum/viewtopic.php?f=4&t=83&start=10>.
Dobkin, D. (2003), *Shanghai Knights*. USA: Touchstone Pictures.
Driver, F. (2001), *Geography Militant*. Oxford: Blackwell Publishers.
Dyer, R. (1997), *White: Essays on Race and Culture*. London & New York: Routledge.
East London Observer (1888), "A reign of terror in Whitechapel," *East London Observer*, 15 September, viewed 11 September 1999, <http://casebook.org/press_reports/east_london_observer/elo880915.html>.
Edwards, J. D. (2005), *Gothic Canada: Reading the Spectre of a National Literature*. Edmonton, AB: The University of Alberta Press.
Elliot, S. (2009), *Victorian Farm*. UK: Lion Television.
Emilsson, W. (2002), "Iain Sinclair's Unsound Detectives." *Critique: Studies in Contemporary Fiction*, 43, 3, Spring, 271–88.
Eng, D. and Han, S. (2003), "A dialogue on racial melancholia", in D. Eng and D. Kazanjian (eds), *Loss: the Politics of Mourning*. Berkeley and Los Angeles, CA: University of California Press.
Faber, M. (2002), *The Crimson Petal and the White*. Edinburgh: Canongate Books.
Fang, K. (2003), "Britain's Finest: The Royal Hong Kong Police", in Burton, A. (ed). *After The Imperial Turn: Thinking with and through the Nation*. Durham, NC: Duke University Press, pp. 293–307.
Favreau, J. (2011), *Cowboys and Aliens*. USA: Universal Pictures.
Ferguson, N. (2005), *Colossus: The Rise and Fall of the American Empire*. New York: Penguin Books. London and New York: Allen Lane.
Fink, J. (2011), *Chester 5000 XYV*. Marietta, GA: Top Shelf Production.
Fisch, M. (2000), "Nation, war, and Japan's future in the science fiction anime film *Patlabor II*," *Science Fiction Studies*, 80, 27, pp. 49–68 March. Viewed 6 February, 2007. <http://www.depauw.edu/sfs/backissues/80/fish80art.htm>.
Fleras, A. and Elliot, L. (2002), *Engaging Diversity: Multiculturalism in Canada*. Scarborough, ON: Nelson Thomson Learning.

Forby, M. (2009), *Princess Kaiulani*. USA: Roadside Attractions.
Fore, S. (1997), "Jackie Chan and the Cultural Dynamics of Global Entertainment" in S. H. Lu (ed.), *Transnational Chinese Cinemas: Identity, Nationhood, Gender*. Honolulu, HI: University of Hawai'i Press, pp. 239–62.
—(2001), "Life imitates entertainment: home and dislocation in the films of Jackie Chan," in E. Yau (ed.), *At Full Speed: Hong Kong Cinema in a Borderless World*. Minneapolis, MN: University of Minnesota Press, pp. 115–42.
Foster, J. W. (1977), "The poetry of Margaret Atwood," *Canadian Literature*, 74, 5–20.
Foucault, M. (1967), "Of other spaces," *Diacritics*, 16, Spring, 22–7.
—(1990), *The History of Sexuality Vol.1*. London: Penguin Books.
Fowles, J. (1969), *The French Lieutenant's Woman*. London: Jonathan Cape.
Frankenberg, R. (1993), *White Women, Race Matters: the Social Construction of Whiteness*. Minneapolis, MN: University of Minnesota Press.
Frayling, C. (1986), "The House that Jack Built: Some Stereotypes of the Rapist in the History of Popular Culture," in S. Tomaselli and R. Porter (eds), *Rape: An Historical and Cultural Enquiry*. Oxford: Basil Blackwell Ltd., pp. 174–215.
Freedman, C. (2005), "To the Perdido Street Station: The representation of revolution in China Miéville's *Iron Council*," *Extrapolation*, 46, 2, 235–48.
Freud, S. (1917), "Mourning and melancholia," in A. Phillips (ed.), *Sigmund Freud: The Penguin Freud Reader*. London: Penguin Books, pp. 310–26.
—(1922), *Beyond the Pleasure Principle* (trans. and ed., J. Strachey). London and New York: W.W. Norton & Co.
Gay, J. (1989), *Around the World in Eighty Days*. USA: NBC.
Ghosh, A. (2008), *Sea of Poppies*. New York: Farrar, Strauss & Giroux.
Gibson, W. and Sterling, B. (1991), *The Difference Engine*. New York: Bantam Books.
Gikandi, S. (1996), *Maps of Englishness: Writing Identity in the Culture of Colonialism*. New York: Columbia University Press, 1996.
Gilroy, P. (1993), *The Black Atlantic: Modernity and Double-Consciousness*. Cambridge, MA: Harvard University Press.
—(2005), *Postimperial Melancholia*. New York: Columbia University Press.
Goetsch, P. (2000), "Margaret Atwood: A Canadian nationalist," in R. Nischik (ed.), *Margaret Atwood: Works and Impact*. Rochester, NY: Camden House, pp. 166–79.
Gordon, J. (2003), "Reveling in genre: an interview with China Miéville," *Science Fiction Studies* 91, 3, 355–73 <http://www.depauw.edu/sfs/interviews/mievilleinterview.htm/>.
Gowariker, A. (2001), *Lagaan: Once Upon A Time in India*. India: Aamir Khan Productions.
Great Steampunk Debate (2010), viewed 14 September, 2010. <http://www.greatsteampunkdebate.com/forum/index.php>.
Green, C. (2001), "Charles Babbage, the analytical engine, and the possibility of a nineteeth-century cognitive science," in C. Green, M. Shore and T. Teo (eds), *The Transformation of Psychology*, Washington D.C.: American Psychological Association.
Gregory, D. (2004), *The Colonial Present*. Malden, MA: Blackwell Publishing.
Grenville, K. (2005), *The Secret River*. New York: Canongate.
Grewal, I. (2007), "Amitav Ghosh: cosmopolitans, literature, transnationalisms," in Krishnaswarmy, R. and Hawley, J. (eds), *The Postcolonial and the Global*. Minneapolis, MN: University of Minnesota Press, pp. 178–90.

Gunew, S. (2004), *Haunted Nations: the Colonial Dimensions of Multiculturalisms*. London & New York: Routledge.
Gutleben, C. (2001), *The Victorian Tradition and the Contemporary British Novel*. Amsterdam: Rodopi.
Hacking, I. (1995), *Rewriting the Soul: Multiple Personality and the Sciences of Memory*. Princeton, NJ: Princeton University Press.
Hadley, L. (2010), *Neo-Victorian Fictions and Historical Narratives*. Basingstoke, UK: Palgrave.
Hall, S. (2005), "Whose Heritage?: Unsettling 'the Heritage,' Re-imagining the Post-Nation" in J. Littler and R. Naidoo (eds), *The Politics of Heritage: The Legacies of Race*. London and New York: Routledge, pp. 23–35.
Hanes, W. T. and Sanello, F. (2002), *The Opium Wars: The Addiction of One Empire and the Corruption of Another*. Naperville, IL: Sourcebooks Inc.
Hansen, R. (2000), *Citizenship and Immigration in Post-war Britain*. Oxford: Oxford University Press.
Hanson, P. (1996), "First Speech in the House of Representatives," 19 September, viewed 29 July, 2011 <http://australianpolitics.com/parties/onenation/96-09-10hanson-first-speech.shtml>.
Hantke, S. (1999), "Difference engines and other infernal devices: history according to steampunk." *Extrapolation*, 40, 1, 244–54.
Haraway, D. (1991), *Simians, Cyborgs, and Women: The Reinvention of Nature*, London: Free Association Books.
Hardt, M. and Negri, A. (2000), *Empire*. Cambridge, MA: Harvard University Press.
Hark, T. (1991), *Once Upon a Time in China*. Hong Kong: Golden Harvest.
Hartigan, J. (2005), *Odd Tribes: Towards a Cultural Analysis of White People*. Durham NC: Duke University Press.
Harvey, D. (2005), *The New Imperialism*. Oxford: Oxford University Press.
Hassall, A. J. (1997), "A tale of two countries: *Jack Maggs* and Peter Carey's fiction," *Australian Literary Studies*, 18, 128–35.
Heilmann, A. and Llewellyn, M. (2010), *Neo-Victorianism: The Victorians in the Twenty-First Century 1999–2009*. Basingstoke, UK: Palgrave Macmillan.
Herman, J. (1992), *Trauma and Recovery*. New York: Basic Books.
Hewison, R. (1987), *The Heritage Industry: Britain in a Climate of Decline*. London: Methuen.
Hewitt, R. (2005), *White Backlash and the Politics of Multiculturalism*. Cambridge: Cambridge University Press.
Higgins, A. (1997), "China's Epic Exorcism: Britain is the arch villain of a film to purge the imperial legacy," *The Guardian*, 12 June, viewed 3 March 2001. <http://www.tsquare.tv/film/Guardian01.html>.
Ho, E. Y. (2000), *Timothy Mo*. Manchester, UK: Manchester University Press.
—(2009), "China abroad: nation and diaspora in a Chinese frame", in E. Y. Ho and J. Kuehn (eds), *China Abroad: Travels, Subjects, Spaces*. Hong Kong: Hong Kong University Press, pp. 3–22.
Ho, E. and Hadley, L. (2010), "The lady's not for turning, new cultural perspectives on Thatcher and Thatcherism," in E. Ho and L. Hadley (eds), *Thatcher & After: Margaret Thatcher and Her Afterlife in Contemporary Culture*. Basingstoke, UK: Palgrave Macmillan, pp. 1–28.

Hodge, B. and Mishra, V. (1991), *Dark Side of the Dream: Australian Literature and the Postcolonial Mind*. Sydney, Australia: Allen & Unwin.

Hofmeyer, I. (2010), 'Universalizing the Indian Ocean,' *PMLA*, 125, 3, 721–9.

Hong, C. (2009), "Flashforward democracy: American exceptionalism and the atomic bomb in *Barefoot Gen*," *Comparative Literature Studies*, 46, 1, 125–55.

Hong Kong Legislative Council (1992), *Official Report of Proceedings*, Wednesday, 22 December, viewed 14 August, 2004, <http://www.legco.gov.hk/yr82-83/english/lc_sitg/hansard/h821222.pdf>.

Howells, C. A. (2003), *Contemporary Canadian Women's Fiction: Refiguring Identities*. Basingstoke, UK: Palgrave Macmillan.

Hudson, W. (2000), "Differential citizenship," in W. Hudson and J. Kane (eds), *Rethinking Australian Citizenship*. Cambridge: Cambridge University Press, pp. 15–25.

Huggan, G. (1987), *Territorial Disputes: Maps and Mapping Strategies in Contemporary Canadian and Australian Fiction*. Toronto: University of Toronto Press.

—(2001), *The Postcolonial Exotic: Marketing the Margins*. New York: Routledge.

Hughes, A. and Hughes, A. (2001), *From Hell*. USA: Twentieth Century Fox.

Hutcheon, L. (1988a), *A Poetics of Postmodernism*. New York: Routledge.

—(1988b), *The Canadian Postmodern: A Study of Contemporary English-Canadian Fiction*. Oxford: Oxford University Press.

Huyssen, A. (2003), *Present Pasts: Urban Palimpsests and the Politics of Memory*. Stanford, CA: Stanford University Press.

Ignatiev, N. (2008), *How the Irish Became White*. London and New York: Routledge Classics.

Jameson, F. (1991), *Postmodernism or, The Cultural Logic of Late Capitalism*. Durham, NC: Duke University Press.

—(2006), "Radical fantasy," *Historical Materialism*, 10, 4, 273–80.

Jeunet, J. (1995), *The City of Lost Children*. USA: Sony Pictures.

"Jha," (2010), "Countering Victorientalism," *Silver Goggles*, blog post, 7 March, viewed 2 December, 2010, <http://silver-goggles.blogspot.com/2010/03/countering-victorientalism.html>.

Jiang, Z. (1997), "Speech made at the SAR Establishment ceremony," reprinted in *South China Morning Post*, 2 July, p. 8.

Johnson, C. (1990), *Middle Passage*. New York.: Scribner Books.

Joyce, S. (2007), *The Victorians in the Rearview Mirror*. Athens OH: Ohio University Press.

Jukić, T. (2000), "From worlds to words and the other way around: the Victorian inheritance in the postmodern British novel," in R. Todd and L. Flora (eds), *Theme Parks, Rainforests and Sprouting Wastelands: European essays on Theory and Performance in Contemporary British Fiction*. Amsterdam: Rodopi, pp. 77–87.

Kaplan, A. E. (2005), *Trauma Culture: The Politics of Terror and Loss in Media and Literature*. Piscataway, NJ: Rutgers University Press.

Kaplan, C. (2007), *Victoriana: Histories, Fictions, Criticisms*. New York: Columbia University Press.

Karl, R. E. (2001), "The burden of history: *Lin Zexu* (1959) and *The Opium War* (1997)", in X. Zhang (ed.), *Whither China: Intellectual Politics in Contemporary China*. Durham NC: Duke University Press, pp. 229–60.

Keating, P. (1992), "Redfern Speech," 10 December, viewed 29 July, 2011, <http://australianpolitics.com/executive/keating/92-12-10redfern-speech.shtml>.
Keen, S. (2001), *Romances of the Archive in Contemporary British Fiction*. Toronto, ON: University of Toronto Press.
—(2006), "The historical turn in British fiction," in J. English (ed.), *Concise Companion to Contemporary British Fiction*. Oxford: Blackwell Publishing, pp. 167–87.
Kelly, P. (2000), *Paradise Divided: The Changes, the Challenges, the Choices for Australia*. Sydney, Australia: Allen & Unwin.
Kendrick, C. (2008), "Monster realism and uneven development in China Miéville's *The Scar*," *Extrapolation*, 50, 2, 258–75.
Kernerman, G. (2006), *Multicultural Nationalism: Civilizing Difference, Constituting Community*. Vancouver, BC: University of British Columbia Press.
Kilbourn, W. (1989), "The Peaceable Kingdom Still," in S. Graubard (ed.), *In Search of Canada*. New Brunswick, NJ: Transaction Publishers.
Klein, B. (2002), "Introduction: Britain and the sea," in Klein, B. (ed.), *Fictions of the Sea: Critical Perspectives on the Ocean in British Literature and Culture*. Burlington VT: Ashgate, pp. 1–12.
Kneale, M. (2000), *English Passengers*. New York: Anchor Books.
Kohlke, M. L. (2008), "Introduction: speculations in and on the neo-Victorian encounter," *Neo-Victorian Studies*, 1, 1, 1–18.
Kohlke, M. L. and Gutleben, C. (eds) (2010), *Neo-Victorian Tropes of Trauma: The Politics of Bearing After-witness to Nineteenth-Century Suffering*. Amsterdam: Rodopi.
Knight, S. (1983), *Jack the Ripper: The Final Solution*. London: Granada.
Kucich, J. and Saddoff, D. F. (2000), "Introduction: Histories of the Present," in J. Kucich, and D. F. Saddoff (eds), *Victorian Afterlife: Postmodern Culture Rewrites the Nineteenth Century*. Minneapolis, MN: University of Minnesota Press, pp. ix–xx.
Kumar, A. (2003), "Introduction," in A. Kumar (ed.), *World Bank Literature*. Minneapolis, MN: University of Minnesota Press, pp. xvii–xxxiii.
Lamb, K. (2005), "Bringing Australia Home: Peter Carey, the Booker, and the Repatriation of Australian culture" in A. Gaile (ed.), *Fabulating Beauty: Perspectives on the Fiction of Peter Carey*. Amsterdam: Rodopi, pp. 17–30.
Laub, D. (1992), "An Event Without A Witness: Truth, Testimony and Survival," in S. Felman and D. Laub (eds), *Testimony: Crises of Witnessing in Literature, Psychoanalysis, and History*. London and New York: Routledge, pp. 75–92.
Lawson, A. (2004), "Postcolonial theory and the 'settler subject'" in C. Sugars (ed.), *Unhomely States: Theorizing English-Canadian Postcolonialism*, Ontario & New York: Broadview Press, pp. 151–64.
Lefèbvre, H. (1991), *The Production of Space*. Trans. Donald Nicholson-Smith. Oxford: Blackwell Publishers Ltd.
Lee, J. and Cardinal, L. (1998), "Hegemonic nationalism and the politics of feminism and multiculturalism in Canada" in V. Strong-Boag, S. Grace, A. Eisenberg and J. Anderson (eds), *Painting the Maple: Essays on Race, Gender, and the Construction of Canada*. Vancouver, BC: University of British Columbia, pp. 215–61.
Lee, V. (1996), "Scaffolders Get Up Nose," *South China Morning Post*, 5 November, p. 8.
Leonard, M. (1997), *Britain™*. London: Demos.
Levy, A. (2010), *The Long Song*. London: Farrar, Straus & Giroux.

Lewis, C. (1985), *The Ripper.* USA: United Entertainment Pictures.
Leys, R. (2000), *Trauma: A Genealogy.* Chicago, IL: Chicago University Press.
Light, A. (1991), *Forever England: Femininity, Literature and Conservatism Between The Wars.* London: Routledge.
Lo, K. (2001), "Double Negations: Hong Kong Cultural Identity in Hollywood's Transnational Representations." *Cultural Studies*, 15, 3–4, 464–85.
—(2005), *Chinese Face/Off: Transnational Popular Culture of Hong Kong.* Champaign, IL: University of Illinois Press.
Longan, M. and Oakes, T. (2002), "Geography's conquest of history in *The Diamond Age*," in R. Kitchin and J. Kneale (eds), *Lost in Space: Geographies of Science Fiction.* London and New York: Continuum, pp. 39–56.
Lonsdale, K. (2000), "Rounding up the Usual Suspects: Echoing Jack the Ripper," in C. L. Krueger (ed.), *Functions of Victorian Culture At the Present Time.* Athens, OH: Ohio University Press, pp. 97–114.
Loomba, A., Kaul, S., Bunzl, M., Burton, A., and Esty, J. (2005), "Beyond What?: An Introduction" in A. Loomba, S. Kaul, M. Bunzl, A. Burton, and J. Esty (eds), Postcolonial Studies and Beyond. Durham, NC: Duke University Press, pp. 1–38.
López, A. J. (2005), "Introduction: whiteness after empire," in A. J. López (ed.), *Postcolonial Whiteness: A Critical Reader on Race and Empire.* Albany, NY: SUNY Press, pp. 1–29.
Lovelady, S. (1999), "'I am telling this to no one but you:' private voice, passing and the private sphere in Margaret Atwood's *Alias Grace*", *Studies in Canadian Literature*, 24, 2, 35–63.
Lowe, L. (1999), *Immigrant Acts: On Asian American Cultural Politics.* Durham, NC: Duke University Press.
Lucas, A. (2005), *The Mysterious Geographic Explorations of Jasper Morello.* Australia: Madman Entertainment.
Lucas, R. (2003), "Narratives, terminable and interminable: literature, psychoanalysis and Margaret Atwood's *Alias Grace*" in J. Damousi and R. Reynolds (eds), *History on the Couch: Essays in History and Psychoanalysis.* Carlton, Victoria: Melbourne University Press.
Mackey, E. (2002), *The House of Difference: Cultural Politics and National Identity in Canada.* Toronto, ON: University of Toronto Press.
Malouf, D. (1994), *Remembering Babylon.* London and New York: Vintage International.
Marchetti, G. (2000), "Buying American, Consuming Hong Kong: Cultural Commerce, Fantasies of Identity, and the Cinema", in P. Fu and D. Desser (eds), *The Cinema of Hong Kong: History, Arts, Identity.* Cambridge: Cambridge University Press, pp. 289–313.
—(2001), "Jackie Chan and the black connection", in M. Tinkcom and A. Villarejo (eds), *Keyframes: Popular Cinema and Cultural Studies.* London and New York: Routledge, pp. 137–58.
McClintock, A. (1995), *Imperial Leather: Race, Gender and Sexuality in the Colonial Conquest.* London and New York: Routledge.
McCloud, S. (1994), *Understanding Comics.* New York: Harper Paperbacks.

McCrum, R. (2001), "Reawakening Ned: Interview with Peter Carey," *The Observer*, 7 January, viewed 25 May 2001, <http://www.guardian.co.uk/books/2001/jan/07/fiction.petercarey>.
McDonald, S. (2000), "A conversation with Matthew Kneale," *Boldtype*, 3, 3, April, viewed 24 May, 2011. <http://www.randomhouse.com/boldtype/0400/kneale/interview.html>.
McHale, B. (1992), 'Difference Engines,' *ANQ*, 5, 4, 220–3.
McLeod, J. (1999), "On the Chase for Gideon Nye: History and Representation in Timothy Mo's *An Insular Possession*," *Journal of Commonwealth Literature*, 34, 21, 61–73.
McMahon, E. (2007), "The centaur and the cyborg: abject becoming on the colonial frontier," *Southerly: A Review of Australian Literature*, 67, 1–2, 211–25.
McPhee, G. and Poddar, P. (eds) (2007), *Empire and After: Englishness in Postcolonial Perspective*. Oxford: Berghahn Books.
Mehta, K. (2005), *The Rising: Ballad of Mangal Pandey*. India: Kaleidoscope Entertainment.
Meyer, N. (1979), *Time After Time*. USA: Warner Brothers.
Miéville, C. (2000), *Perdido Street Station*. New York: Del Rey Books.
—(2002), *The Scar*. New York: Del Rey Books.
Mitchell, D. (2004), *Cloud Atlas*. New York: Random House.
Mitchell, K. (2010), *History and Cultural Memory in Neo-Victorian Fiction: Victorian Afterimages*. Basingstoke, UK: Palgrave, Macmillan.
Mitchell, M. (1936), *Gone With the Wind*. New York: Warner Books.
Mizuno, H. (2009), *Science for the Empire: Scientific Nationalism in Modern Japan*. Stanford: Stanford University Press.
Mo, T. (1986), *An Insular Possession*. London: Picador.
Monk, C. (2000), "Underbelly UK: The 1990s underclass film, masculinity, and the ideologies of New Britain" in A. Higson and J. Ashby (eds), *British Cinema, Past and Present*, pp. 274–87.
Moodie, S. (1852), *Roughing It In the Bush*. London: Richard Bentley. Available at: <http://digital.library.upenn.edu/women/moodie/roughing/roughing.html>.
—(1854), *Life in the Clearings Versus the Bush*. Toronto, ON: McClelland & Stewart.
Mooers, C. (2006), "Introduction: the new watchdogs" in C. Mooers (ed.), *The New Imperialists: Ideologies of Empire*. Oxford: Oneworld Publications.
Moore, A. (1999), *From Hell: Being a Melodrama in Sixteen Parts*. Ill. E. Campbell. Marietta, GA: Top Shelf Production.
—(2002), *The League of Extraordinary Gentlemen, Vol. 1*. Ill. K. O'Neill, La Jolla, CA: America's Best Comics.
—(2004), *The League of Extraordinary Gentlemen, Vol. 2*. Ill. K. O'Neill, La Jolla, CA: America's Best Comics.
Moorthy, S. and Jamal, A. (eds) (2009), *Indian Ocean Studies: Cultural, Social and Political Perspectives*. London and New York: Routledge.
Moretti, F. (1998), *Atlas of the European Novel 1800–1900*. London: Verso.
Mori, K. (2002–8), *Emma: A Victorian Romance*. La Jolla, CA: Wildstorm Productions.

Morley, D. and Robins, K. (1995), *Spaces of Identity: Global Media, Electronic Landscapes and Cultural Boundaries*. London and New York: Routledge.
Morris, J. (1997), *Hong Kong: Epilogue to an Empire*. London and New York: Penguin.
Morrison, T. (1997), *Beloved*. New York.: Vintage Books.
Mote, A. (2003), *Over Crowded Britain: Our Immigration Crisis Exposed*. Hampshire, UK: Tanner Publishing.
Munich, A. (1987), "Queen Victoria, Empire and Excess," *Tulsa Studies in Women's Literature*, 6, 2, 265–81.
—(1998), *Queen Victoria's Secrets*. New York: Columbia University Press.
Murray, A. (2007), *Recalling London: Literature and History in the work of Peter Ackroyd and Iain Sinclair*. London: Continuum.
Murray, J. (2001), "Historical figures and paradoxical patterns: the quilting metaphor in Margaret Atwood's *Alias Grace*," *Studies in Canadian Literature*, 26, 1, 65–83.
Nakazawa, K. (1973–85), *Barefoot Gen* [reprint]. San Francisco, CA: Last Gasp.
Nasta, S. (2002), *Home Truths: Fictions of the South Asian Diaspora in Britain*. Basingstoke, UK: Palgrave Macmillan.
Naumetz, T. (2004), "Many doubt multiculturalism policies working," *The Gazette*, 18 July. Available from: http://www.lexisnexis.com. Viewed on 16 May, 2007.
Neo-Victorian Studies (n.d.), <http://www.neovictorianstudies.com/>.
Ng, K. (1997), "Role of Opium Remembered." *South China Morning Post*, 28 April, p. 5.
Niu, G. (2008), "Techno-orientalism, nanotechnology, posthumans, and post-posthumans in Neal Stephenson's and Linda Nagata's science fiction," *Melus*, 33, 4, Winter, 73–96.
Nixon, S. (2001), "Resignifying masculinity: from 'new man' to 'new lad," in D. Morley and K. Robins (eds), *British Cultural Studies: Geography, Nationality and Identity*. Oxford: Oxford University Press, pp. 373–86.
Nora, P. (1989), "Between memory and history: *les lieux de memoire*," *Representations*, 26, Spring, 7–24.
Nunn, H. (2001), "Running wild: fictions of gender and childhood in Thatcher's Britain." *EnterText*, 1, 3, Autumn, 15–41.
—(2002), *Thatcher, Politics and Fantasy: The Political Culture of Gender and Nation*. London: Lawrence and Wishart.
O'Brian, P. (1970), *Master and Commander*. London and New York: W. W. Norton & Co. Ltd.
O'Conner, E. (2003), "Preface for a post-postcolonial criticism." *Victorian Studies*, 45, 2, Winter, 217–46.
Ong, A. (1999), *Flexible Citizenship: The Cultural Logic of Transnationality*. Durham, NC: Duke University Press.
Otomo, K. (2004), *Steamboy*. Japan: Bandai.
—(1998), *Akira*. Japan: Bandai.
Pagliasotti, D. (2010), "Against VictOrientalism," blog post, *Dru Pagliasotti: The Mark of Ashen Wings*, 10 March, accessed December 2, 2010, <http://drupagliassotti.com/2010/03/10/against-victorientalism/>.

Palmer, C. (2009), "Saving the city in China Miéville's Bas-Lag novels," *Extrapolation*, 50, 2, 224–38.
Pan, L. (1990), *Sons of the Yellow Emperor: A History of the Chinese Diaspora*. Boston and London: Little, Brown & Co.
Parker, J. (2010), "David Mitchell's Cloud Atlas of narrative constraints and environmental limits," in J. Parker, A. Harris and C. Steineck (eds), *Time: Limits and Constraints*. Leiden, the Netherlands: Koninklijke Brill BV, pp. 201–17.
Parks, S. (1996), *Venus*. New York: Theatre Communications Group Inc.
Pearson, M. and Shanks, M. (2001), *Theatre/Archeology*. London and New York: Routledge.
Penney, S. (2008), *The Tenderness of Wolves*. New York: Simon & Schuster.
Perera, S. (1996), "Claiming Truganini: Australian national narratives in the year of indigenous peoples," *Cultural Studies*, 10, 3, 393–410.
Perry, A. (1997), "'Fair Ones of a Purer Cast': White women and colonialism in Nineteenth-Century British Columbia," *Feminist Studies*, 23, 3, Autumn, 501–24.
Phillips, C. (1993), *Cambridge*. London: Vintage.
Pick, D. (2000), *Svengali's Web: The Alien Encounter in Modern Culture*. New Haven, CT: Yale University Press.
Pierce, P. (1999), *The Country of Lost Children: An Australian Anxiety*. Cambridge: Cambridge University Press.
Plant, S. (2000), "On the matrix: cyberfeminist simulations," in D. Bell and B. M. Kennedy (eds), *The Cybercultures Reader*, London and New York: Routledge, pp. 325–36.
Porter, B. (2006), *Empire and Superempire: Britain, America and the World*. New Haven, CT: Yale University Press.
Poulter, G. (2009), *Becoming Native in a Foreign Land: Sport, Visual Culture and Identity in Montreal, 1840–85*. Vancouver, BC: University of British Columbia Press.
Priest, C. (2009), *Boneshaker*. New York: Tom Doherty Associates.
Redhill, M. (2007), *Consolation*. New York: Little, Brown and Company.
Rhys, J. (1966), *Wide Sargasso Sea*. London and New York: W.W. Norton & Company Ltd.
Robox Studios (2007), *Orphan Feast* [flash game]. Adult Swim. Accessed 13 December 2011 from http://games.adultswim.com/orphan-feast-adventure-online-game.html.
Roof, J. (2000), "Display cases," in J. Kucich and D. F. Saddoff (eds), *Victorian Afterlife: Postmodern Culture Rewrites the Nineteenth Century*. Minneapolis, MN: University of Minnesota Press, pp. 101–22.
Rowse, T. (2000), "Indigenous citizenship," in W. Hudson and J. Kane (eds), *Rethinking Australian Citizenship*. Cambridge: Cambridge University Press, pp. 86–95.
Rudd, K. (2008), "'Apology to Aborigines' speech," *BBC News*, 12 February, viewed January 15, 2009. <http://news.bbc.co.uk/2/hi/asia-pacific/7242057.stm>.
Rushdie, S. (1992), *Imaginary Homelands: Essays and Criticism 1981–91*. London: Granta Books.
Rushdy, A. H. A. (1999), *Neo-Slave Narratives: Studies in the Social Logic of a Literary Form*. Oxford: Oxford University Press.
Said, E. (1979), *Orientalism*. New York: Vintage Books.

Samuel, R. (1992), "Mrs. Thatcher's Return to Victorian Values" in T. C. Smout (ed.), *Victorian Values: Joint Symposium of the Royal Society of Edinburgh and the British Academy, December 1990*. Oxford. Oxford University Press, pp. 9–29.

—(1994), *Theatres of Memory, Vol. 1*. London: Verso.

—(1999), *Island Stories: Unravelling Britain* (Theatres of Memory, Vol. II). London: Verso.

Sardar, Z. (1996), "Alt.Civilizations.FAQ: Cyberspace as the Darker Side of the West," in Z. Sardar and J. Ravetz (eds), *Cyberfutures: Culture and Politics on the Super Information Highway*. New York: New York University Press, pp. 1–13.

Seltzer, M. (1998), *Serial Killers: Death and Life in America's Wound Culture*. New York and London: Routledge, 1998.

Sexton, D. (1985), "Interview with Peter Carey," *Literary Review*, 84, June, 38–41.

Shiller, D. (1997), "The redemptive past in the neo-Victorian novel," *Studies in the Novel*, 29, 4, 538–61.

Shinoda, T. (2006), "Japan's top-down policy process to dispatch the SDF to Iraq," *Japanese Journal of Political Science*, 7, 1, 71–91.

Sinclair, I. (1987), *White Chappell, Scarlet Tracings*. London: Granta.

—(1997), *Lights Out for the Territory: 9 Excursions in the Secret History of London*. London: Granta.

—(2002), "Jack the Rip-Off." *The Observer*, 27 January, p. 8, viewed 24 April, 2003, <http://www.guardian.co.uk/film/2002/jan/27/features.historybooks>.

—(2003), *Downriver, or, The Vessels of Wrath: A Narrative in Twelve Tales*. London: Granta.

Sinnema, P. (2003), "Around the world without a gaze: Englishness and the press in Jules Verne", *Victorian Periodicals Review*, 36, 2, Summer, 135–52.

Skeldon, R. (1994), "Reluctant Exiles or Bold Pioneers: An Introduction to Migration from Hong Kong", in R. Skeldon (ed.), *Reluctant Exiles?: Migration from Hong Kong and the New Overseas Chinese*. New York: M. E. Sharpe, pp. 3–18.

Snow, P. (2003), *The Fall of Hong Kong: Britain, China, and the Japanese Occupation*. New Haven, CT: Yale University Press.

Sonnefeld, B. (1999), *Wild Wild West*. USA: Warner Brothers.

Spencer, N. (1999), "Rethinking ambivalence: technopolitics and the Luddites in William Gibson and Bruce Sterling's *The Difference Engine*," *Contemporary Literature*, XL, 3, 403–29.

Spenser, E. (1590), "The Faerie Queene," in Abrams, M. H. et al (eds), *The Norton Anthology of English Literature* 5th ed. Vol. 1. New York: W. W. Norton & Company.

Stanley, S (2003), "The eroticism of class and the enigma of Margaret Atwood's *Alias Grace*", *Tulsa Studies in Women's Literature*, 22, 2, 371–86.

"The Steampunk Scholar" (2010), "Leaving London, arriving in Albion: the future of steampunk," blogpost, *The Steampunk Scholar*, viewed 29 April, 2010. <http://steampunkscholar.blogspot.com/2010/04/leaving-london-arriving-in-albion.html>.

The Steampunk Workshop, Website, viewed 12 July, 2010. <http://steampunk-workshop.com/>.

Stein, M. B. (1997), "Improving the process of constitutional reform in Canada: lessons from the Meech Lake and Charlottetown constitutional rounds," *Canadian Journal of Political Science*, 30, 307–38.

Steiner, T. (2008), "Navigating multilingually: the chronotope of the ship in contemporary East African fiction." *English Studies in Africa*, 51, 2, 49–58.
Stephenson, N. (1996), *The Diamond Age, or, A Young Lady's Illustrated Primer*. New York: Bantam Books.
Stirling, S. M. (2003), *The Peshawar Lancers*. New York: ROC/Penguin Books.
Sturken, M. (1997), *Tangled Memories: The Vietnam War, The Aids Epidemic and the Politics of Remembering*. Berkeley, CA: University of California Press.
—(1999), "Narratives of recovery: repressed memory as cultural memory", in M. Bal, J. Crewe and L. Spitzer (eds), *Acts of Memory: Cultural Recall in the Present*. Hanover, NH: University Press of New England, pp. 231–47.
Sugden, P. (1994), *The Complete History of Jack the Ripper*. London: Carroll and Graf.
Sungenis, P. (2006 – present), *The New Adventures of Queen Victoria*, webcomic, viewed September 14, 2011, <http://www.newadventuresofqueenvictoria.com/>.
Sussman, H. (1994), "Cyberpunk meets Charles Babbage: *The Difference Engine* as alternative Victorian history," *Victorian Studies*, 38, Autumn, 1–23.
Talbot, B. (2011), *Grandville*. New York: Random House.
Tasker, Y. (1993), *Spectacular Bodies: Gender, Genre and the Action Cinema*. London and New York: Routledge.
Taylor, M. and Wolff, M. (2004), *The Victorians Since 1901: Histories, Representations and Revisions*. Manchester: Manchester University Press.
Tenszen, M. (1985), "'Melting pot' concept not right for Canadians, minister say," *The Globe and Mail*, 14 May, viewed 16 May, 2007. Available from: http://www.lexisnexis.com.
Thieme, J. (2001), *Postcolonial Con-texts: Writing Back to the Canon*. London: Continuum.
Thomas, D. M. (2000), *Charlotte: The Final Journey of Jane Eyre*. London: Duckworth Literary Entertainments, Ltd.
Thompson, H. (2005), *To The Edge of the World*. San Francisco: MacAdam/Cage.
Toboso, Y. (2007 – present), *Black Butler*. New York: Yen Press.
Treat, J. W. (1994), "Hiroshima's America," *boundary 2*, 21, 1, Spring, 233–53.
Turner, G. (1993), "Nationalising the Author: The celebrity of Peter Carey." *Australian Literary Studies*, 16, 2, 131–9.
U.K. Steampunk Convivial (n.d), <http://steampunk.synthasite.com/>.
The U.K. Steampunk Network (n.d.). Website, viewed 13 September, 2010. <http://www.steampunknetwork.co.uk/>.
Valpy, M. (1994), "The myth of Canada as a cultural mosaic," *The Globe and Mail*, 21 June, viewed 16 May 2007. Available from: http://www.lexisnexis.com.
Voigts-Virchow, E. (2009), "'In-yer-Victorian-face:' a subcultural hermeneutics of neo-Victorianism," *Lit: Literature Interpretation Theory*, 20, 108–25.
Wachtel, E. (1993), "We really can make ourselves up: interview with Peter Carey," *Australian and New Zealand Studies in Canada*, 9, 103–5.
Walcott, D. (1979), "The Sea is History." *The Star-Apple Kingdom*. New York: Farrar, Strauss & Giroux.
Walkowitz, J. (1982), "Jack the Ripper and the Myth of Male Violence." *Feminist Studies*, 8, 3, Autumn, 542–74.
—(1992), *City of Dreadful Delight: Narratives of Sexual Danger in Late-Victorian London*. London: Virago Press.

Walkowitz, R. (2006), *Cosmopolitan Style: Modernism Beyond the Nation*. New York: Columbia University Press.

Wallen, D. (1997), "Hong Kong 'will bury ageing Beijing elite'," *South China Morning Post* 2 July, p. 10.

Wallhead, C. and Kohlke, M. K. (2010), "The neo-Victorian frame of Mitchell's *Cloud Atlas*: temporal and traumatic reverberations," in M. L. Kohlke and C. Gutleben (eds), *Neo-Victorian Tropes of Trauma: The Politics of Bearing After-Witness to Nineteenth-Century Suffering*. Amsterdam: Rodopi, pp. 217–452.

Wan, M. (1996), "The artist who saw red: interview with Pun Sing-lui." *South China Morning Post*, 10 October, p. 15.

Wang, G. (2003), "Foreword," in L. Jayasuriya, D. Walker, and J. Gothard (eds), *Legacies of White Australia: Race, Culture and Nation*. Crawley, Western Australia: University of Western Australia Press, pp. vii–ix.

Ward, S. (ed.) (2001), *British Culture and the End of Empire*. Manchester: Manchester University Press.

Warf, B. (2002), "The way it wasn't: alternative histories, contingent geographies," in R. Kitchin and J. Kneale (eds), *Lost in Space: Geographies of Science Fiction*. London and New York: Continuum, pp. 17–38.

Warner, M. (1985), *Monuments and Maidens: The Allegory of the Female Form*. Berkeley, CA: University of California Press.

Waters, S. (1999), *Affinity*. London: Penguin Group.

—(2009), *The Little Stranger*. London: Virago Press.

Weir, P. (1975), *Picnic At Hanging Rock*. Australia: Australian Film Commission.

Wetmore Jr., K. J. (2006), "From *Scaretto* to *Kaze to tomo ni sarinu*: musical adaptations of *Gone with the Wind* in Japan," in D. Jortner, K. McDonald and K. J. Wetmore Jr. (eds), *Modern Japanese Theatre and Performance*. Lanham, MD: Rowman & Littlefield Publishers, pp. 237–49.

"What are the most popular fictional Ripper books?" (n.d.), *Casebook: Jack the Ripper*, viewed 5 June, 2002, <http://www.casebook.org/ripper_media/book_reviews/fiction/reader_av.html>.

Wickberg, E. (1999), "Localism and the organization of overseas migration in the nineteenth Century", in G. Hamilton (ed.), *Cosmopolitan Capitalists: Hong Kong and the Chinese Diaspora at the End of the Twentieth Century*. Seattle, WA: University of Washington Press.

Wickes, D. (1988), *Jack the Ripper*. UK: Euston Films.

Williams, R. (1973), *The Country and the City*. Oxford: Oxford University Press.

Wilson, R. (2005), "Spectral critiques: tracking 'uncanny' filmic paths towards a biopoetics of trans-pacific globalization", in M. Morris, S. L. Li and S. Chan (eds), *Hong Kong Connections: Transnational Imagination in Action Cinema*. Hong Kong: Hong Kong University Press.

Winter, A. (1998), *Mesmerized: Powers of Mind in Victorian Britain*. Chicago, IL: University of Chicago Press.

Winter, B. H. (2010), *Android Karenina*. Philadelphia, PA: Quirk Books.

Wolfreys, J. (1998), *Writing London: The Trace of the Urban Text from Blake to Dickens*. London: Macmillan Press.

Wright, P. (1985), *On Living in an Old Country: The National Past in Contemporary Britain*. London: Verso.

Wu, H. (1997), "The Hong Kong clock – public time-telling and political time/space," *Public Culture*, 9, 3, Spring, 329–54.

Xiao, Z. (2000), "The opium war in the movies: history, politics and propaganda," *Asian Cinema*, 11, 1, 68–83.

Xie, J. (1997), *The Opium War (Yapian Zhangzheng)* (1997). China: A Shanghai Film Studio Production.

Index

Abbas, Ackbar   113–14, 117, 124, 211n. 1
Ackroyd, Peter,
   Dan Leno and the Limehouse Golem   22, 31, 37–8, 40–3, 205n. 4
   and psychography   52
Alias Grace see also Canada
   and Britishness   91
   and civility   84, 90–1, 95, 97, 99, 101
   and criminality   81, 98
   and domesticity   84, 97, 109–10
   and "double consciousness"   104–5
   feminism   101–2
   and Irishness   82, 84–5, 91–2, 94–6
   and "memoro-politics"   102–3
   and multiculturalism   83–4, 87, 96, 99–102, 106–7
   multiple personality disorder   105–7
   and trauma   85, 88, 102, 104, 106, 108–9
   and U.S.   91–4, 108
   and white guilt   110–11
   and whiteness   24, 82–5, 90–2, 94–7, 110–11
Android Karenina   145
Ang, Ien   58, 73, 102, 137, 207n. 4
Atwood, Margaret   11, 23–4, 201, 208n. 1
   on Canadian past   81, 85, 100, 110
   on multiculturalism   87, 96, 106
   Susanna Moodie   86–7, 89–90, 105, 209n. 6
   on victimization   88–90, 111
Australia   5, 11, 13, 21, 73, 80, 107, 177
   see also Carey, Peter
   and aboriginal dispossession   23, 56–7, 64–5, 78
   and 'bastard complex'   65–6
   and citizenship   23, 58, 64, 79–80
   convicts   23, 58, 60, 64–7, 69, 78
   and England   12, 22–3, 61–3, 67, 73, 80
   and illegitimacy   66
   multiculturalism   12, 23, 56–8, 65, 67, 78, 80
   and national literature   21, 57, 68–9, 72

   rhetoric of 'home'   59–60, 63
   'Stolen Generations'   56, 66, 78
   and trauma   57–8
   White Australia Policy   56–7, 60, 63, 68, 207n. 3

Bal, Mieke   16
Barrett, Andrea,
   Servants of the Map   174
   Ship Fever   173
   Voyage of the Narwhal   173, 188
Baucom, Ian   17, 49
Beyond Victoriana (website)   147–8, 161, 213n. 5
Bhabha, Homi   76–7, 123, 128, 136, 168
   see also hybridity; mimicry
Black Butler   6, 162
"The Black Line"   181
Blair, Tony   21, 29, 53, 214n. 9
   'Cool Britannia'   29
   New Labor   29, 52
Booker Prize, Man   4, 6, 11, 21, 57, 68–72, 86, 118, 200, 204n. 17, 208n. 9
Britain   6, 16, 21, 24, 26, 52–3 *see also* Ripperature
   and Englishness   21–2, 29, 31–3, 36, 41, 44–52
   and heritage   17, 22, 29, 31–2, 38–44, 205n. 3, 206n. 13
   as imperial center   8, 11–12
   and post-imperial melancholia   16–17, 22, 42
   and neo-Victorian fiction   6, 17
   and New Labor   21–2, 29
   and Thatcherism   21–2, 34, 36, 52
British Empire,
   comparison to United States imperialism   13, 25, 90, 149, 151, 154, 204n. 8

as recalled by neo-Victorianism 5–6, 7, 10, 12, 14, 25, 51, 113, 139, 147, 171, 174, 184, 194
Byatt, A. S.,
  Possession: A Romance 4, 9, 20–1, 28, 160, 178, 204n. 16
Burton, Antoinette,
  "imperial turn" 12, 16, 61

Canada 11–13, 21, 23–4, 81–5 *see also* Atwood, Margaret
  Arctic Policy 172–3
  and Canada First movement 90, 210n. 9
  multiculturalism 12, 23–4, 81–7, 90–1, 96–102, 105, 107, 111
  as schizophrenic 87, 104–6
  and US 23, 82, 90–1, 93, 96, 108, 110–11
  as victim 24, 82, 85, 88–90, 103, 106–7, 109–11
  and whiteness 24, 81–111, 208n. 1
Carey, Peter 11–12, 22–3, 55, 57, 201, 208n. 8 *see also* Australia
  and Booker Prize 68–72, 204n. 17
  Jack Maggs,
    and Australia as "home" 59–60, 64
    and Australian authorship 67–72
    and citizenship 79–80
    and convict ancestry 23, 55, 60–1, 64, 67, 69, 78–9
    and England as "home" 58–64
    and Englishness 23, 62, 67
    and legitimacy 64–7
    and mesmerism 72–6
    and mimesis 77
    and orphan figure 66, 208n. 3
    revising Dickens 55, 64–5
    and trauma 12, 14, 57, 61, 72, 76–9
  Oscar and Lucinda 55, 68, 204n. 17, 207n. 2
  The True History of the Kelly Gang 69, 204n. 17, 207n. 2, 208n. 10
Carriger, Gail,
  Parasol Protectorate 146
cartography *see also* psychogeography
  failure of 187–9, 191, 199
  neo-Victorianism's reordering of 12–13, 144, 147, 151–2, 161–2, 169

Caruth, Cathy 18–19
Chan, Jackie 24, 114, 116, 121, 130, 139–40
  see also Hong Kong; Opium War (1839–42)
  Around the World in Eighty Days (2004) 25, 124, 141–4, 152, 159, 166
  as cyborg 143
  as global icon 124–5, 144
  Project A 24, 114, 124–31, 212n. 14
  and self-orientalization 144
  Shanghai Knights 24, 114, 124, 130, 134–40
  Shanghai Noon 24, 114, 124, 130–4, 139
Chester 5000 XYV 4
China 6, 13, 25, 113–16, 119–23, 127–8, 131–3, 135, 137, 139, 184, 186 *see also* Hong Kong; Opium War (1839–42)
  and imperialism 3, 13, 24–5, 113–14, 116
  and "Victorientalism" 144, 156–9
Chineseness 24, 118, 122, 128, 130–1, 133–40, 142, 212
Chow, Rey 10, 24, 114–15, 130, 132, 142
  on Hong Kong 24, 115, 130, 136, 140, 211n. 2
City of Lost Children 145
Clavell, James,
  Tai Pan 116–18
coolie 132, 184–5
Cowboys and Aliens 145
cyborg 143, 151, 153, 158, 164, 167–8

Derrida, Jacques 17, 188
diaspora,
  Chinese 24, 116, 118, 124, 129–39, 171
  Indian 176, 184–5
  and neo-Victorian-at-sea 181
Dickens, Charles,
  Great Expectations 23, 55, 64, 68
Dirlik, Arif 144, 262, 164
Dyer, Richard 24, 82–3, 85, 92, 84, 110

Emma: A Victorian Romance 6, 162

Faber, Michel,
  The Crimson Petal and the White 4

Fowles, John,
  The French Lieutenant's Woman 4, 9, 164
Franklin, John Sir 172–3
From Hell (film) 53–4

Ghosh, Amitav 200
  Sea of Poppies 25, 116, 174, 177, 183–9
    and "coolitude" 185
    and trauma 184
Gibson, William and Bruce Sterling,
  The Difference Engine 25, 144, 146, 149–55, 161, 213n. 7
Gikandi, Simon 5, 10, 19
Gilroy, Paul 174, 195, 198–9
  and postcolonial melancholia 17, 42–4
  The Black Atlantic 25, 175, 184–5, 197
globalization 105, 124, 154, 158, 204n. 11
  and neo-Victorian-at-sea 171, 175, 177, 189–200
  neo-Victorianism's response to 5, 9, 13–14, 26, 169
  nineteenth century as precursor to 115, 121–2, 145, 176–7, 199
Great Exhibition (1851) 145, 162–4, 167
Great Steampunk Debate, The (website) 148, 190, 213n. 3
Gregory, Derek 11
Grenville, Kate,
  The Secret River 57, 204n. 17, 208n. 9

Hacking, Ian 103, 105, 210n. 12
  and "memoro-politics" 17, 103
Hanson, Pauline 56–7, 60, 63–4, 111, 208n. 5
Haraway, Donna 153, 158, 168
Hardt, Michael and Antonio Negri
  "Empire" 149, 154–5, 159, 161, 171, 188, 204n. 11
Heilmann, Ann and Mark Llewellyn 4–5, 8–9, 203n. 6
heritage film 125, 262
historiographic metafiction 4, 7
Hong Kong 1–5, 13–14, 24–5, 131, 205n. 19 *see also* Chan, Jackie; Clavell, James; Mo, Timothy; Opium War (1839–42); Xie, Jin
  and British Nationality Act, 1981 136–7
  "one country, two systems" 113, 126, 140

  and opium 115–16, 121, 140
  as port 130–1
  and reunification (with China) 24, 113–15, 117–18, 135, 139, 212n. 14
Hung, Sammo 127, 212n. 1
Huyssen, Andreas 15
hybridity 117, 120, 123, 129–30, 134, 168, 177, 191
hypnosis 74–8, 102–7

immigration 15, 52, 56–7, 60, 63, 76, 83, 90, 94–5 116, 131, 135–40, 209n. 6, 212n. 13
imperialism,
  compared to globalization 5, 9, 13–14, 169, 174, 177, 192, 194, 199
  and cosmopolitanism 198–9
  and "Empire" 154–5, 159, 161, 188
  and feminism 101
  and Japan 162, 167
  legacy in the present 3, 7, 11–12, 19, 101, 116, 132
  and neo-imperialism 6, 9, 13, 25–6, 90, 131, 160–1, 169, 171, 190, 194, 200
  and neo-Victorian texts 5
  and neo-Victorian-at-sea 25–6, 174, 180
  neo-Victorianism as critique of 7, 9, 14–15, 19, 26, 99, 169, 171, 187, 195
  nineteenth century as memory of 5, 10–13, 171, 188, 190, 192–3, 198
  and psychogeography 49
  and Ripperature 54
  and steampunk 25, 144, 148–9, 149–61
  United States 5, 13, 90, 139, 154, 160
  and whiteness 12, 82, 84
  within diaspora 131
Irishness 24, 57, 64, 74, 82–3, 91–2, 94–6, 173, 207n. 2

Jack the Ripper 22, 145, 205n. 1 *see also* Ackroyd, Peter; Moore, Alan; Sinclair, Iain; Ripperature
  as English icon 31–3, 53
  and misogyny 31, 33, 36–8
Jameson, Frederic 7, 189

Japan 6, 152–4, 161–9, 171, 213n. 6, 214n. 13 *see also* Otomo Katsuhiro
 and imperialism 13, 165
 and military 169
 and "scientific nationalism" 166–7
 and steampunk 152–5, 161–9
 and "techno-orientalism" 153–4
 and trauma of Hiroshima 164–6
 and the West 5, 25, 152
Joyce, Simon 9
Jukic, Tatjana 7

Kaplan, Cora 7, 8, 203n. 4
Keating, Paul 56
Kneale, Matthew,
 English Passengers 25, 173, 177–83, 187–9, 197
Kucich, John and Dianne F. Sadoff 7, 146

Lagaan 6, 215n. 5
Last Exile 162
Lefebvre, Henri 47
Levy, Andrea,
 The Long Song 175
Leys, Ruth 75–7, 108

McClintock, Ann 10, 49, 209n. 3
McCloud, Scott 40
McHale, Brian 147
Malouf, David 57, 69
melancholia 15–17, 22, 42, 131–3
 postcolonial melancholia" 17, 42–3
 "racial melancholia" 131–2
mesmerism 23, 58, 72–9, 102
Miéville, China 201
 The Scar 26, 189–94, 215n. 6
mimicry 76–7, 128, 140, 143
Mitchell, David 201
 Cloud Atlas 26, 189, 194–200
Mitchell, Kate 15
Mitchell, Margaret,
 Gone With The Wind 164, 214n. 11
Mo, Timothy 120
 An Insular Possession 116, 118–20
Moodie, Susanna 86–90
Moore, Alan *see also* Jack the Ripper; Ripperature

From Hell 22
 anxiety about history 40–1, 43–4
 and Englishness 36, 44–52, 54
 and 'enterprise culture' 27
 and *From Hell* (film) 53–4
 and gender 33–6, 44, 48–9
 graphic novel and temporality 27, 41
 and heritage industry 28, 29, 31–2, 34, 38–41, 44
 and Margaret Thatcher 33
 and New Labor 29, 31, 52–3
 and psychogeography 44–52, 206n. 14
 and Queen Victoria 34–5
 and scopophilia 40
 and Thatcherism 29, 31
 and 'Victorian values' 29
 The League of Extraordinary Gentlemen 145, 160–1
Mori, Arinori 152, 164, 213n. 6
Mysterious Geographic Explorations of Jasper Morello, The 146

neo-slave narrative 175, 204n. 16
Neo-Victorian Studies (journal) 10, 203n. 9
neo-Victorian-at-sea 25–6, 171–201 *see also* Ghosh, Amitav, Kneale, Matthew, Miéville, China; Mitchell, David
 and cosmopolitanism 187, 194–200
 definition of 174–7
 and Englishness 178–9
 and genre-death 188–9
 and globalization 171, 175, 177, 189–200
 and heterotopia (Foucault) 176, 185
 and multilingualism 180, 186–7
 and trauma 184
neo-Victorianism,
 as alternate history 25, 41, 137, 140, 142, 147–51, 189
 definition of 4–7
 and ethics of appropriation 10, 44, 145, 148–9
 as global phenomenon 5–6, 8, 11–14, 18–19, 21, 24, 26, 31, 41, 113–17, 164, 171–201
 and "improper postcolonialisms" 10–14, 113, 140

Index

and nation 12, 15, 17–18, 23, 26, 54, 97, 99, 114, 138, 171, 177, 193
and neo-Victorian studies 10, 26, 163, 173, 175, 177, 184, 188
as politics of memory 15–19
postcolonial examples of 5–6
as postcolonial strategy 1–6, 10, 14–16, 18–26, 32, 81–3, 111, 169, 171–4
and postmodernism 6–8
and race 12, 25, 50, 54, 58, 85, 134, 136, 140, 148 *see also* whiteness
as recovery from the past 3–6, 14–19, 23, 43–4, 64, 72–9, 102–7, 149, 171, 184, 186, 199
and settler postcolonialism 11, 23, 54, 85, 107, 111, 171, 198
New Adventures of Queen Victoria, The 4
Nora, Pierre 49
nostalgia 3, 15, 17, 22–3, 36, 42–3, 125, 149, 153

O'Brian, Patrick 175
Opium War (1839–42) 24, 113–17, 120–1, 193
orientalism 144, 148, 153
Orphan Feast 4
Otomo Katsuhiro *see also* Japan; steampunk
Steamboy 25, 144, 152, 161–9, 214n. 10

Pacific Rim 153, 161–2, 164, 174
Penney, Stef,
The Tenderness of Wolves 81
Phillips, Caryl,
Cambridge 175
Priest, Cherie,
Boneshaker 145
Princess Kaiulani 6
Pun Sing-Lui 1–5, 14, 18, 20–1, 34

Queen Victoria 3, 9, 206n. 6
comparison to Margaret Thatcher 33–8
depictions of 34–5, 121–2, 136–7, 142
statues of 1–4, 21

Rasputina 5
Redhill, Michael 88
Consolation 6, 86, 204n. 17

resistance to Blairism 29
and "Ripperology" 31, 38
Rhys, Jean,
Wide *Sargasso Sea* 6, 164, 175
Ripperature *see also* Ackroyd, Peter; Jack the Ripper; Moore, Alan; Sinclair, Iain
countermovement to Thatcherism 22, 29, 34, 36, 49–50
definition of 22, 29
and Englishness 22, 31–3, 39, 41, 43, 54
and heritage 22, 29, 31–2, 36, 43
and male bonding 34
and melancholia 42–4

Said, Edward 148
Samuel, Raphael 32, 40, 47, 206n. 13
screen memories 125, 137, 140, 165
Shiller, Dana 4
Shonibare, Yinka 6
Sinclair, Iain,
on *From Hell* (movie) 53
and psychogeography 44–5, 48, 50–2
White Chappell, Scarlet Tracings 22, 31, 36–8, 40, 43, 50–2, 206n. 10
slavery 175, 184–5, 187, 197, 204n. 16
Space: 1889 5
steampunk *see also* Gibson, William and Bruce Sterling; Otomo Katsuhiro; Stephenson, Neal
and anxiety over technology 146–7, 153, 164–9
comparison to neo-Victorianism 25, 142–3, 144–9
and geography 143–5, 147, 151–3, 163
and imperialism 148–61
and Japan 152–5, 161–9
and neo-imperialism 25
and race 143–4, 147–8, 152–4, 156–9, 161–8
and "techno-orientalism" 153–4, 158
and "Victorientalism" 25, 144, 147–9, 213n. 5.
Steampunk Network, The UK 148–9
Stephenson, Neal,
The Diamond Age 25, 144, 149, 154–60
Stirling, S. M.,
The Peshawar Lancers 147

Sturken, Marita 88–9, 125
Sweeney Todd 4

Talbot, Bryan,
  Grandville 161
Tasmania 177, 180–3
Thatcher, Margaret 17, 21–2, 29, 33, 113, 120, 124, 137
  and comparison to Queen Victoria 33–8
  and enterprise culture 28
  and psychogeography 45, 50, 52
  and Ripperature 29, 31, 36–7
  "Victorian values" 29, 205n. 3
Thomas, D. M.,
  Charlotte: The Final Journey of Jane Eyre 6
Thompson, Harry,
  To The Edge of the World 173
The Tiger Lillies 5
trauma *see also* Caruth, Cathy; Leys, Ruth
  neo-Victorianism as response to 11, 18–19, 72–9, 113, 181, 198, 204n. 14
  nineteenth century as 12, 57, 61, 64, 85, 99, 148, 198
  politics of 16–19, 88, 102–7, 197

and postcolonial theory 19
as present's relationship to the past 15–16, 17–19
Truganini 182

Verne, Jules,
  Around the World in Eighty Days 25, 124, 141
Victorian Farm 4
Victorian Studies 5, 9, 145

Walkowitz, Judith 31, 33, 37–8
Walkowitz, Rebecca 195
whiteness *see also* neo-Victorianism and race
  and Australia 57, 67
  and Canada 24, 85–111, 208n. 1
  and Englishness 31, 45, 120, 130–1, 136, 181
  and neo-Victorianism 12, 82–5, 92, 97, 111, 130, 140, 160, 181
Wild Wild West 145

Xie, Jin,
  The Opium War 116, 120–3, 131, 133

Printed in Poland
by Amazon Fulfillment
Poland Sp. z o.o., Wrocław